FRIED EGGS
AND RIOJA

Also by Victoria Moore

The Wine Dine Dictionary

FRIED EGGS AND RIOJA

What to Drink with Absolutely Everything

Victoria Moore

GRANTA

Granta Publications, 12 Addison Avenue, London W11 4QR
First published in Great Britain by Granta Books, 2021

Much of the material in this book has previously appeared in *The Wine Dine
Dictionary* by Victoria Moore, published by Granta Books in 2017.

A CIP catalogue record for this book is available from the British Library.

1 3 5 7 9 10 8 6 4 2

ISBN 978 1 78378 790 6
eISBN 978 1 78378 791 3

Illustrations by Hannah Daniel
Text design and art direction by Clare Skeats
Typeset in Scala and Scala Sans by M Rules
Printed and bound by CPI Group (UK) Ltd, Croydon, CR0 4YY
www.granta.com

MIX
Paper from
responsible sources
FSC® C020471
FSC
www.fsc.org

Contents

Introduction

This book is about finding a glass of wine that will taste good with the food you like to eat at home. Because the bottle that you open makes a difference to the way you experience and enjoy your food. Perhaps the best way to understand this is to consider a notoriously *bad* match: freshly squeezed orange juice after toothpaste. I've yet to find anyone who enjoys that experience. Good matches are hard to quantify but what you find in them is a kind of harmony. Each complements the other. The first time I had this experience was in the kitchen of the flat I was living in as an au pair in Italy. The family had gone out. I poured myself a glass of red wine (sangiovese, I was in Florence), grabbed a chunk of Parmesan and stood by the fridge having a sip and then taking a bite. It was a match. The grainy savour of the cheese demanded the dust and juice of the wine and vice versa.

The qualities that make a good match aren't always the same. There are wines I like to pour before I eat because they go so well with the smell of the food that's cooking even if they're not so great with the food itself. Marlborough sauvignon blanc with Thai green curry is a good example of this. I love it beforehand but not so much with it, when the chilli in the food has a habit of stripping the fruitiness out of the wine. Then, when it comes to bottles for the table, some good matches sit alongside the flavours on your plate, others act as a sauce or relish, cutting across them. It means there's always lots of choice and I hope that this book will offer many good choices.

It's arranged like a dictionary to enable you to look up a dish (for instance, gazpacho) or a key ingredient (such as duck) and find suggestions for what wine might work well with it, such as fino sherry for the gazpacho and pinot noir or mourvèdre for the duck (unless you're making duck à l'orange when falanghina, a white Italian grape, would be good).

I have also included twenty recipes for food I make a lot at home, though I should say as a disclaimer that I am not a big cook. I am one of those time-poor people who needs to be able to make dinner in ten minutes but likes to have a glass of wine with it that tastes good. These are the recipes I make because they are simple, (mostly) speedy and work well with wine.

Much of the material here has been published before, in *The Wine Dine Dictionary*, and in response to some of the feedback I had from that book, I wanted to say a word about missing ingredients. My A to Z of food could not possibly contain every dish or every ingredient in existence. You will find omissions. However, what I have tried to cover are popular dishes and also those ingredients that either have a major influence on the flavour of the finished dish, or are likely to be the main anchor in a meal. So you will find entries for red peppers, for example, but not for carrots; for chilli but not for nutmeg.

One of the biggest wrestles with any book that follows a dictionary format is figuring out how to make the material easily searchable without being repetitive. The index is a key part of this function, so please do use it. Think of it as as essential a part of the experience as a corkscrew or a plate.

And with that I will let you get on to planning your next plate of food and glass of wine.

VICTORIA MOORE
November 2021

Taste, smell and what we mean by flavour

What is going on when we smell the grassy scent of sauvignon blanc wafting out of the glass, or when we chew a salty, garlicky piece of lamb? What do we mean by flavour? The way we talk about smell and taste, as if smelling is what happens before we eat or drink and tasting is what we do once something is in our mouth, obscures what is actually happening.

THE SENSE OF TASTE

Much of what we think we taste, we actually smell. If you've never tried it, the jelly bean test is a good demonstration of this: shut your eyes so that you can't see what colour you're taking, pick a jelly bean from a bag of sweets, pinch your nose closed with your fingers, pop the jelly bean in your mouth, and chew. You will find that you can't tell what colour – what flavour of jelly bean – it is until you release your nose, and breathe. Breathing creates an internal airflow that wafts scent molecules to your olfactory receptors, and gives you the information you need to identify lime, bubble gum or orange. Without the input of our sense of smell, all we notice of the jelly bean is a mixture of sugar and acidity.

We have about 10,000 taste buds, located on our tongue, palate, pharynx and larynx, which are activated when they encounter food dissolved in saliva. It used to be thought that the taste buds were capable of detecting just four basic tastes: salt, sweet, sour and bitter. In the Western world these are all very familiar flavour-enhancers, and can be represented by the white flakes of sea salt we sprinkle over our plates of food; the sugar we add to tea, or a bowl of straw-berries; vinegar shaken over fish and chips or lemon squeezed over tuna carpaccio; and the bitterness of dark chocolate or quinine in tonic water.

In 1908, the Tokyo chemist Kikunae Ikeda identified a fifth taste, umami, in seaweed dashi, and proposed that the molecule responsible for it was glutamate. Umami is best described as the deep, savoury quality that makes food taste intense and moreish. It is found in high quantities in soy sauce, tomatoes (it's especially intense in oven-dried tomatoes), mushrooms, beef, yeast and yeast extracts (such as Marmite), Parmesan, fish sauce and shellfish. The question now is – how many more are there?

Fat is considered by most experts to be the sixth basic taste. Metallic is another. If you have ever undergone an operation, you might have been warned by the anaesthetist to expect a metallic taste in the mouth just as you go under; in normal life it's the taste you find if you lick blood from a cut.

The evolutionary argument is that basic tastes developed and survived because they helped to guide us towards the right foods. So, the theory goes, a taste for sweetness, steers us towards the calorie-heavy carbohydrates we need for fuel. Salt draws us to replace lost minerals. Umami may be a protein signal. Bitterness is thought to warn us away from hazardous plants, from unripe fruit to poisonous roots and berries. A liking for bitterness usually develops later, by which time we have learnt which plants may do us harm.

It's clear, then, that when we talk colloquially about 'the taste' of food or drink, we're actually talking about much more than that. If you ask me what a wine 'tastes' like, or to describe its flavour, and all I mention are its acidity, sweetness, bitterness, saltiness and any metallic qualities (they do exist in wine: I find an iron tang in fer servadou), you might feel a bit short-changed. The assumption is that flavour encompasses more than the information given to us by our sense of taste.

THE SENSE OF SMELL

Occasionally I stick my nose in a glass of wine, inhale and am surprised to find a freeze-frame image dropping down in front of my inner eye. It's rarely a neat picture, more like an accidental mobile snap – a view across a field towards some mountains, say; or the wooden legs of a picnic table buried in deep grass. But I can usually place the picture straight away, and, as I do so, I'm also able to identify the wine because I know that smell and picture come from the same place.

This demonstrates two of the quite extraordinary powers of our olfactory system. Our sense of smell has the ability to differentiate accurately between the many hundreds of thousands of different odours it encounters each year – from foods to perfumes, people, environments and, in my case, bottles of wine. Our mind is also able to take the scent of that individual wine and file it away, linking it to other memory traces that are retrieved the next time the brain encounters the same, very particular, smell.

For a long time much of the medical establishment has treated the sense of smell as a luxury, perhaps because, without it, it is possible to navigate modern life unaided. The mass anosmia – both temporary and permanent – caused by COVID-19 has given this under-appreciated sense a much higher profile. Many, suddenly losing their sense of smell, realized for the first time how much they used it. And not just for eating and drinking but also as a navigation tool, for cooking, feeling close to friends and family and rooting themselves in their surroundings (not being able to smell what's around you creates a sense of dislocation).

Our olfactory system is a truly remarkable thing, second only to our highly complex visual system in its number of sensory receptor cells. Until recently scientific literature estimated that humans could differentiate between about 10,000 different odours. Now it is thought that this is likely to be an underestimate, although no one can agree on what the true number might be.

In order for us to perceive an odour, a tiny molecule of a substance must float through the air to make contact with our olfactory receptors, which are located in the nasal cavity, behind the nose. There are two routes to the olfactory receptors: through the nostrils (orthonasal), which is how we process smoke, perfume, and other environmental odours such as the smell of food as it's cooking on the stove, or the aroma of coffee on the street; and in through the 'back entrance' (retronasal) via our mouth and throat, which is how we smell (or taste, as we inaccurately call it) food as we eat. The retronasal route is only activated when you breathe out through the nose, which is why the jelly bean test is so effective, and why we can't taste food properly when we have a cold.

An interesting thing is that the two different routes to our olfactory receptors do not appear to give the same results. A good example of this is the stinky cheese paradox. As lovers of pongy cheese will be aware, the pungent smell of a ripe piece of Epoisses is often quite unpleasant and yet the cheese is delicious to eat – it appears to smell different, or we have a different response to it, when it is sampled orthonasally rather than the retronasally. With coffee, the effect is reversed: the smell of freshly ground coffee always seems better when you sniff it in the air than when you have it in your mouth. Studies using fMRI scans have confirmed the orthonasal/retronasal effect, showing that the two routes can result in different patterns of brain activity for the same smells.

FLAVOUR AND THE SOMATIC SENSES

I've talked about the impact of smell and taste on flavour, but when we describe food and drink we refer to other qualities too. The soma-tosensory system – which covers not just touch, but also temperature and pain – has a huge role to play.

The feel of a food or wine has a big impact on the way we perceive it. A friend can't abide oysters – 'Like eating snot,' as he says. It's not just the immediate sensation of slime or ruggedness on our tongue and against the roof of our mouth that contributes to the way we feel about food, but also how hard our jaw has to work, what muscles have to get involved, because mastication, too, is part of the eating and drinking experience.

One particularly important sensation when it comes to wine (as well as tea and plain chocolate) is the drying, puckering effect caused by tannin. Is this a taste? Or a feel? Even the scientists are divided on the question.

Chilli is another – very vigorous - contributor to the flavour of any dish that contains it. The perception of chilli is also mediated by the somatosensory system. We feel its burn as pain, which is picked up by the nociceptors (pain receptors) and conveyed via the trigeminal nerve to the brain. Aspects of garlic (its heat) and cinnamon (its jagged texture) are sensed in a similar way. These condiments and spices would taste like a shadow of themselves if we ignored this somatosensory input.

So, it seems fairly clear that it's wrong to talk only about taste when we talk about taste. At least three of the senses play a vital role in flavour.

FLAVOUR AND THE OTHER SENSES

Could we go further? The impact of hearing and vision on the perception of flavour is less direct but it certainly can't be ignored. Our brain doesn't simply rely on the input from our mouth and nose, it grabs any information that comes in to help build up a picture.

For instance, if I were to deepen the shade of a rosé wine by adding a few drops of red food colouring, the chances are that it would taste 'more pink' to you – that is, more of red fruits and berries – because your brain would be primed to look for and be receptive towards those flavours.

Charles Spence is an Oxford psychologist who has done a lot of work in this area. His book *The Perfect Meal: The Multisensory Science of Food and Dining* is a good read for anyone interested in learning more about the way all of our senses feed into what we feed ourselves.

Spence looks, among other things, at the way that our perception of flavour is affected by what we can see and hear. For instance, he has found that strawberry mousse will taste ten per cent sweeter if eaten out of a white rather than a black container and that if there is yellow in our sightline then the lemon we squeeze on our smoked salmon will taste more intense.

One of his most famous experiments is known as The Sonic Chip. For this one, Spence had volunteers eat crisps while wearing headphones that played the sound of their own crunchy munching back to them. Unbeknown to the subjects, he manipulated the crunching sound to see if the noise they heard affected the way the participants appreciated the crisps. He found that a crisp that emits (or appears to emit) a louder, higher-pitched sound is rated as being more crispy by the person eating it than one with a quieter, lower-pitched sound.

All of this suggests that when we 'taste' wine and food we're not just tasting but using all of our senses at once. We really need a new verb to describe the act of trying food and drink – to flave, perhaps?

Simple guidelines

Some people have such an innate and creative grasp of flavour that they are able to make unexpected food and wine matches that inspire gastronomic fireworks. There are also a handful of quick tricks you can use to help you choose a wine without fuss. These are outlined below.

PICKING BY MOOD

Some wines and foods evoke certain moods, so choosing wine and food becomes instinctive. I'm thinking barbecued meat with heavy reds; light summer salads with pristine, chilled whites. If you can imagine the wine and the food in the same setting that's a good start.

PICKING BY WEIGHT

Think about texture and weight. Ask: how heavy is this wine going to taste? How powerful is the food I am eating? Am I setting a shout against a whisper? Look for an even balance so that the food does not drown out the wine, or vice versa. For instance, a thunking great Aussie shiraz with an abv of 15% isn't the best pick for Dover sole. Likewise, it's not fair to pitch a tremulous and faded old claret up against spicy barbecued meat.

PICKING BY PLACE

Go local is the best short cut I know. That is, local to the food, not to wherever you happen to be. Take a cassoulet from Gascony. You might either set this hearty, peasant stew next to a thick black Cahors, or play the other way and open an acidic red Marcillac to cut through the rich meat and fat. Either way, both are wines found not so far away, in the same corner of south-west France. And both work.

Sitting in a restaurant overlooking Sydney Harbour ordering crispy soft shell crab? (Well I wish I were.) Then try a semillon from the Hunter Valley a couple of hours north. As for salade niçoise, it is not just south of France holiday longing that makes me say it never tastes better than with a pale pink rosé or a white rolle from Provence. Well, perhaps it is a bit, but it's true anyway.

Putting place with place, region with region, is a trick that works partly because food and wine cultures grow together. It's not just that a winemaker's taste is influenced and shaped by what he eats every day (although it is); over the centuries wine has been made to go on the table beside local food and the popular styles would have been the ones that matched the local palate.

Climate also comes into play. Wine made with grapes that have seen a lot of sun has a richer, warmer taste, a sweet ripeness, that can work with food that has also seen a lot of sun.

FINE WINE AND FINE FOOD

With fine wine, I like to go as simple as possible with the food. It sometimes feels like a better idea not to bother with food at all on the grounds that, if you have a very complex drink in your glass, anything else is just a distraction, though I would never turn down the chance to eat a plate of truffles and pasta with a glass of even the most perfect nebbiolo.

I take a similar view when it comes to choosing what to drink with very fine food: the dance of flavours in a complex plate of precision-cooked food is better enjoyed for what it is than matched to a competingly spectacular wine. I tend to stick with water, or order an easy session wine on the rare occasions when I eat this type of food.

It took me a long time to understand that this is the reason why serious wine drinkers are often contemptuous of the idea of wine and food matching. For them, the wine is everything. And they are right – if you have uncorked a 1982 Margaux, frankly whatever else is going on had better not take up too much of your attention.

KEEPING AN EYE OUT FOR GAME-CHANGER INGREDIENTS

A bottle of bright, cherryish dolcetto is a good match for a plate of bresaola and bitter rocket salad. But what if you add goat's cheese (or curd) and vinaigrette to the plate? Both these are what I call game-changer ingredients. They insinuate themselves in a dish with force and cannot be ignored. A better match now is a fleshy but acidic white wine – probably an oaked sauvignon blanc from Bordeaux or the Loire or maybe a Savennières.

Other powerful game-changer ingredients include *chilli, garlic, herbs* of all kinds, *lemons* (and even the tiniest amount of *preserved lemons*), *artichokes, vinegar* and spices. I've flagged them up and explained how to deal with most of these in the food A to Z because they make a huge difference to the way you perceive the wine.

GETTING MORE TECHNICAL: THE BIG SIX

Nearly everything we think of as taste – from the flavour of a pink raspberry squashed against the roof of your mouth to that of rosemary roast lamb – is actually smell. Remove our sense of smell, and we are reduced to managing solely on the data conveyed by our taste buds, which are only sensitive to salt, sweetness, bitterness, acidity, umami, fat (and, it is emerging, a few other flavours, such as metallic).

These basic six tastes have a huge impact on how a mouthful of wine is perceived. If picking a wine to go with a plate of food it helps to take them into account.

SALT As any cook who has ever put too much vinegar in a sauce, and then added salt to mitigate the mistake, knows, salt reduces the impact of acidity (and vice versa). In wine and food terms, this means that salty food will make a wine with low or middling acidity taste flat, but get on famously with a screamingly acidic wine. So with salty food, look for a sharp white – I think we all like drinking champagne with salty snacks. Many Italian reds can be pleasingly brisk too.

A second strategy is to look for sugar, which can also taste good with salt: think of salted caramel, or a juicy Charentais melon with prosciutto. Sweet wines often match well with salty cheeses, too.

Another way of looking at this is to think that, if you have very salty food, then whatever you drink is going to taste as if you've put salt in the glass too. If the thought of doing this is very unappealing, then don't serve that wine with that food. Heavy salt can make oaked wines taste odd – this is why oaky chardonnay isn't great with a bag of crisps but a brisk glass of unoaked sauvignon blanc is.

SWEETNESS Sugar can kill wine. If going to a professional tasting I don't eat anything sweet for at least an hour beforehand. Sweetness skews the palate. It can make wine taste almost bitter, as anyone who's ever tried to return to a glass of dry wine while eating apple crumble or ice cream will know.

If putting a wine with pudding, pick one that is sweeter than the food. If there's a touch of sweetness – from luscious fruit, say – in a main course, consider a slightly off-dry wine, or at least a rich-tasting wine: a ripe chardonnay, say, rather than a skinny sauvignon blanc.

BITTERNESS A bitter ingredient such as radicchio, chicory or rocket can also throw a wine. I like to put bitter food with bitter wine or, if you can't find bitter wine, then with astringency (tannin) and acidity. For instance, charred bitter radicchio tastes much better with a young Chianti whose fresh acidity and tannin give it a bit of edge. Drinking a ripe, soft, smooth wine with a bitter food can leave the wine looking isolated and helpless, like a child caught in a fierce political debate.

ACIDITY Acidity might not sound appealing but it's a good thing – a quality that gives wine mouthwatering bite and vim. Acidic food needs acidic wine. If you have a sharp vinaigrette, or a lot of citrus, on the plate, match that acidity with a sharp wine. The reason for this is that we adapt to tastes very quickly, and eating an acidic food has the effect of knocking out the acidity of the wine (at least, as we perceive it). If the wine is gentle to start off with, it will taste flabby and flaccid after a mouthful of lemon juice.

UMAMI The most potent source of umami is soy sauce, which is rich in the flavour-enhancer monosodium glutamate. This meaty, savoury taste is also found in *dashi*, the broth made from kelp and dried bonito flakes that is a building block of many Japanese dishes. Human tasters identify a similarly rich taste in mushrooms (particularly shiitake), yeast, aged Parmesan, anchovies, tomato products and Marmite, though laboratory testing for umami does not always back this up. Sake, of course, made from fermented rice, is what you will find on the table in Japanese restaurants. The oxidative taste of dry sherry, or of vin jaune from the Jura also works well with many of these foods.

FAT With fatty food, pick a wine with either good acidity or good tannin or both, to slice through the fat. An example of this is a young nebbiolo with onions stuffed with a creamy, cheesy mixture. Or a lively young claret with a fatty roast goose.

What to drink with ...
an A to Z

A

ABALONE This prized mollusc, also known as ormer and ear shell, or oreja de mar (in Spain), is held in particular esteem in Asia and everywhere commands very high prices. A member of the genus haliotis (I can't read that word without seeing halitosis), the herbivorous sea snail lives in a shell with a dull surface and a glistening mother-of-pearl lining. Abalone can grow up to 12 inches across and attach themselves to rocks via a single, muscular foot – which is the bit that is edible. The meat is chewy, often described as having a texture that is a cross between squid and conch. In Japan it is eaten raw, as sashimi, and its marine flavours taste good with a gentle, unoaked chardonnay from Chablis or New Zealand. Abalone that is simply cooked and dressed (say, steamed or grilled) takes on a more meaty taste and texture. Light, fresh wines such as sauvignon blanc and lighter chardonnays still work well. If the abalone is dressed with rice wine and soy sauce, then a lighter sake or the more complex flavours of an oaked, maturing chardonnay are better. In Chinese cuisine, abalone is often braised and may be prepared with shiitake, soy sauce, oyster sauce, spring onions and ginger. These dishes are good with sparkling wines that have been made by the classical method, with a secondary fermentation in the bottle: richer champagnes, English sparkling wine and chardonnay, pinot noir and pinot meunier sparkling blends from Australia and New Zealand.

AIOLI This garlicky mayonnaise is often served as a starter with a plate full of crunchy crudités. A dry pale rosé from Provence will happily wash the whole lot down, and complete the picture of a summer evening, but a neutral white wine with firmer acidity might be better if the garlic is fierce. Try needle-sharp aligoté; the clean, Alpine jacquère from the Savoie; or lemony arneis, pecorino or cortese from Italy.

See also garlic.

ALIGOT After holidaying in the Aveyron in the south of France I acquired a serious addiction to this potato purée made with garlic and a lot of Tomme cheese. It is superb with magret de canard and with herby, garlicky sausages and in both cases I wouldn't look much further than wines from nearby. The food is rich and you could go with something that either provides a sharp contrast or that packs a similar punch. Marcillac, made from fer servadou, which tastes of iron, a bit like the blood licked from a cut, is the sappy, cut-across choice. Cahors is the match-heft-with-heft alternative.

ANCHOVIES These salty little brown cured fish appreciate a refreshing wine. If they're on a pizza, a good savoury match would be a light Bardolino, Valpolicella or simple Chianti (all from Italy) or a red made with the Spanish mencía grape (look to the regions of Bierzo and Ribeira Sacra). With anchovies on bits of toast or toast and gentleman's relish as a nibble, then a glass of chilled manzanilla or a sparkling wine with some nerve (English or Loire fizz or cava or Franciacorta or a pinot noir-chardonnay sparkling blend from New Zealand or South Africa) goes well. Another killer aperitif with brown anchovies is the olive martini: ice-cold gin (or vodka) with a briny olive is very good indeed with the rich, flaky pastry and savoury fish of an anchovy twist, which is why you so often find these pastries in sleek hotel bars.

The fleshier white boquerones, drenched in olive oil and eaten as tapas, are good with bright white wines such as verdejo, unoaked white Rioja and young Australian Hunter Valley semillon; salty-iodine manzanilla/fino sherry; gentler albariño; rosé; Provence whites; or that ultimate fish wine, Muscadet.

ANTIPASTI In Italy you can expect to eat the classic cluster of prosciutto, fennel-seed salami, chunks of grainy Parmigiano, tomato-and-basil bruschetta, insalata tricolore, chicken liver crostini, and all the rest, with either a glass of sparkling prosecco, if everyone is feeling festive, or the local wine, whatever that happens to be. Prosecco is light and airy enough to wash down all of these and with people milling around, picking at this and that while they chat, this is a classic case of a mood match being more important than a food match. I like the softness of prosecco, but there is no need to constrain yourself to Italy when excellent casual fizz is also made in New Zealand, Tasmania, the Loire, Limoux, South Africa, Germany, Spain and England. Anything that would be good at a picnic gets my vote.

ARTICHOKES GAME-CHANGER The artichoke is an illusionist among vegetables. It is thought to contain a substance that effectively hacks our taste buds and cons us into thinking that whatever we eat or drink immediately afterwards is sweeter than it actually is. This phenomenon, which has long been familiar to cooks and artichoke-eaters, received scientific attention in 1935 when Albert Blakeslee reported in the journal *Science* that, at a biologists' dinner attended by nearly 250 people, 60 per cent of those who had eaten globe artichokes found that water tasted different afterwards and 'to most, this taste was sweet'.

In 1972, the eminent food psychologist Linda Bartoshuk set out to investigate these taste-modifying properties. In her experiments, she replicated the finding that eating artichokes made water taste sweet and noted that this sweet sensation was unusual in that it didn't arise from having anything in the mouth that was actually sweet, but was an effect apparently caused by temporarily altering the taste receptors on the tongue. Bartoshuk has since speculated that the most plausible explanation for this effect is that a substance found in artichokes (probably cynarin) inhibits the sweet receptors in the mouth. When the taste buds are rinsed by water or another liquid (such as wine), the inhibition is removed, and a message is sent to the brain through the pathways that convey sweet taste, giving rise to a phantom sensation of sugar.

So what to drink with artichokes? It depends how you're eating them. I find the Artichoke Effect is most extreme when you mix artichokes and acid – say, by squeezing lemon juice over them or adding vinaigrette. Try it for yourself by eating a tinned artichoke heart with a bit of lemon juice on it and taking a mouthful of wine afterwards – you get a faint, metallic-sweet taste in your mouth through which it's almost impossible to taste the wine at all. To help counter this, whenever artichokes are part of a dish or salad, whether as raw shavings of hearts or roasted, almost-whole vegetables, look for a white with some astringency and/or acidity. The job is done very well by one of the increasingly fashionable orange wines – white wines that have been left in contact with the skins so that they develop some astringency and a beautiful amber hue. Alternatively, try something Italian and white with a slight hint of bitterness – for instance, vermentino, carricante, vernaccia, ribolla gialla or verdicchio. Manzanilla or fino sherry is another good choice. Reds tend to clash – particularly if they are heavy and oaky. I wouldn't pick a red if artichokes were the main ingredient on the plate, but where red wine fits in best with the other ingredients, you can assuage the artichokes by picking one with a bit of elbow – young and acidic, say Marcillac, Beaujolais or dolcetto or tannic and acidic, like nebbiolo or lagrein.

When artichokes are eaten as a course on their own – boiled and nibbled, leaf by vinaigrette-dipped leaf – I don't serve wine, on the grounds that it's not possible to handle a glass of wine with all that going on. If you do, it had better be something with fierce acidity the better to cope with the vinegar – try aligoté, or a determined, unoaked assyrtiko, or an English white wine (sparkling or still).

PATATAS CON ALCAUCILES
(Potatoes with artichokes)

SERVES 4

3 medium (about 300g) potatoes, peeled
    and sliced ½ cm thick
olive oil
1 large Spanish onion, halved and sliced
4 cloves of garlic, sliced
2 bay leaves
a small bunch of flat-leaf parsley, chopped
2 × 180g cans or jars of artichoke hearts in
    olive oil, drained and thickly sliced
175ml fino
salt and freshly ground black pepper
2 tablespoons breadcrumbs

Drop the potatoes into a pan of boiling salted water and simmer for 3–4 minutes until just tender. Heat the oven to 190°c/Fan 170°c/Gas 5/ 375°F. Heat 3 tablespoons olive oil in a large, wide, ovenproof pan. Add the onions, garlic and bay leaves and cook until the onions are soft and golden, about 10 minutes. Add the parsley, artichoke hearts and the fino and season. Simmer for 5 minutes. Discard the bay leaves before adding the potatoes and turning them around in the pan. Spread everything out evenly, then sprinkle with breadcrumbs and a little more olive oil. Transfer the pan to the oven and bake for 30 minutes until golden.

ASPARAGUS

green Deep green spears of asparagus have an insistent flavour that is well matched by grassy, acidic wines: English bacchus with its taste of hedgerows; Sauvignon de St Bris (the sauvignon blanc from Burgundy); young, razor-sharp, unoaked Bordeaux Blancs; bright young semillon from Australia's Hunter Valley; Austrian grüner veltliner; podded-pea-like sauvignon blancs from Chile; vermentino, arneis or verdicchio from Italy; or herbaceous Loire sauvignon blanc (for specific Loire sauvignon blancs, see the sauvignon blanc entry in 'Wine Portraits').

Green asparagus has such a clear, soaring flavour that just a few discs of it thrown into a plate of pasta or salad will skew the direction of the dish towards these clean white wines.

white Pale cream asparagus doesn't have the chlorophyll edginess of green. It tastes less grassy, more rounded and tender, like white cabbage compared to green. This softer taste goes well with a simple Saumur Blanc from a ripe vintage (especially one that has been in bottle for a year or so to mellow out a bit). The toasty flare of an aged Australian or South African semillon (which sometimes smells a bit like white asparagus, and often smells like salad cream) also goes well. A dry weissburgunder (German pinot blanc) will give the asparagus a bit of punctuation. A just-off-dry German riesling also works very well; pick one from the Nahe, as these rieslings have a taste reminiscent of soft sunshine or backlighting that melds with the soft, alabaster-white fleshiness of the asparagus, or one of the dry but fleshily fruity rieslings made by Joachim Flick in the Rheingau, which have lemony rather than limey acidity, along with a juicy taste of pears and oranges.

AUBERGINE The noble aubergine's finest and foremost features are its plush texture and unctuous richness (at least by the time it's been cooked in lots of oil). These allow it to be drunk with quite weighty wines. Aubergine is a chameleon ingredient, though: it may be cooked with uplifting summer accents that make you want to reach for a fragrant white, or it may be cosied up and made so wintry that only a heavy red will do.

in a dip Aubergine dips are usually eaten as part of a spread of meze and there are wine suggestions in that entry, but a hoppy craft beer like Beavertown Neck Oil will play against the thickly silky, smoky flesh of the blackened aubergine.

with feta and mint If aubergines are being sliced and rolled with feta and mint then, with the chalky cheese in your mouth and the scent of the leaves in your nostrils, a white wine feels fresh as a late spring day. Sauvignon blanc from the cool of the Adelaide Hills is calmer and less attention-seeking than many versions of this grape, a gentle wash of lemon with the herbs. Slightly fuller, more aromatic whites are fun too. Malagousia is a native Greek grape that was virtually extinct until being revived in the late twentieth century. It smells of peaches, prickly pears and jasmine. Greco and fiano, two white grapes found in the vineyards of Campania, also fit the bill; or try an unoaked southern white Italian blend, incorporating fragrant malvasia.

in a salad In a Middle Eastern aubergine salad the squelchy, charred flesh of the star ingredient is combined with fragrant olive oil, tahini, translucent pomegranate seeds, mint or flat-leaf parsley, tomatoes, garlic and lemon juice. As part of a vegetarian meal, I would try this with one of the whites listed directly above. The glorious, burnt, smokiness is also brilliant with a young, barrel-fermented sauvignon blanc or assyrtiko, both of which gleam with the rapier thrust of citrus and, thanks to the oak, have a smoky taste themselves. If the aubergine salad is to accompany grilled lamb or spicy sausages and you prefer to go red, then look for a wine with some pleasingly dirty flavours and a bit of spice. I'm thinking a central Italian sangiovese with a touch of cabernet added to the blend to give it punch; a red from the Dão or Douro in Portugal; a Côtes du Rhône with plenty of syrah in the blend; the baroque syrah that Alain Graillot makes in Morocco; a Lebanese red; or one from Greece or Turkey.

In an Italian salad, the aubergine is more often griddled, and might be put with creamy mozzarella, raw tomatoes, fresh basil and sticky balsamic vinegar. A good match with the sweet-sour of the thick vinegar is Valpolicella Ripasso. If the salad is dressed only with olive oil, you could try one of any number of lighter Italian reds (say, a nero d'avola or simple sangiovese) or a simple Italian white. Moving away from the Italian peninsula, the fragrant breadth of malagousia would be superb here too.

See also aubergine parmigiana, ratatouille.

AUBERGINE PARMIGIANA Flopping out of the dish in great slabs of melted cheese, olive oil, garlicky tomato sauce and soft aubergine, this is comfort food of the highest order. It is great with any of the dusty, earthy wines I affectionately call 'dirty reds' (red blends from the Dão or Douro in Portugal, agiorgitiko from Greece, Lebanese blends, rustic Chianti). Valpolicella from northern Italy is excellent too; a light version cuts through the stodge, while a ripasso, which has been enriched by passing over the skins from an Amarone ferment, has a baroque, cherryish, dusty warmth with a bit of a clip on the finish that is perfect here. Oaked reds from central Italy have plushness but also a mouth-cleansing acidity that makes you ready for the next mouthful – try a Rosso di Montalcino for breadth and spice or a Chianti Classico or a Montepulciano d'Abruzzo. Reds from southern Italy are equally good but perform a different service – warming more than punctuating – try the ripe warmth of primitivo from Puglia, the mineral drive of feral aglianico, or the mulberry swoosh of a nero d'avola from Sicily.

With more modern versions of this dish, like the 'Baked aubergines with tomatoes, tarragon and crème fraîche' in Skye Gyngell's book *A Year in My Kitchen*, in which gooey cheese is replaced with crème fraîche and tinned tomatoes with fresh, it can be nicer not to weigh it down with one of the heavier wines and instead go for a simple Valpolicella or Beaujolais, an unoaked Chianti, or, better still, a Chianti Rufina, which is lighter, edgier and fresher than a Classico. A Douro white would go well too.

AVOCADO Lustrous and green and full of good fat, avocado is surprisingly subtle. If it's the main ingredient in a dish, be careful to pick a wine that doesn't get in the way of its cashmere-soft texture. The smooth curves and luminosity of a warmer-climate chardonnay make a good match. Pinot grigio may not be as fashionable as the avocado right now but it is ideal to drink with it: smooth enough to provide a neutral frame, but with a subtle, lemony wash. In my student days the best meal I could afford to eat out was salad made with frisée lettuce, smoked bacon, avocado, grated Emmental and hot vinaigrette warmed up in the bacony frying pan. We drank it with a Pinot Grigio delle Tre Venezie that made me think of a stream running over stones and lemons. The combination still tastes good. Other simple, pure wines that work well with avocado include picpoul, Muscadet, aligoté, Soave, Lugana or a very young and inexpensive Chablis.

dressed with balsamic vinegar An off-dry riesling from New Zealand is one option: it has a tinge of sweetness and vibrant acidity that reflects and meets those qualities in the vinegar with quite a crackle.

on toast The whites in the general avocado introduction above will work, of course. However, what I really love to drink with avocado on sourdough, sprinkled with chilli flakes and dressed with good olive oil and a squeeze of lemon, is a piercing sauvignon blanc from Marlborough, New Zealand. The wine brings a luminous uplift to each forkful and its hints of nectarine and passion fruit take avocado out of a dimly lit room and back into the sun. My second choice would be a calmer sauvignon blanc from Australia's Adelaide Hills or an exuberant, green capsicum-scented sauvignon blanc from Leyda in Chile.

B

BACALAO Salt cod is eaten throughout Spain and Portugal and served in so many different ways, with so many different sauces, that it is most straightforward to say the best wine to go with it is usually the local one. Does that sound like a cop-out? Then I'll add that if you have a soft spot for bacalao with waxy yellow boiled potatoes, Vinho Verde and verdejo are both good.

Or Maria José Sevilla has another option. The cook, writer, broadcaster and wine expert is a bountiful fount of information on Spanish food and drink, with a laser-like instinct for finding the best restaurants in any town – I have never eaten badly in her company. She says: 'One drink is better than anything with bacalao. And that is cider. In the Basque country, after they press the apples but before they bottle the cider, in December, they taste it, and there are three dishes that are always cooked by the cider houses where Basques go to eat and taste. First, bacalao fritto – salt cod just fried in a bit of flour and egg. Second, tortilla, which is made by making a soffritto of chopped onions with little bits of red pepper and then breaking pieces of salt cod into crumbs and stirring them into it and using that mixture in the tortilla. I make this at home using fresh cod, because you can get such good cod in London. I salt it for just two or three hours beforehand; then it gets that magic that bacalao has when it's salted, but it's more delicate. And thirdly, pil-pil sauce, made with cod and garlic and olive oil, where the gelatin in the fish creates an emulsion with the oil in the pan. All of these are good with cider.'

BAGNA CAUDA Bright young dolcetto is delicious with this pungent garlic and anchovy dip from northern Italy. Gavi and arneis – two white wines from the same area – are good, refreshing alternatives.

BAKED BEANS Beans on toast and a quick glass of wine is up there on the 'too exhausted to cook but in need of a break' list of dinners. Baked beans are so sweet and so processed that it can be best if the wine is too. Just go for a cheapo supermarket red, which is likely to have a smidge of sugar in it. Otherwise open something fantastic and treat yourself. But drink it before and after the beans on toast, not while you eat.

BANITSA A Bulgarian dish made by layering a mixture of eggs whisked with spinach and feta cheese between sheets of filo pastry and baking until risen and golden. I love eating this with simple, lemony white wines such as Soave or Gavi or pecorino, which cut across the fat, but it also works with heavier, oaked Bordeaux Blanc or assyrtiko. Rustic reds from Bergerac (for something heavier); from Marcillac or Beaujolais (for something light-bodied); or from Greece, Turkey or Bulgaria itself turn it into a more picnicky and casual meal. And I can testify that banitsa, which goes quite solid when it cools and sets, is very good food for a picnic or eating in the car on a long drive back from Cornwall.

BARBECUES At big barbecues where all kinds of meat, vegetables and fish will be thrown on to the coals, and there's a long table covered in bowls full of colourful salads, wine essentially needs to behave like a good guest: to have something to say for itself, to rub along well with everyone.

Barbecued food is usually strongly flavoured: smoky from the fire, pungent from the spices and rubs. And it's not just the food that is smoky. If you're standing around waving bellows and tongs, you'll have smoke in your eyebrows and the smell of burning charcoal up your nose. It's not like sitting in the cool of an immaculate restaurant eating food that someone else cooked out the back. It's like standing at a sweaty, shouty rock concert and being handed a hip flask. If what's in the flask is subtle, you won't even notice it under such sensory onslaught. To meet the heat and olfactory noise of a barbecue, go for bold reds from Chile, Argentina, California, Australia, Portugal or South Africa. Or play it the other way and pick a contrast: a refreshing light red, such as Beaujolais, marzemino or a cabernet franc from the Loire, maybe serving it slightly chilled to counteract the brawn of the food.

My go-to barbie red is the Mullineux Kloof Street Rouge from Swartland, South Africa – a loosely knit, open-hearted, liquoricey blend of syrah, carignan, mourvèdre and cinsault. It's not a total party monster, but it doesn't arrive wearing a lounge suit either.

Rosé is always a good barbecue swiller too. If the barbecue flavours are very robust, I like to go for a deeper-coloured rosé; if they are hot, perhaps a raspberry-coloured rosé that is not perfectly dry. This is a book about wine but, of course, it's not just wine that's good at barbecues. For instance, cider is great with juicy pork burgers; a golden ale such as Harviestoun Bitter & Twisted is beautiful with lemon-charred prawns; and a happy jug of sangria will tie the whole thing together.

Marc Kent of Boekenhoutskloof in South Africa, a country where they are rightly proud of their barbecues – or rather, braais – gave me the following recipe for a fiery barbecue sauce. He adapted it from a spicy sauce he first tasted in a rib shack in Anguilla. It can be used as a marinade for chicken wings, ribs or steak, or served as an accompaniment to barbecued meat. It is hot and it is full on and Marc recommends eating it with his Chocolate Block wine – a full on, sock it to 'em bottle of red made in the Cape from grenache, cinsault and syrah, whose tannins will aggravate the chilli in this sauce, which is why Marc likes the two together.

MARC KENT'S SPICY SMOKED BBQ SAUCE

MAKES 1.5 LITRES

20 medium tomatoes (preferably Roma)
2 onions, peeled
fresh chillies, to taste
8 tablespoons olive oil
250ml tomato ketchup
250ml tomato purée
375ml cider vinegar
4 tablespoons aged dark rum or brandy
125ml orange juice
4 tablespoons mild molasses
100g light brown sugar
2 tablespoons smoked Spanish paprika
4 teaspoons freshly ground black pepper,
    or to taste (*ingredients continue overleaf*)

8 large cloves of garlic, peeled and crushed
ground chilli (optional)
salt

Cut the tomatoes in half and scoop out the seeds. Place the tomatoes, cut side up, in a smoker on the opposite side to the heat source. Put the onions and chillies in with them and smoke until tender. Remove from the smoker. Peel the chillies and the tomatoes, saving as much juice as you can. Roughly chop the tomatoes, onions and chillies. Put the oil in a large cast-iron pan and heat until smoking. Add the tomatoes, onions and chillies and all the other ingredients and bring to a gentle simmer. Simmer for 2 hours, stirring occasionally, until the sauce has thickened. Allow to cool, then transfer to a blender and liquidize (you may have to do this in batches) until smooth. Season to taste, adding ground chilli if you want it hotter.

See also beef: barbecue sauce, burgers, chilli, five-spice, sausages.

BEEF Real traditionalists drink cabernet with lamb and pinot noir with beef, but bordeaux (and other cabernet-merlot blends) is also a favourite with Sunday roasts and chargrilled steaks – as are nebbiolo, Tuscan reds, Napa cabernets, Aussie syrahs, malbecs from Argentina ... I could go on. In truth it's hard to go wrong when it comes to beef and a bottle of red, but some wines do seem more delicious with some plates of meat than others. The cuisson and the cut both have an impact on the type of wine I like to pick. Beef that is well-done tends to be enhanced by juicy, young wines and richer, riper reds from sunny climates that act as a flavour-boosting sauce for the drier meat. At the other end of the spectrum, the squidgy flesh of rare beef is good with more tannic and also with older wines. So with a well-cooked rump steak I might choose a soft, warm-climate cabernet-merlot to help bring some succulence to the meat, but with a rare sirloin perhaps a prickly young claret or maturing Chianti Classico. I'd put Barossa Shiraz with either.

As far as the cut goes, the fattier the meat the more it suits wines with good acidity and tannin that refresh the mouth in between forkfuls of food. But here are a few more specific ideas.

Cuts and cooking styles

bresaola I often put this salty, air-dried beef with a juicy Italian red such as dolcetto or Lambrusco, but its intense beefiness also goes well with the leather-and-red-berries taste of South African pinot noir. Then again, when it is served on an antipasti plate with rocket and mozzarella it tastes good with white sparkling Franciacorta, and if it's made into a salad with spinach or rocket and goat's curd, then I'd pick an oaked sauvignon blanc with the weight to meet the beef and the lithe fruitiness and acidity to suit the cheese.

carpaccio If there's lemon juice squeezed over the meat, pick a red with good savour, tannin and acidity – a softer red will taste oddly sweet and lacklustre. Italian reds usually have good bite that works well with lemon juice. Young claret is good too.

chargrilled steak Amplify the smoky-sweet vibe of those caramelized black stripes by pouring a red that tastes of smoky oak.

cold roast beef Leftover beef tastes drier and more solid than it did half an hour after it came out of the oven, so I like to choose a more juicy wine to liven it up. Dolcetto is a favourite with cold roast beef with salads. Pinkish-crimson slices of cold roast topside eaten outside on a hot summer's day are very good washed down with a gorgeously ample, red-berry-scented garnacha from Campo de Borja in Spain; I love the generosity of the garnacha with the tender, cold meat, and this is a brilliant summer wedding combo too. With a dinner of cold roast beef and hot home-made chips, I often open a cosy Aussie cab-shiraz or a Côtes de Bordeaux, Castillon.

daubes, stews and casseroles Long, slow-cooked beef in a rich gravy sauce is one of the most 'friendly to red wines' dinners in existence. Choose any red you like, or look to marry the wine with the other ingredients in the casserole. I often slow-cook beef with thyme and anchovies, and love to eat it with fragrant Mediterranean red blends, such as Minervois, St Chinian, or wines from Corsica. One of my favourite ever dinners was a beef casserole eaten on a cold November night in a Cotswolds gastropub, with a bottle of Côtes du Roussillon that smelt of old leather, bonfires, autumn leaves and dried herbs.

See also boeuf bourguignon and boeuf à la gardiane.

fillet The tender softness of a fillet of beef is beautiful with pinot noir. Pick a luscious pinot from the Mornington Peninsula or Sonoma to boost the juicy sweetness of a medium-cooked fillet, or a youthful red burgundy to add a slight prickle to one that is crimson in the middle. However it is cooked, fillet of beef also goes well with plush, velvety reds, such as those from Pomerol in Bordeaux, Bolgheri in Italy or Priorat in Spain. Fillet cooked with rosemary or bay leaves or served with redcurrant jelly suits one of the more floral, silky, blueberry-and-violet-scented malbecs from Argentina. This cut is also good with cinsault, and with Loire cabernet franc (Chinon, or Bourgueil or St Nicolas de Bourgueil) from a warm year, particularly if green spring vegetables are an accompaniment.

rib, rib-eye and tomahawk With the feral, earthy, bony flavours of a plainly cooked aged rib of beef; a rib-eye steak; or a tomahawk (a rib-eye steak with the full bone attached), I like an older wine that also has vestigial tastes of blood, soil, decay, tobacco, old leaves or mushrooms. Maturing bordeaux (all kinds of it) comes into its own here. Leathery Madiran, brooding Cahors, top-notch Chianti, Brunello di Montalcino, Barolo and mature northern Rhône reds or earthy syrah from elsewhere are excellent too, as are the malbecs made in Argentina by the likes of Mendel and Achaval Ferrer, which speak more of cedar and smoke than of luscious, bright fruit. If the rib of beef is to be served with sweet roasted root vegetables, or if the meat has less of a feral taste, then a good Rioja or Ribera del Duero will also make a fine accompaniment.

sirloin Sirloin accommodates more or less any red wine you throw at it. Personally, though, I favour wines with savoury notes. Sirloin steak usually has a thick ribbon of yellow fat that flavours the meat and cabernet-merlot blends and also sangiovese go well with this taste.

steak tartare The first time I ordered steak tartare I had no idea what I was doing. After the little patty of raw meat arrived at the table with all its condiments and a raw egg yolk, I politely sat and waited for the chef to come and cook it for me. It was about fifteen minutes before I nervously began to eat it, all the while expecting to be hounded out of the restaurant as a savage. With its capers, shallots, spices, and completely uncooked meat, steak tartare is the beef dish most suited to the firm edges of a claret from the

Médoc, ideally one at Cru Bourgeois level. I once had a brilliant steak tartare at the elegant Le Colombier in London, washed down with my share of a bottle of Château Poujeaux. Young, unoaked or barely oaked nebbiolo is another good option.

tagliata Steak (usually either rib-eye or sirloin) that is served the Italian way – chargrilled, sliced, and mixed into a plateful of rocket and Parmesan, dressed with olive oil and lemon juice – needs wine with good acidity and tannin. First choice is a robust red from central Italy – Chianti, Brunello, Sagrantino di Montefalco. Second choice is a red from elsewhere in Italy.

topside (roast) Topside is the cut most commonly used for roast dinners and for me the colour of the meat, the temperature at which it's being eaten and the rest of the dinner play the biggest part in picking the wine.

See also cold roast beef.

B

Accompaniments, rubs and seasonings

barbecue sauce The sticky sweetness of barbecue sauce, often used as a marinade for beef ribs, needs a loose, fruity wine such as Californian zinfandel or Chilean merlot.

béarnaise The tarragon flavour in béarnaise can be quite strong. It works just fine with cool-climate cabernet blends and is brilliant with the herbal scent of maturing wines from the southern Rhône – Vacqueyras, Sablet, Gigondas, Châteauneuf-du-Pape and so on.

black peppercorn crust Steak cooked with a black peppercorn crust has a beautiful spicy aroma that is reminiscent of violets. Please try this with a bottle of syrah, a grape that can also have a hauntingly floral, black-peppery scent. This profile is (famously) most often found on syrah from and around the Rhône, but I have also found it on syrah from Argentina, Australia, Chile and elsewhere.

celeriac purée The green notes of celeriac taste better with savoury rather than sweetly rich reds – Chianti rather than zinfandel; claret rather than Chilean cabernet sauvignon.

coriander, teriyaki, chilli and garlic rub This is a favourite marinade for either sirloin or a big rib of beef. I make it by mixing equal quantities of teriyaki sauce with Kikkoman less-salt soy sauce, a dash of sesame oil, finely chopped garlic and ginger root, and plenty of roughly chopped fresh coriander, and serve it with either a robust pinot noir from Australia, New Zealand, South Africa, the US or Chile, or with a cool-climate Australian shiraz.

green peppercorns With fiery peppercorns I avoid softer, richer, sweetly ripe reds and look for those with good tannin and acidity – wines from Bordeaux and Tuscany are usually good. With a creamy green peppercorn sauce, there's more latitude, and you can go for herbal reds such as those from the Rhône.

horseradish Fiery accompaniments like horseradish steer me towards cooler-climate red wines, such as cabernet-based bordeaux or rustic Buzet or Bergerac.

mustard Mustard reduces the impact of tannin in a wine, so you can get away with a harsher, greener red – for instance, a tannic, green bordeaux tastes much fleshier and fruitier when you drink it with mustard.

See also barbecues, beef Wellington, boeuf bourguignon, boeuf à la gardiane, burgers, chilli con carne, Chinese, cottage (or shepherd's) pie, meatballs, mustard, ragù alla bolognese, Thai beef salad.

BEEF WELLINGTON The classic accompaniment is pinot noir, a grape that goes well with both the beef and the mushrooms inside the pastry case. Pick a pinot noir that is savoury rather than sweet. I often see this dish served with St Emilion, perhaps partly because 'beef Wellington' and 'St Emilion' are phrases that have immense celebratory menu appeal – you can just feel Christmas and festivities around the corner. The two do go well together. The slightly fruit-cakey right-bank bordeaux has a richness that marries well with the rich food.

BEETROOT Beetroot's earthy taste is good with earthy versions of pinot noir and it can also go well with those dusty styles of cabernet sauvignon that make you think of the brown husk at the tip of a blackcurrant. There aren't many meals so big on beetroot that you'd be looking to find a wine that went with it, though, as the other ingredients tend to take over. For instance, one popular beetroot dish is beetroot and goat's curd salad, but I'd usually open a sauvignon blanc or a breezy white from the Savoie in France to placate the insistent goat's curd. One plate of food that does very definitely taste of beetroot is beetroot risotto, like the one that Vanya Cullen of Cullen Wines in Margaret River, Australia, makes to eat with her very good biodynamic cabernet sauvignon.

BEETROOT RISOTTO

SERVES 4

The amount of stock you need will depend
    on the rice you use, so you may need
    a little less or a little more.
400g beetroot
olive oil
1.25 litres vegetable or chicken stock
butter
1 large onion, finely chopped
4 anchovy fillets in olive oil, drained and
    chopped (it's fine to omit these)
175g Arborio or Carnaroli rice
a small glass of red or white wine
10 black olives, quartered
2 tablespoons chopped chives
1 handful of flat-leaf parsley, chopped
1 handful of sage leaves
salt

Preheat the oven to 200°C/Fan 180°C/Gas 6/400°F. Peel the beetroot and cut into 1cm dice. Put half on a non-stick roasting tray, drizzle with a little olive oil and season, then roast until tender, about 20–30 minutes. Put the rest of the beetroot in a pan with the stock, bring to a simmer and cook until just tender, then scoop out with a slotted spoon. Leave the stock on a low simmer. Heat a tablespoon of olive oil and a knob of butter in a wide, shallow sauté pan. Add the onion and cook until soft and translucent, then add the anchovies and cook for another couple of minutes. Add the rice and cook for 3 minutes, stirring until it is coated in the buttery mix. Tip in the wine and bubble away until it has almost gone. Add the simmering stock a couple of large ladlefuls at a time. Keep stirring now and again until the liquid is absorbed, then add more stock. When the rice is almost tender stir in the boiled and roasted beetroots. To finish the risotto stir in the olives, chives and parsley, a splash of stock or water, and another knob of butter and season. Put on a lid and leave for 5 minutes. Heat another knob of butter in a small frying pan until foaming. Add the sage leaves and fry until crisp. Serve the risotto in warm bowls topped with the sage leaves.

BEURRE BLANC I never like to let friends see how much butter has gone into this classic French sauce, which has just four ingredients: shallots, vinegar, white wine and a *lot* of butter. In her *Garden Cookbook* Sarah Raven uses it over egg tagliatelle with a purée of broad beans mixed with tiny, peeled broad beans, the colour of new leaves. I always eat this with Sardinian vermentino because I love the gentle, green flavours in the wine with the rich sauce and the tender beans, but another vermentino would do just as well. When beurre blanc is served with fish, try Chablis; grüner veltliner; Limoux or new-wave Australian chardonnay; sauvignon-semillon from Australia's Margaret River, or a white bordeaux from France. Failing that, find a good version of the consummate fish wine, a Muscadet sur lie, to bring out the more saline, oceanic qualities in the fish.

BLINIS Buckwheat pancakes with fishy toppings and crème fraîche go down best with ice-cold vodka, knocked back in a shiver of shots. If wine is called for, look for a knife-sharp white, such as aligoté, or a lean, lemony white from Greece, or try Muscadet, a white that likes fish and smells of a cold grey sea. The sur lie versions, matured on their lees, have more texture and a yeasty flavour that works well here.

BOEUF BOURGUIGNON Don't get into a stew about what to drink with boeuf bourguignon. As its name suggests, this beef casserole is traditionally made and served with red burgundy, but in practice any country-style French red will do the trick, from Fitou or Corbières to a basic claret or Bergerac to a Costières de Nîmes or Côtes du Rhône.

BOEUF À LA GARDIANE This slow-cooked beef, red wine and black olive casserole is from the Gard département of France, which takes in the towns of Nîmes and Uzès, as well as the magnificent Pont du Gard Roman aqueduct. It is not only a delicious dish but also a brilliant backdrop to all kinds of French red wine. When I have to do a tasting of different reds from Bordeaux, the Languedoc, Provence, the Rhône or south-west France, I routinely make Elizabeth David's version from *French Provincial Cooking* to eat with whichever bottle I decide to drink for dinner at the end of it.

I cooked boeuf à la gardiane for a wine merchant, Tom Ashworth, one evening, because he had promised to bring a mystery bottle of wine and I knew that this magical dish would see the wine right. Tom told me that his stepfather, Robin Yapp, the founder of Yapp Brothers, which specializes in wines from the south of France, makes the exact same dinner when cooking for friends, and for the same reasons. The stew has a salty herbiness that plays into the wilder nature of those reds that taste of the tinder-dry thyme and olive leaves of the garrigue; sits well with the dark nature of northern Rhône syrah; and allows the emotive fire of a Châteauneuf-du-Pape to flare. And it's kind to the more architectural, structured wines of Bordeaux, which taste calm and intelligent beside it.

BOLOGNESE see *ragù alla bolognese*.

BONE MARROW 'I wanted to live deep and suck out all the marrow of life,' wrote Henry Thoreau. Eating bone marrow is an atavistic activity. There is a flavour that stirs something deep within. Eating it with wine that has the vibe of mall music, or a boyband hit, is a horrible thing to do. Open rosé if you want, but make it a rosé from Provence – these wines are more thoughtful than frivolous, even when they are easy to drink. I don't mind white wine either if it's simple and saline, or one of those French country wines that are impossible to describe. But the best wines with bone marrow are reds that taste of the earth and the land, that have a savour or a feel of the farmyard, that taste as if they were made by hand rather than on gleaming production lines. You might find this in the Côtes du Roussillon, in Bordeaux, Chianti, Montalcino, St Chinian or the Douro, among other places.

BOQUERONES see *anchovies*.

BOTTARGA The Mediterranean delicacy of salted, pressed and sun-baked roe of the tuna or grey mullet is great with whites such as falanghina, greco di tufo or fiano, which bring out its fruitiness. Ribolla gialla, Verdicchio di Matelica or vermentino will emphasize its marine salinity. These are all Italian wines, but if you want something a bit different go for a fiano made by one of the more experimental Australian producers (Coriole and Fox Gordon both do one). This grape smells of pine nuts, orange blossom and basil and in Australian hands it becomes more rounded and generous, adding an extra swish and a more contemporary feel to the dish.

BOUILLABAISSE This Mediterranean fish stew, a speciality of Marseilles, works well with limpid rosé from Provence; a deeper-coloured and more robust rosé from the Languedoc; or the soft curves of a Rioja Rosado. Spanish verdejo or Portuguese Vinho Verde are thirst-slaking white options. For a wine that gently meets some of the complexities of the seafood broth, try a glass of local Cassis – not a blackcurrant liqueur but a white wine made from marsanne, clairette, ugni blanc and sauvignon blanc. Wines from the AOP Cassis can taste delicate and drily herbaceous at first, but they have concealed might and staying power. Along similar lines, the garlic, saffron and tomatoes in the stew work well with white blends from the Rhône, also made with marsanne and roussanne; and sometimes also with floral viogniers, which taste of almond kernels and hay and waxy white flowers. The nutty, sourdough scent of a dry sherry, or a vin jaune from the Jura, riffs along nicely with the rich seafood broth too. With all those confident flavours, bouillabaisse is forceful enough to survive a red wine such as a young, inexpensive Bandol (don't go for too good a name as the robustness of the young wine will then overpower the food). Tomato-based fish stews also work well with cheaper, rustic reds, such as those from the Dão or the Douro in Portugal, or even a simple Chianti.

BOXING DAY LEFTOVERS, AKA THE GREAT TURKEY BUFFET Now is the moment to pull out the aromatic pinot gris that goes so well with turkey and trimmings, but that you didn't feel like drinking on Christmas Day itself. Suddenly, the day after the excess, a gently perfumed, chilled white, perhaps off-dry (yes – sugar is always a welcome hangover aid), is much more appealing.

'Pinot gris is definitely Boxing Day wine,' says Tim Adams, who makes wine in Clare Valley, Australia. 'On Christmas Day we drink magnums of The Fergus – our grenache, tempranillo, shiraz, mourvèdre blend – and on Boxing Day we open pinot gris.'

Of course, if you've got Christmas dinner wines as well as food to spare they will taste great all over again. Otherwise, bright, young, refreshing reds are good with the firmer consistency of cold meat – think cheap young claret, dolcetto or Beaujolais Villages. In our family, with Christmas Day turkey sandwiches and Boxing Day leftovers, we like to drink white wines from the Rhône (Côtes du Rhône or white Châteauneuf). These are wintry whites with a hint of warmth, and a subtle taste of ripe pears, white peaches, sushi ginger and heavy blossom, that have a celebratory feel and go well with all the pork products (spicy sausageballs, sausagemeat and chestnut stuffing, chipolatas wrapped in bacon) that we have on our plates alongside the turkey and creamy, clove-scented bread sauce. Failing all those, pull out the prosecco. Its gentle bubbles and slight sweetness are a real perk-up.

See also turkey sandwiches.

BRAAI see *barbecues.*

BRILL If it is simply grilled or fried and plated up with lemon, then chardonnay will do the trick. Brill is often served with a red wine sauce (and sometimes also roasted root vegetables) or with lentils and in this case a good accompaniment is a red wine such as Bierzo from Spain.

BROAD BEANS Pale yet also intensely verdant, double-podded broad beans are one of life's great luxuries. The time invested in the second peeling is considerable but worth it. As with peas, wines that work well are those that taste green (of leaves, herbs and grass) and of cool citrus and that remind you of spring. With a broad bean and pea risotto, good options are sauvignon blanc – from the Loire, the Awatere Valley in Marlborough or Leyda in Chile; the scything edge of an Awatere riesling; verdejo from Spain; grüner veltliner from Austria; vermentino, verdicchio, cortese (used to make Gavi) or pecorino from Italy. These wines also go well with crostini piled with mashed broad beans mixed with gratings of Pecorino cheese and mint and olive oil (though I suspect you've probably got the prosecco out for that – good choice).

When eating broad beans with creamy cheeses like ricotta, I lean more towards slightly creamier wines: for instance, a Lugana from north-east Italy or a super-Soave. With the recipe below, a taut, lean, brightly lemony contemporary Australian chardonnay is also good and will illuminate the freshness of the spring vegetables. If you choose a wine that's oaked or, when you open it, marked by the struck-match characteristic known as reduction often found in these wines, then that will also underscore the toasty tang of the sourdough.

B

BROAD BEAN, PEA SHOOT, ASPARAGUS AND RICOTTA BOWL

SERVES 2

225g frozen broad beans
about 10 spears of asparagus
4 handfuls pea shoots
125g fresh garden peas
2 sprigs of mint, leaves removed from stems
4 generous tablespoons fresh ricotta
grated zest of half a lemon
2 tablespoons good olive oil
4 slices sourdough toast
salt

Put the broad beans into a heatproof jug or bowl, cover with boiling water, leave for a minute, then drain. Slip the beans out of their skins and put to one side. Trim the hard base of the asparagus stalks and then cook on a hot griddle pan, turning occasionally, until slightly charred but still crunchy. Arrange the pea shoots, raw peas, broad beans, asparagus and mint leaves in two bowls with a couple of spoonfuls of ricotta on the side of each. Mix the lemon zest and olive oil and drizzle over the top. Serve with a couple of slices of sourdough toast per bowl, drizzled with olive oil and salt to taste.

Broad beans also go with red wines that taste of spring, such as young, unoaked cabernet franc from the Loire or a sappy light gamay, perhaps from Touraine, where an edge of earth kicks in with the green.

BUBBLE AND SQUEAK My friend, wine hurricane Joe Wadsack, always says that leftovers taste better if you eat them with the person who shared the original dinner. I feel the same way about the wine that might go with this fry-up of mashed potato, leftover sprouts, cabbage and bacon. It should just be something that's knocking around in your kitchen.

BURGERS (BEEF) Arguably the ultimate food for red wine, the (beef) burger makes nearly every type look good. Especially if it is home-made with decent, 20 per cent fat, butcher's mince (except for salt and pepper, I don't put anything else in my burgers). And even more especially if it is cooked rare, then its soft, pink middle will snuggle down with whatever delicious bottle you feel like opening, be it a roasted-fruit-scented Central Otago pinot noir, a slightly wild Sicilian nero d'avola, a lightweight Beaujolais or a chunky South African cabernet. If anything provides more of a steer on what you might want to be drinking, it's the garnishes, sauces and side salads.

Melted cheese and fruity ketchup can still handle more or less any red. As soon as you add smoky barbecue sauce, the heat of chilli, blue cheese, punchy gherkins or crunchy slaw made with chipotle mayonnaise, you'll need a red that can match the intensity of these rich flavours. Bigger, fruitier, riper reds that fit the bill include carmenère-cabernet sauvignon-merlot from Chile (I absolutely love Casa Silva's version with home-made burgers); sun-baked reds from Puglia, Italy's heel (for instance, Salice Salentino); and malbec from Argentina. Relaxed American zinfandel, with its high alcohol and smell of raspberries, brambles, cough mixture and dust, is particularly good with chipotle and barbecue sauces, as is carmenère, which has quite a rugged texture. And if you're intending to blacken the meat on a barbecue and use very intense, shouty sauces, then pinotage from South Africa is probably the loudest wine of all.

BURRATA Indulgently soft burrata is a cheese made from mozzarella and cream. It's good with wines that enhance its luxurious texture. Top-end Soaves (or wines from Anselmi, which opted out of the Soave classification) have a savoury custard and nutty-pear taste that adds a touch of gilded grandeur to the plate. An always-discreet Lugana, also from north-east Italy, slips in quietly alongside it. Deep-coloured, just-off-dry rosé will meld beautifully with the burrata and amplify its pillowy texture. At a 'Wine Wars' dinner at Arbutus restaurant in Soho that kicked off with a burrata and compressed watermelon starter, Wine Car Boot founder Ruth Spivey poured a glossy, watermelon-pink Monferrato Chiaretto from Villa Sparina, made from dolcetto and barbera, to go with it. It was a huge hit.

B

BUTTER Even I would not eat just a slab of butter for dinner, though if you've ever seen how much I put on toast you may argue that I come close. Still, buttery (and creamy) sauces have a richness that leads you away from poky-elbowed, shrill wines like sauvignon blanc or verdejo and towards a more curvaceous chardonnay (oaked or unoaked), marsanne, roussanne or oaked chenin blanc. For instance, sole meunière (cooked in a brown butter sauce) is much better with a white burgundy than with a fresh Loire sauvignon blanc.

An exception is beurre blanc, the classic French sauce made by reducing vinegar with chopped shallots and stirring in huge quantities of melted butter, because the acidity of the vinegar counters some of the richness. The acid in the vinegar needs to be taken care of, so you can still do chardonnay – it needs to be a vibrant one, such as a new-wave Australian chardonnay (low in alcohol, bright with acidity, yet still with curves) – but fresher wines often work better.

See also beurre blanc.

C

CAJUN Cajun food is a very broad term that covers a whole spectrum of dishes but, as a general rule, its warmth, in which bell peppers, onions, celery, shrimp and pork mingle with the red heat of Tabasco, doesn't work at all well with cool northern European reds. It prefers the more laid-back, throaty flavours of American zinfandel, primitivo from Italy's heel, Chilean carmenère-cabernet, bonarda from Argentina, the Rhône Ranger wines (red or white) from California, or a Rioja with lots of American oak and ideally a graciano component. Fried shrimp and crab do go well with albariño, though, and spicy fish and white meat can, as ever, work well with off-dry riesling. Beer is also a good bet.

CAKE A slice of cake really belongs with a good cup of tea or coffee, in my view. But there are a few occasions on which you might want to drink wine with cake, and also a few glorious cake and wine couplings, most of them involving sweet fortified wine. So here is a quick guide.

birthday cake If you are drinking wine and eating cake on a birthday, then you probably have fizz in your glass. The sweeter the better, as dry wine tastes odd after sugar, so prosecco over cava and a sweeter champagne (ideally a demi-sec) over a zero dosage.

chocolate cake A very simple chocolate cake (no icing, no cream) or brownie is lightened by the refreshing neroli scent of a Muscat de Beaumes de Venise. For ideas of what to drink with richer chocolate gateaux and dessert-like tortes, see *chocolate*.

Christmas cake Sweet oloroso sherry has a rich, raisin and roasted nut taste that combines well with dense fruitcake. For celebratory occasions, try a demi-sec champagne.

fruitcake Fruitcake of all kinds, not just the rich Christmas version, is good with sweeter sherries. Cakes that are more cake than fruit are also lovely with a glass of Madeira.

Madeira cake Plain Madeira cake, made with butter and baked so that the top erupts and crusts over, is good with tawny port, sweet sherries, Marsala and with bual or malmsey Madeira. The simple flavours of the cake act as a canvas for the richer, dried fruit and nut echoes in the glass.

seed cake The St John chef Fergus Henderson introduced the excellent habit of drinking a glass of old Madeira (the proper stuff, not the cheapo supermarket cooking wine) with seed cake at elevenses.

wedding cake All the same suggestions apply as for *birthday cake* and *Christmas cake* above.

See also tarte tatin.

CALAMARES FRITOS see *fritto misto*.

CAMEMBERT This cheese makes red wine taste terrible. Or 'oh-fule', as one Frenchman once put it to me. As in, 'The French tradition of baguette Camembert with red wine is oh-fule.' I'm actually quite happy if there's a big mouthful of crusty baguette in between a tumbler of rustic red, me and the Camembert, but it's not much fun eating a polite little cheese plate of Camembert while drinking red wine. The two seem to curdle in the mouth. A low-acid wine such as a rosé from Provence is a happier option. A creamy chardonnay also works.

CANNELLONI For beef cannelloni try the same wines as those that work with lasagne or ragù alla bolognese. Ricotta and spinach cannelloni baked in a tomato sauce is also rich and will work with all the same reds as well as being good with fiano or pinot grigio.

CAPERS The salty, vinegary pinch of a pickled caper will floor any wine that does not meet it with confident acidity. Oaked, high-alcohol chardonnay, for instance, tastes fat and flabby and uncomfortable if you encounter it straight after a mouthful of capers. As a quick rule of thumb, you can usually rely on Italy to provide wines with good acidity, both red and white.

CAPSICUM see *red pepper*.

CARBONARA Eggy pasta (spaghetti or penne, ideally) with garlicky bacon bits and black pepper is one of the great dishes of Lazio. A relatively neutral white is cleansing against the deep yellow egg yolks and cheese. The local option would be Frascati. A Soave, or a pinot grigio from Italy or Hungary fulfils the same role. The sharp little bubbles of a sparkling wine are also refreshing in between cheesy, eggy mouthfuls. I would go for something like a Graham Beck from South Africa, or for a dry red Lambrusco, which isn't a conventional match by any stretch but hits a mood.

CASSOULET This one-pot Gascon dish incorporating haricots blancs, pork, duck or goose confit, Toulouse sausages, lamb and goose fat is French slow-cooking at its best. The local wine options offer a paradigm for food and wine matching guidelines. Want to pick a wine that refreshes and rinses your mouth in between forkfuls? Try a young Gaillac Rouge or a Marcillac, a light-bodied, acidic red made in the Aveyron from fer servadou, which tastes of blood and iron. Prefer a wine that matches the heft and mass of the plate of food? How about a Cahors, young or old, made from malbec, once so dense and dark the wines were known as 'the black wines of Cahors'? Doug Wregg, a buyer at the wine importer Les Caves de Pyrène, is particularly eloquent on this match. In the company's wine list, he writes: 'Eating cassoulet without a glass of wine is like trying to carve your way through the Amazonian jungle with a pair of blunt nail clippers. We should accept that some combinations are meant to be. Cahors is renowned for its medicinal, iodine flavour; it expresses notes of tea, fennel, dried herbs and figs; it has a pleasant astringency and a lingering acidity. Cassoulet is crusty, oozy and gluey, beans bound by fat. The food requires a wine of certain roughness and ready digestibility. Sweet, jammy oaky reds and powerful spicy wines lack the necessary linear quality.'

I also like drinking natural wines with this slow food: as a group, they have an atmosphere and gentle, steady rustic sensibility that work very well here. A syrah or gamay from the grower Hervé Souhaut would be just about perfect. Or a Morgon – Beaujolais's meatiest cru – from Julien Sunier, Domaine M. Lapierre or Jean Foillard.

CAULIFLOWER CHEESE There are two ways to go with cauliflower cheese. For maximum snugness, and to emphasize the cosy-blanket aspect to this nursery food, pick a chardonnay whose creamy texture will meld into the cheesy white sauce. It doesn't matter whether the chardonnay is Australian, Chilean, or an inexpensive white burgundy. Go for your comfort chardonnay, and if you don't have one get one. Mine is Domaine Mallory et Benjamin Talmard Mâcon-Villages. For an (arguably) more sophisticated combination that feels like wrapping up in a puffa jacket and woolly bobble hat (that bit's the cauliflower cheese) and going out into the cold snow (that bit's the wine), pick a light red wine with a bit of cut and serve it chilled. Suitable reds here include trousseau or ploussard from the Jura in France; an inexpensive Bourgogne Rouge; gamay; Marcillac; Bardolino; a very light Valpolicella; and Fronsac, that lightest and greenest of wines from Bordeaux.

C

CAVIAR Vodka, poured ice cold from the deep freeze, is the classic accompaniment to caviar and it does matter what sort. A friend once complained about being given vodka that 'cut my mouth to ribbons'. Was he maybe being a bit hysterical? Well, we are talking about a food that is classically served on special mother-of-pearl spoons, so I think we can also be pernickety about the vodka. It must be wheat vodka, which has a creamy, broad, gentle texture and does not interrupt the sensation of silky little balls moving smoothly across your tongue until they burst in an explosion of salt and sea spray. Rye vodka (Polish vodka is typically made with rye) has a sharper, needling texture. It might not *quite* cut your mouth to ribbons, but it does spoil the luxurious flow. Very good champagne with a high pinot noir/meunier content (for instance, Bollinger) is the celebratory alternative.

CELERIAC Even when it's only a vegetable with a main, or in a salad, the green flavours of celeriac steer my choice away from sweet or jammy reds or blowsy whites and towards wines with savour and acidity. With roast beef, say, the undergrowth flavours of celeriac would lean me towards claret over a richer, riper cabernet sauvignon or merlot.

Celeriac remoulade with Bayonne ham This is particularly good with
reds that have some edge and, again, acidity. Examples: Beaujolais

Villages, simple young bordeaux, Marcillac. It also goes well with nervy whites. Examples: grassy semillon-sauvignon blends; sauvignon blanc with a touch of oak for body – the ham will thank you for it; grüner veltliner; or, my favourite in this instance, petite arvine which grows in Alpine regions.

CEVICHE This dish of raw fish, cured in lemon or lime juice and served with chilli and maybe also chopped spring onions, coriander or avocado, needs an acerbic wine to handle the citrus. When guacamole and coriander are involved, aromatic torrontés from Argentina is a good breezy, floral option. Young semillon from the Hunter Valley in Australia works well, as do the rich sauvignon blancs from Marlborough, New Zealand and colombard-ugni blanc blends from Languedoc.

CHARCUTERIE A plate of cured ham or a wooden board set out with salami and a sharp little knife so you can hack off chunks screams for a glass of wine. It is hard to pick badly but, as ever, local is always good. A few suggestions: with Teruel ham, a red from Aragon – perhaps a Calatayud; with fatty wild boar salami, a sharp little Chianti; with saucisson sec, the wild buck and kick of a young Cahors; with chewy biltong, the leathery flavours of old-school South African pinotage or cabernet sauvignon. Part of the joy of red wine with charcuterie is that protein softens its tannins and, if you have a feral young red, its acidity is offset by any fattiness in the meat.

White wine is often overlooked as a partner for charcuterie, though, and it is excellent with cured ham. Pick a white that is glossy and has bounce as well as freshness (none of your mean little razor-blade whites) and it will bring out the succulence of the meat. Whites that go particularly well with cured ham include white Rioja (oaked or otherwise); petite arvine (this one's a big favourite – it's an Alpine grape found in Switzerland as well as the Val d'Aosta region of Italy around Mont Blanc); godello; Jurançon sec (from the Pyrenees in France); and Jura whites.

Of course, one of the great cured ham wines is sherry. The salty, iodine riff of manzanilla; the sourdough punch of fino; the intensity of palo cortado . . . Take your pick.

CHEESE Cheese is eaten enthusiastically with wine but the two are not always the happiest of bedfellows: the creamy fat that coats your mouth can make it hard to taste the wine at all. Often a pint of beer is a much better bet than a glass of wine – especially with the English cheese, vinegary pickled onions and slab of fatty pork pie in a ploughman's lunch. However, beer is not always what you want, so here are a few guidelines to getting the most out of cheese and wine.

cheesy dinners For many dishes that are rich in cooked cheese (for instance, fondue, macaroni cheese, spaghetti carbonara, banitsa), a white wine with good acidity is the natural choice because the acidity will slice through the gloop. Think bright Gavi or Frascati rather than oaked chardonnay. Light, acidic reds such as Bardolino, Marcillac or Valpolicella will do the same job. With richer cheese and tomato dishes, such as aubergine parmigiana or baked and stuffed onions, try reds with grainy tannins as well as fresh bite, such as nebbiolo, lagrein or sangiovese. I love the prickly feel of acid and tannin as they cut through the cheese.

Some raw cheeses, such as feta or goat's curd, have such a tang that red wine – especially oaked and/or tannic reds – can seem to curdle in the mouth. These cheeses tend to settle better with a sharp white. Think of this if you are adding cheese to a plate of food, because the cheese may change the colour of wine that brings out the best in the food. For instance, I'd probably pick a juicy, cherry-ish red like dolcetto to drink with an autumn salad of lightly dressed spinach, rocket, bresaola and quartered figs. Stick a goat's curd dressing on there and suddenly the red isn't as appetizing as the glossy grapefruit taste of an oaked sauvignon blanc.

If you want to wallow in cheesy dinner with wine, then friends recommend visiting Bernard Antony at Fromagerie Antony in Alsace, where you can book a special dinner at which cheese is served in every course, and wine carefully selected to match. One friend says, 'We often have a first course of Crottins and Cotat. Then we tend to move into Burgundy, and the Rhône, through Alsace, there's always a bit of Vendange Tardives. You might have one with potatoes, with sublime, wonderfully salted butter ... It's a genius place.' And one that would give you greedy cheesy tummy, I am sure. But probably be worth it.

the cheeseboard The fantasy of cheese and wine is that a cheese plate is a civilized way to carry on drinking once the main bit of dinner is over. The reality is that much cheese murders much red wine (or vice versa). There are times when this can be a good thing. The old wine trade saying 'Buy on an apple, sell on cheese' isn't based on the idea that cheese flatters wine, more that cheese flatters ropy wine by dulling your ability to taste it at all, which is extremely helpful if you're trying to flog a duff bottle. It's also part of the reason why the field labourer or beach picnicker's lunch of a hunk of cheese with a tin mug of very rough red is such satisfying sustenance.

Once you move up the scale with the wine, the problems begin. Strong cheese is particularly hard on mature fine wine. Hugh Johnson talks about delicate old wine opening out like a peacock's tail, but this is often entirely obliterated by the pong, the acid and the fat, so uncorking a bottle of precious old red with the cheeseboard is not necessarily the greatest plan.

Here are a few guidelines, followed by a short and very far from comprehensive list of happy combinations.

1. Local cheese and local wine often taste great together – for instance, burgundy is good with Époisses – but don't open a special bottle, as the cheese will overpower it.
2. White wine is almost always better than red.
   Eric Monneret, director of Château La Pointe, fulminates that, 'There are only three kinds of cheese for red wine. Old Gouda. St Nectaire from the Massif Central. And Brebis, from the Pyrenees is not bad, though it's better with white.' That's a very Francocentric view. I can think of a handful more, from inside and outside France (including Comté, see below), but the point is well made.
3. Sweet and fortified wines are good with cheese.
   a) The salty pungency of a blue cheese often works well with the luscious, fruity quality of, say, an off-dry pinot gris or riesling, or a properly sweet Muscat de Beaumes de Venise.
   b) Just as dried fruit and nuts go well with certain cheeses, so (with the same cheeses) do the fortified wines that also taste of fruit and nuts. Think sherry (especially

amontillado, palo cortado and oloroso), Madeira, tawny port and Marsala.

A few good partnerships:

- grainy Parmesan with old Valpolicella or Amarone
- Mont d'Or and savagnin
- blue cheese with blanc de blancs champagne
- proper Cheddar with white burgundy
- Comté or grainy Mimolette with claret
- Munster with gewürztraminer
- mozzarella's creamy texture is good with succulent wines – try a darker rosé, such as a Chiaretto

See also banitsa, burrata, Camembert, cauliflower cheese, Comté, fondue, Greek salad, jacket potato, macaroni cheese, omelette, soufflé, Stilton.

CHESTNUTS When these starchy nuts are used to flavour a stuffing or polenta I would be more likely to veer towards a fuller-flavoured, earthy wine. They are rarely the dominant flavour in a meal, but wines that go well with chestnuts include reds from Piemonte and the Languedoc.

CHICKEN Roast chicken is anything goes territory. No wine is able to spoil the enjoyment of a good roast chicken (and vice versa). Stick a bird in the oven, baste it every so often with some fat and its own juices, uncork a bottle of a wine you love, and you are off. There is no need to keep to white, either, especially if the roast is a Label Anglais or proper free-range farm chicken that's had lots of chance to run around.

There are a few notably good roast chicken combinations:

- chardonnay with chicken slathered in butter so that the skin is crispy and golden and the juices are sticky and buttery
- white burgundy or oaked semillon-sauvignon from Margaret River or Bordeaux with chicken roasted with tarragon butter massaged under its skin
- light red (Valpolicella; light Chianti; Bourgogne Rouge; Bierzo) with chicken roasted with thyme

- Italian red with chicken roasted River Café 'festive' style, with nutmeg and wrapped in prosciutto
- left-bank bordeaux with roast chicken cooked to Thomas Keller's recipe (it is in his *Bouchon* cookbook), which calls for the bird to be roasted with thyme and then served with a slab of ice-cold unsalted butter and mustard on the table. You eat each morsel with butter and mustard.

Mostly, though, with roast chicken the mood of the drinkers dictates the wine and with other dishes it's the sauces and other ingredients that inform the choice.

coronation chicken This Seventies-tastic dish with its curry spices and sweet raisins really does work with Seventies wine – a medium-dry riesling from Germany.

with forty cloves of garlic An aromatic French classic in which a jointed chicken is cooked slowly with forty whole unpeeled cloves of garlic, thyme, white wine and carrots, so that when the lid is lifted from the pot all the fragrance pours out. Brilliant with a white from the Rhône in France, for choice a simple Côtes du Rhône. These blends of varieties such as marsanne, roussanne, viognier, grenache blanc and clairette tend to be forgotten, but they are gentle, textured and subtle, often with a mild almond-blossom fragrance.

griddled chicken More or less any white, rosé or light red goes (depending on what you're eating the chicken with), but the smoky taste of an oaked sauvignon blanc-semillon blend from Margaret River in Australia or Bordeaux is good with those black grill lines.

Kiev Oozing with garlic butter and covered with crispy breadcrumbs, chicken Kiev goes well with a crisp white such as vermentino, sauvignon blanc or picpoul. A bright young chardonnay, with lowish alcohol and good acidity, will also cut through the fat.

liver For fried chicken livers, still pink on the inside and tossed in a peppery watercress, spinach and bacon salad, dressed with olive oil and vinegar that has also been used to deglaze the pan, open a bottle of light sangiovese (such as a young and inexpensive Chianti, but not one that is heavily oaked or a riserva style). This grape has the acidity to cope with the salad dressing and the earthiness to meet the liver, and it's refreshing too.

smoked chicken Oak-aged chardonnay has the toasty edge that will go with the smoky chicken.

See also coq au vin.

CHICKPEAS Sangiovese and chickpeas both have an earthy taste and grainy feel and they go well together. Zuppa di ceci – chickpea soup, a kind of thick, granular purée eaten with toasted bread drizzled with olive oil – is a classic Tuscan dish and it tastes good with a simple Chianti (made from sangiovese). Chickpeas also turn up a lot in Middle Eastern and Spanish food, such as hummus; salads; and casseroles with chorizo, spinach, squid, garlic, chicken and/or potatoes. They are robust, so a red such as a simple tempranillo, Côtes du Rhône or Bierzo, or a more gutsy wine from Lebanon, Rioja, or Ribera del Duero, often seems more appropriate than a white – particularly if the stew is flavoured with smoked paprika. If opting for a rosé with a chickpea casserole, steer away from delicate pinks from Provence and towards a fuller, weightier Rioja Rosado or Languedoc pink.

CHILLI GAME-CHANGER It's no exaggeration to say that we don't so much taste chilli as feel it as a blaze of pain. The active ingredient in a jalapeño, Dorset Naga, Trinidad Scorpion or any other kind of chilli pepper (as well as the pepper spray used in riot control) is a compound called capsaicin. It's capsaicin that is responsible for the sensation that your mouth is on fire and it does not activate the taste buds but the nociceptors (pain receptors).

Thanks to the work of Professor David Julius at the University of California in San Francisco, we know that the part of our sensory network that responds to capsaicin is a specific ion channel on sensory nerve endings in the mouth called TRPV1 (it's pronounced 'trip vee one'). This same channel is also part of our warning system for potentially dangerous levels of heat: TRPV1 is sparked into life when it encounters tissue-damaging temperatures above 43.25°c, which is why, when it's activated by chilli (and also, to a lesser extent, garlic), we're tricked into experiencing it as a burn.

The stinging sensation of heat that chilli brings to the mouth, tongue and lips has a strong effect on the perception of everything else we taste while under its influence. Take a sip of wine while your mouth is on fire and you'll barely recognize it as the one you were drinking two minutes earlier. The fruitiness seems to drop out, leaving the wine stripped, featureless and flat. Chilli also heightens perception of tannins, so that even a relatively gentle red wine suddenly acquires a drying astringency and rough sinew.

The question is: when picking a drink to sip with chilli, what do you want to achieve?

Extreme chilli
To up the burn factor, go for big, tannic red wines
Aggression in the form of a red-hot, full-on mouth attack. Is this appealing? The ultra-runners of chilli-eating know who they are. They don't think twice about ordering a dish in their local Indian if it is plastered with heat warnings and pictograms of multiple red chillies. Very likely, they board planes with a travel-size bottle of Tabasco rattling around with the toothpaste in their plastic liquids bag. A crime reporter friend of mine munches bags of raw bird's-eyes – I'm talking chillies, not fish fingers – like the rest of us snack on edamame. He would stare at me in slack-jawed incomprehension if I tried to have a discussion about choosing a drink to mitigate the effect of the burn. I mean, what burn? What's the problem?

If ultra-chilli-eaters care at all about what they wash the chilli down with, it's all about stoking the discomfort. To square the burn by adding a clash of violent astringency, then choose a big, tannic red wine. You know how tea tastes less tannic when you add milk? Well, drinking tannic red wine with chilli in your mouth is like taking the milk out of the tea – and then some. Let that astringency loose. A young cabernet sauvignon, spiky syrah or malbec should do it.

Softly, softly
To cool things down, there are a couple of options
Yoghurt-based drinks such as lassi I once popped a padron pepper into my mouth while hosting a food and wine class. It was a hot one. A very, very hot one. I had no choice but to bolt to the fridge, pour myself a large glass of full-fat milk and drink until it was finished. As it turned out, almost all the peppers were hot. Man by woman, my class tried to contain themselves before flinging away their pride and making a grab for the milk carton. One or two tried to tough it

out, but the tears streaming from their eyes gave them away. It's the casein – a protein – in milk and yoghurt that soothes the fire of chilli by interfering with the reaction between the pain receptors and the capsaicin. This is why traditional Indian lassi – a yoghurt-based drink that may be flavoured with mango or simply drunk plain – is such a good idea with curried food. And, indeed, why yoghurt-based sauces such as raita are often served on the side.

Wines: lighter reds, fruity whites and rosés, and sweetness For a more harmonious approach with wine, steer away from tannin and oak and seek out sugar, as this will help to counteract some of the stripping effect of the chilli. For reds, that means softer, lighter-bodied wines, such as inexpensive New World pinot noir, or smooth, fruity wines like bonarda from Argentina, tempranillo, and plush Chilean merlot. Look out, too, for natural reds that have been made using whole-bunch fermentation which often have a rounded, gentle glow that can sit well with the mild warmth of, say, a rich chilli con carne. Cheap supermarket reds often have their fruitiness boosted by a small, hidden quantity (about 5g per litre to be technical) of sugar, and this makes it easier to taste the wine when you are eating chilli.

For whites and rosés, round and fruity is better than piercing and narrow. Chilli blocks out much of a wine's rounded succulence – it can turn a brisk white into a howl of barbed wire, or simply make it disappear altogether, which is not ideal. As with reds, a touch of sweetness, just a little, helps the wine to hold its own. It won't so much taste sweet as leave the wine feeling nicely filled out.

If you want sauvignon blanc, for example, try picking a sweetly fruity example from Chile or New Zealand rather than a stern and steely Sancerre. Whites that have texture and body tend to sit more comfortably against spice than linear whites that are all about citrus and refreshment. Try pinot gris rather than pinot grigio (it's the winemaker's shorthand for the sweeter, more floral style of the same grape). Consider off-dry German riesling – say, a kabinett style, which is sweet like biting into a melon is sweet and can be a real hit with Thai-influenced salads and curries. And don't write off Mateus Rosé, which also has a bit of sparkle (see below) and goes extremely well with Indian takeaways, as well as Vietnamese salads and Thai curries.

the fizz phenomenon

Fizzy drinks of all kinds – lager, G&T, sparkling water, soft drinks,
or wine from Vinho Verde to prosecco – also mitigate the burning
effect of chilli

Bubbles – a G&T, sparkling wine or lager – are a classic Indian restaurant fallback option and the science behind how we taste helps
to explain why. I had always presumed that fizz went well with
curry because the physical sensation of bubbles bursting against
your tongue acted as a refreshing respite to the heat. This is completely wrong. Carbonated drinks react in the mouth in a number
of ways. They taste slightly sour because, when the carbon dioxide
reacts with water, carbonic acid is created. But that gentle nipping
and pinching at your tongue is not bubbles bursting, it's the carbon
dioxide stimulating our pain receptors – and involving the same ion
channel (TRPAı) that is used to detect mustard oil and wasabi – to
create a pleasing tingle. You could say that we experience the fizz in
fizzy drinks in a similar way as we experience some forms of spice,
and perhaps that's why it feels so good to drink fizzy beer, wine or
soft drinks with hot, spicy food. For specific recommendations, see
individual dishes.

CHILLI CON CARNE The combination of spice, tomatoes and a
meaty sauce enriched with plain chocolate makes chilli con carne a
gleaming, bold oil painting of a dish. A similar bold intensity is found
in reds that ripen under a warm Chilean, Argentine or South African
sun. I like those which have that enveloping richness but also a bit
of earthiness to mirror the grainy dust of the red kidney beans. The
dried-herbs-and-loose-leaf-tea scent of a rugged Chilean carmenère
(or carmenère blend) riffs along with the cumin in the chilli. The
smoky, biltong-and-leather smell of an old-fashioned South African
cabernet sauvignon makes you feel as if you're ready to saddle up and
hit the dusty road after a hearty refuel. An oaked Chilean merlot will
bring out the chocolatey smoothness of the sauce; a Chilean cabernet
will play up to the meatiness. A South African blend of mourvèdre,
syrah and grenache also works well here. As does an easy-going,
vibrant bonarda from Argentina or zinfandel from the States. For a
more refreshing option, try a Côtes du Rhône, although it risks being
drowned out by the fire of the chilli. I usually eat chilli con carne

just with rice. If you're going for the full array of guacamole, grated cheese and tortilla, a malty old-school strong ale looks good – how about Fullers 1845, Brains SA or Hogs Back T.E.A.?

This is my brother's recipe for chilli con carne. He adds a square of plain chocolate, which gives a beautiful depth and gloss to the sauce. He also makes it with chunks of meat rather than the traditional mince. I've tried the same recipe with both braising steak and mince and it's much better his way.

JONNY'S CHILLI CON CARNE

SERVES 4 OF MY FRIENDS, OR 2 OF MY BROTHER

2 tablespoons olive oil
2 medium onions, finely chopped
2 sticks of celery, finely chopped
4 cloves of garlic, peeled and chopped
1 red chilli, deseeded and finely chopped
1 heaped teaspoon ground cumin
1 heaped teaspoon paprika
450g braising steak, trimmed and cut into small
    pieces the size of the tip of your little finger
1 × 400g tin whole plum tomatoes
1 beef stock cube
red chilli flakes
1 square 85% plain chocolate
1 × 200g tin red kidney beans, drained
natural yoghurt
fresh coriander, chopped
seasoning to taste

Heat half the olive oil in a small, cast-iron casserole dish on a low heat on the hob. Add the onions and celery and cook, stirring from time to time, until almost soft and translucent. Add the garlic and chilli and continue to fry until the garlic is cooked. Add the cumin and paprika and cook for a further 30 seconds, stirring to mix. Remove the vegetable mixture from the pan and set to one side.

Put the second tablespoon of olive oil in the pan and fry the meat quickly in batches to brown it. Return all the meat and the onion mixture to the pan and add the tomatoes and their juice. Use a pair of scissors to chop the tomatoes in the pan. Crumble in the stock cube, then rinse the empty tomato tin with water and pour this into the pan too. Stir well. Add more chilli flakes to taste. Simmer gently for 2 hours, or until thickened and glossy, stirring occasionally. Add the chocolate and stir in.

The casserole can now be put to one side until you are ready to eat. Add the drained kidney beans just before reheating and when the chilli con carne is hot all the way through, serve with brown rice, chopped coriander and yoghurt on the side.

CHINESE Cantonese is the best-known and most prevalent type of Chinese cuisine outside China. It comes from the Guangdong province (formerly called Canton). Christine Parkinson, former Head of Wine for the Hakkasan group of restaurants, knows more than most about how Cantonese food works with wine from all over the world. She ran the wine operation for Hakkasan's restaurants, from London to Shanghai to San Francisco to Mumbai, for years, and is one of the most talented and also punctilious restaurant tasters I have encountered. Parkinson was careful to search out good wines, and meticulous when it came to trialling them with Hakkasan's food, holding a tasting meeting every Tuesday at which any new candidates vying for a place on the wine list, as well as new vintages of current wines, were tested with at least eight different dishes from the restaurant kitchen, selected to cover the different styles of food (spicy, light and so on). If it tasted bad with any single dish – and, said Parkinson, many did – it was out.

'The single biggest problem with Cantonese food when it comes to wine is that there's a lot of sweetness – a lot of sugar or honey or malt or whatever – and that's a real enemy to tannin and to green notes in red wines,' she says. 'And then of course the flavours are very big. Cantonese cuisine is not particularly shy or delicate. It has robust flavours, which means some wines can get completely lost.'

The heavy use of spice, from ginger to chilli to sichuan pepper to yellow chives, is also an issue, as is acidity in the food, not just with sweet-and-sour dishes, where you might expect it, but also with others that have a strong vinegar component. Chinese chive is also tricky, says Parkinson: 'It's a different variety to the English one. When you see green dim sum wrappers, that's Chinese chive and it is another enemy to wine.'

It's normal to have several different dishes on the table at once, and to be picking and sharing across all those sweet, sour, spicy, vinegar, bold flavours. The chances are you'll be following a mouthful of one with a mouthful of wine with a mouthful of another. So the challenge is to find a wine that still tastes good whether you're eating black pepper rib-eye beef, silver cod in champagne honey, or spicy prawns.

I find the vibrant alertness of English sparkling wine works particularly well with Chinese food, both with dim sum and with main courses. Bob Lindo, who makes wine at Camel Valley in Cornwall, agrees that English sparkling is a good match for the variety of Cantonese food, but even he points out, 'You don't want to drink sparkling wine all the way through a dinner, there has to be still wine in there somewhere.'

From her long years of experience at Hakkasan, Christine Parkinson recommends three mainstream wine styles that can generally (though not always) be relied on to work well: barrel-fermented chardonnay; riesling with a little bit of residual sugar (that is, off-dry riesling); and pinot noir. I find that herbaceous, lean styles of pinot noir – say, from Baden in Germany or a basic Bourgogne Rouge – work particularly well with the umami component in a non-sweet Chinese dish such as beef in oyster and black bean sauce. Off-dry rieslings come into their own with the sweetness of, say, sticky lemon chicken. Barrel-fermented chardonnays are also good with umami, and the texture and spice brought by the wood mean they can deal with richer flavours.

Other wines that work are:

- Lugana from north-east Italy, which is soft, broad and neutral, sometimes with the flavour of savoury custard and orchard fruit. The high-quality wines made by Ca' dei Frati are particularly good.
- ribolla gialla, a white grape grown on the Slovenian border in the mountains of north-east Italy whose wine is tenacious, precise and grips on to your tongue.
- koshu, a white Japanese grape whose wine makes me think

of origami. Sipped on its own, it seems as neutral as a sheet of white paper – like a cross between a very quiet sauvignon blanc and pinot grigio. A bit dull. Sipped with the right food, it pops into shape: you can actually taste it more, as if it has reserves of power that are uncovered only when they are needed. The transformation surprises me every time. Koshu is particularly good with dim sum, but less good with more spicy or sweet food.

- champagne, white or rosé, but non-vintage (NV) – the subtlety of anything finer would disappear amidst the other flavours.
- deep-coloured rosés that are not perfectly dry and which work across the board.
- albariño is great with dim sum but not with dishes that have too much heat or sugar.
- old-vine carignan from Chile is good with heavier meaty dishes and can even take some spice. For example, it works well with star anise.

See also crispy duck pancakes.

CHOCOLATE Wine and chocolate together sounds indulgent and hedonistic. I can almost feel the squish of sofa cushions just thinking about it. And that's exactly how it can be, provided that you follow two main guidelines: go high alcohol and, unless the alcohol is so high that you're actually drinking a spirit, go sweet.

Almost any drink that tastes good inside a chocolate truffle is equally good in a glass beside a rich chocolate mousse, creamy chocolate cake or nemesis, chocolate soufflé, chocolate tart or a piece of plain or milk chocolate.

With *spirits*, this means brandy (including, of course, Cognac and Armagnac); rum – especially aged rum, which has a special affinity for chocolate as the sweet fruitiness and the smoky-nutty flavours of the spirit bring out all the cocoa richness; finally, at a pinch, if it's quite a bitter, restrained chocolate, try whisky.

Fruit-flavoured liqueurs work well too – it's almost too obvious to say, but if you pick ones whose fresh fruits you would put with chocolate, that seems to do the trick. The electricity between the bluffness of plain chocolate and the intense tang of bitter oranges is well known, and both Cointreau and Grand Marnier are gorgeous with straightforward chocolate desserts and those with a glimmer of orange. Kirsch, as everyone knew in the Seventies, is brilliant with cream and chocolate. Framboise, too – chocolate seems to exaggerate the berry flavours.

Ordinary sweet wine rarely works with chocolate, though there are exceptions to this rule, such as Brachetto d'Acqui, the sparkling red wine from northern Italy. Usually it's better to look for a wine that has been lightly fortified. Young vintage port has a red-fruited, velvet strength, like the fabled iron fist in a velvet glove, that is especially delicious with, for instance, chocolate mousse cake. Late bottled vintage (LBV) shares the same affinity for rich chocolate puddings. Meanwhile, tawny port, which has been aged in oak, brings a caramelized nuttiness.

Marsala and Madeira can be good too, but when it comes to Madeira pick your wine with care: the drier, lither styles of sercial and verdelho would be buried by some chocolate desserts, but richer, sweeter bual and malmsey can manage almost anything. Sweeter sherries, such as sweet oloroso, cream sherry or PX, are good with chocolate too.

Vins doux naturels are made by adding a small amount of grape spirit to wine before it has finished fermenting, so that it tastes sweet but also grapey. Many of these are gorgeous, but it's an overlooked category, so you can actually feel you are paying the gastronomic world a courtesy when you get out the chocolate and crack open a bottle.

A few examples: Maury is made in the south of France using grenache and it tastes like a pom-pom of liquidized dried figs and plums with a gentle flame of alcohol. Banyuls is another red sticky wine, made in the Roussillon from a blend of grapes, aged in oak, and often very complex.

White vins doux naturels are more refreshing; they lift chocolate in the same way that crystallized kumquats lift a bitter chocolate sorbet. Muscat de Beaumes de Venise and Muscat St Jean de Minervois, for instance, are both reminiscent of orange blossom and honey, while Muscat de Rivesaltes is pale and fresh when it's young, and grows more intense, like honey with baked apricots, as it gets older.

Liqueur Muscat is a classic Australian sweet wine that is good with chocolate too. Mahogany in colour, it tastes of figs, dates, treacle cake, molasses and raisins. Try it with chocolate refrigerator cake, chocolate mousse or vanilla ice cream with a chocolate sauce.

The Aztecs believed chocolate was a gift of the gods, who drank it themselves. Wine also has plenty of its own gods – Dionysus and Bacchus, for a start – looking after it. So it seems fair to imagine that putting the two together might sometimes cause hostility. This clash is immediately apparent when you try to drink ordinary dry wine with chocolate. Sweet chocolate has a withering effect on the taste – it sucks the joy out of it, leaving behind an alcohol and acid shell. Eating a smooth, sleek truffle and finding your gulp of red has turned it into an angry tangle, like crash wreckage, is not at all appealing.

Despite this, many producers of red wines remain convinced that their wines go well with chocolate. I think this might be because certain red wines actually taste of chocolate. At least, they do a bit. Putting sweet food and dry wine together never really works, in my view, but if you want to taste chocolate-ish flavours in a dry wine, then have a look at some of the big malbecs from Argentina; southern hemisphere cabernet francs, which are often reminiscent of powdery drinking chocolate; riper St Emilions and also Chilean cabernet sauvignon and carmenère blends, which sometimes have flavours similar to intense, bitter cacao nibs.

Australian shiraz is sometimes also a little bit chocolatey, though it's the taste of cooked raspberries I find more here – which might explain why sparkling shiraz is often enthusiastically matched with chocolate. Raspberries and chocolate are great together. Shiraz and chocolate, not so much, although it does help that sparkling shiraz is often a little sweet.

If you are really intent on eating chocolate and drinking dry wine together follow the advice of Sarah Jane Evans, a Master of Wine who is also a committed chocolate expert and author of the book *Chocolate Unwrapped*, which offers a guide to the top eighty chocolate producers, with tasting notes. She advises picking bars of chocolate 'that have texture: nuts, sea salt, a very fine layer of fruit jelly – this mitigates the tannin disaster'. It does make the combination sit together more happily.

drinking with chocolate at a glance

to lift and refresh the chocolate The light dance and orange blossom of Muscat de Beaumes de Venise or Muscat St Jean de Minervois.

to snuggle into the chocolate Young vintage port, LBV port, ruby port, Maury, Australian Liqueur Muscat, malmsey Madeira.

to pay it the compliment of firewater Rum and brandy.

good combinations

chocolate mousse with prunes The rustic fire of Armagnac sparks off the earthy prunes. This is proper winter fireside, iron-hard frost outside stuff.

nuts (and raisins) and chocolate Those sweet wines that have an intrinsic nuttiness mesh well here. So, chilled tawny port, malmsey or bual Madeira, Australian Liqueur Muscat, sweet oloroso sherry, Moscato di Pantelleria.

sea salt chocolate The iodine smokiness of Islay whisky plays to the marine element in the salty chocolate.

white chocolate bars studded with freeze-dried strawberries Oddly specific, I know, but I have Sarah Jane Evans and her extensive chocolate and wine tasting to thank for this one. 'A delightful girly combo with this chocolate is Californian white grenache from Gallo [a sweetish rosé wine],' she says. 'Great fun.'

frozen berries with hot white chocolate sauce A more sophisticated take on the white chocolate and strawberries bar above, I'd put this with Brachetto d'Acqui.

See also cake.

CHORIZO The presence of chorizo in a dish immediately moves me across to red wine. Its sweet softness and paprika spiciness particularly suit Spanish wine. In contrast, say, to Italian, which is all elbows, wine made in Spain from tempranillo, cariñena or garnacha is smooth and juicy when young and, as it ages, suggests sweetness, like cooked strawberries, that mirrors that of the chorizo. So with squid and chorizo casserole, I would drink a mellow Rioja. With chorizo sliced into a butter bean and tomato salsa and topped with a lamb chop, I might drink Rioja again, or garnacha from Campo de Borja or a Priorat or a Montsant. If white is preferred – perhaps with chorizo eaten alone as a nibble, or a chorizo, spinach and poached egg salad – then make it succulent and rounded, and consider looking for wine with oak. Oaked white Rioja is the obvious choice. Godello, with its juicy rounded orchard fruits, fits the bill too. The crackle of an oaked chardonnay from Australia, South Africa or Chile would also be gorgeous with a poached egg and chorizo dish, not least because chardonnay is good with eggs too.

COD, CANNELLINI BEAN, CHORIZO AND TOMATO STEW

SERVES 2

This nourishing child-friendly recipe demands little more prep time than it takes to chop and fry an onion. Everyone has their own version of this dish. Some use chickpeas but my daughter prefers the creaminess of cannellini or butter beans so I go with that. In summer when I've grown tomatoes and have a glut I make it with fresh tomatoes but usually use tinned. Serve with crusty bread and green beans. Add more paprika for a meat-free version and if you're taking out the cod too then wilt handfuls of spinach in at the last moment and serve with a little gem salad. In your glass, I'd go with fino sherry, young Rioja (or other tempranillo) or Bierzo.

75g cooking chorizo sausage, chopped
    into chunks
olive oil (if needed)
1 onion, peeled and chopped
¼ teaspoon sweet smoked paprika
pinch chilli flakes
bay leaf
1 400g tin plum tomatoes
1 400g tin cannellini beans
240g cod fillets
seasoning
flat leaf parsley to serve

Heat the oven to 160°C/Fan 150°C/Gas 3/320°F. Put the chorizo in a stove-proof casserole dish (I use a Le Creuset) and cook on a hob until the fat has melted out and the sausage is beginning to brown. Use a slotted spoon to remove the chunks of sausage and put in a bowl to one side. Put the onion into the chorizo pan and sauté in the orange fat, stirring occasionally, until it is soft and translucent. You can add a slug of olive oil if you need more fat. Add the chorizo, paprika, chilli flakes, bay leaf and tomatoes to the casserole dish along with around 100ml water which you have swilled around the empty tomato can to get out the rest of the juice. Break up the tomatoes, bring to a boil and simmer gently for 10 minutes uncovered. Remove the bay leaf then add the beans and stir into the sauce. Check and adjust the seasoning. Use a spoon to pull the bean sauce to one side. Place the fish in the bottom of the casserole dish then cover it completely with the bean sauce. Cook in the oven, covered, for 20 minutes. After this time remove the lid, cook for another 10 minutes and serve.

CHOWDER This dish is more solid than liquid, so works better with wine than most soups. With a mild, creamy vegetarian corn chowder, try a chardonnay. With spicy seafood chowder, consider the texture of a marsanne, the toasty quality of an aged semillon or the cut of a semillon-sauvignon blend from Australia.

CHRISTMAS DINNER From a food matching point of view, the best way to pick a wine to go with Christmas dinner is to think of it as one more element – a sauce or dish of stuffing – on the crammed table. The turkey may ostensibly be the centrepiece, but it's also a blank canvas. It's the cranberries, the fruity stuffings, the chestnuts, the spicy sausage balls, the prunes wrapped in bacon – all of the other brightly coloured, joyful rattlebag of dishes that need to get along with the wine. Wines that will fall in with this crowd? An aromatic white, such as pinot gris; or a red with cranberry sharpness and bright berry fruit, perhaps a youthful pinot noir (maybe from Central Otago or Martinborough in New Zealand), a Beaujolais Cru, an unoaked carignan, a gaudy garnacha from north-east Spain, or a carignan from Chile.

However. Unless you are particularly in the mood for those wines, picking one would be to miss half the point. Christmas dinner is like the big box of decorations in the cupboard under the steps, filled with gaudy baubles, tasteful baubles, ugly baubles, matching baubles and clashing baubles: a big hotch-potch of family tradition, colour and whim. When you sit down at the Christmas table, the first duty of the wine is not actually to go with the food but to go with your mood: it must be festive and celebratory. The best advice is therefore to drink the wine you quite fancy at the time. Maybe it's classic, reassuring claret, or maybe it's a sturdy, hairy Chilean carmenère.

A good balance between wines that suit the food and the mood might also be struck. How about a richly Christmassy blend of syrah, grenache and mourvèdre from the southern Rhône, Languedoc, California or Australia? Or an Australian bordeaux blend, which will be more vibrantly fruity and hedonistic than a real bordeaux and so go better with the fruity vitality of stuffings and sauces. I love to drink young nebbiolo (ideally a Langhe Nebbiolo) or sangiovese (in the form of a Rosso di Montalcino or Chianti Classico) on Christmas Day, and often tweak the trimmings in a more savoury direction to fit. It's easily done: make stuffings more herby (use thyme and rose-mary) than sweetly fruity; use raisins, cranberries and dried cherries rather than apple and apricots; put Parmesan and cream in with the sprouts; and make sure there are plenty of chestnuts, ideally cooked with bacon; and there it is – reimagined for Italian wine.

See also Boxing Day leftovers, cake: Christmas cake, turkey sandwiches.

CLAMS see *fish* for good, generic seafood wines; also *chowder*; *pasta: vongole.*

COD Cod is a firm-textured fish and when cooked simply its snowy-white flesh suits medium-weight whites that have some freshness: for instance, Chablis, top-notch Mâcon, godello, white Rioja or Douro whites. Grüner veltliner approaches cod with less roundness and a more chiselled edge.
battered cod see *fish and chips.*
black miso cod Silky and umami-rich, black miso cod has a sweetness that is good with champagne. Daiginjo sake would be another obvious choice. Mid-weight pinot noir also works well, as does a nutty white burgundy, say a good-value St Aubin or a Meursault.
brandade of cod This creamy dip is made using salt cod and olive oil. Brisk, salty manzanilla sherry is a pretty perfect match, or try a Rhône white.

cod with green lentils and/or wrapped in air-dried ham Earthy green lentils and/or meaty ham make a light red wine more tempting than a white. Try Bardolino; a light and mineral-edged pinot noir (for instance, one from Germany; or a simple Bourgogne Rouge); zweigelt from Austria; gamay (from Touraine or a Beaujolais); Irouléguy ; or a vin de pays de l'Ardèche.

cod with red peppers, tomatoes and onions Once red peppers and onions come into the equation, red wine tastes better than white. Make it a young Bierzo or Ribeira Sacra or a bright Rioja Joven.

xató This tip comes from Ferran Centelles, the Spanish food and wine expert who for a long time was head sommelier at El Bulli. I asked him for an example of a traditional Spanish food that matches well with a non-Spanish wine. He said, 'Cod fish salad with anchovies and romesco [locally known as xató] is a delicious Catalan dish that I love to match with high-acidity and delicate aromatic wine. I had a great experience combining this really savoury food with a verdicchio from Marche in Italy.'

See also bacalao, esqueixada.

COMTÉ If you invite someone who works as a sommelier or wine buyer for dinner and ask them to bring the cheese, there is a very good chance that they will turn up with a slab of this hard, unpasteurized cheese made on the French side of the border between France and Switzerland. Comté is known as one of *the* cheeses that tastes really good with red bordeaux. As always in wine, not everyone agrees. Eric Monneret, director of Château La Pointe in Pomerol, shook his head when I suggested eating grainy Comté with tannic claret. 'Ah, non, I'm from the Jura and so I would have to say that Comté is best with a vin jaune, which also comes from there.' I'd happily drink either.

COQ AU VIN Almost any red blend from southern France, a red burgundy, or a red Côtes du Rhône is good with this bistro classic. My personal favourite is a pitcher of good Beaujolais Cru. On a cold winter's night the combination of piping hot (the coq au vin) and chilly (the wine) feels as comforting as standing by a fire while watching snow fall on the other side of the window. Beaujolais has a slight tang of stone and graphite – girding against the darkness outside.

CORIANDER The leaves of coriander are widely used in Latin American cuisine, and the seeds and leaves in South Asian food. Its smell is divisive; while some experience coriander as a woody and pleasantly fragrant herb, to others it is soapy and metallic. Research suggests that genetic variants in olfactory receptors could contribute to this polarizing effect, and the olfactory receptor gene OR6A2, which is involved in the detection of particular aldehydes, has been implicated. Loathing for coriander is highest among East Asians (21 per cent), those of European descent (17 per cent) and those with African ancestry (14 per cent), according to one study, which also found that the approval rating for coriander was much higher among those from South Asian, Middle Eastern and Latin American backgrounds. For those who dislike coriander, perhaps only an overpowering pinotage can help to remove its sudsy taste. For others, fresh coriander leaves often work well with grüner veltliner, especially when lemongrass, lime juice and cool basmati rice are also involved. The spicy rattle of the seeds might suggest either a spicy and robust red or its antithesis, a soothing off-dry rosé. You need to take into account the whole dish, however.

COTTAGE (OR SHEPHERD'S) PIE Comfort food – and it is perfect with comfort wine. The boldness of a chunky, inky Chilean red (ideally cabernet sauvignon or carmenère, but merlot will do too) suits the rich mince base, all the more so if it's laden with Worcestershire sauce. In the Chilean version of this dish, mashed sweetcorn replaces potatoes, which is lovely with the sweetly fruity ripeness of these southern hemisphere wines. You could also open a Côtes du Rhône, Corbières, Fitou or an inexpensive, chunky Australian or South African red. If the mood takes you, a vigorous young bordeaux or a sumptuous Ribera del Duero would work well too.

COURGETTE 'What wine might go with courgettes?' is a thought that has never crossed my mind. Dinner is never about this subtle green vegetable, it's about everything else – the garlic, the herbs, the tomatoes, the cheese ... whatever. So there are some dishes to consider.
fried with garlic and tomatoes, scattered with Gruyère, and grilled to melt the cheese Rosé from Provence; the cut of a pecorino from Italy; the freshness of a white from the Savoie.

ribboned, with pine nuts The lemon-rind flavours of a Gavi di Gavi will bring cool freshness (and underscore the crunch of the courgette if you are serving this as a raw salad). A grillo or greco di tufo will emphasize the more exotic, richer texture of the pine nuts.

roasted and added, with oven-dried tomatoes and parsley, to a garlic and raw tomato sauce for pasta A light sauvignon blanc from Italy or France; Gavi; verdicchio.

stuffed with rice, tomatoes, garlic and thyme An aromatic red (say, meaty Bandol) or white (Cassis or a Côtes de Provence blanc) from Provence or a Provençal rosé hits the spot. Clean Italian whites such as verdicchio or vermentino are palate-cleansing too. If you flip the herb from woody thyme to pungent oregano, however, the French wines are suddenly less happy. The herbaceous Italian whites still play well, as do stonily calm, unoaked whites from Crete.

COURGETTE FLOWERS (STUFFED AND FRIED) Again, it's not about the courgette flower, it's about the ricotta, pine nuts, citrus peel, herbs – whatever you have in there. To slice through the fat of cheese and frying oil, and pick up on the brightness of the lemon rind, pick a sharp white that tastes of lemons: Gavi di Gavi, pecorino, assyrtiko, or carricante from Sicily. Other clean whites will have the same refreshing effect: pinot grigio from the north-east of Italy or from Hungary, vermentino, verdicchio or vernaccia. Those 'v' wines also have an astringency that adds a herbal twist. Clean falanghina has an orange-blossom scent that brings another citrus dimension. For a more *Arabian Nights*, perfumed exoticism, choose the crystallized-fruit-tinged fiano, grillo or greco di tufo or the florality of zibibbo – Sicilian muscat. The wine doesn't have to be Italian; Australian fiano or the almond-kernel-and-citrus-peel taste of marsanne from either Australia or France is good too.

CRAB Chablis – which smells of damp sea fossils and has a glow, as if it's backlit – underscores the marine qualities of the crab while also offering a hint of the lemon you might squeeze into your crab mayonnaise. It particularly suits crab with new potatoes and a little gem salad.

Gently peachy albariño, from Spain's Atlantic coast, is also brilliant with crab, whether the crab is fried in croquettes, freshly picked out of the claws, mixed into a mayonnaise (perhaps with finely chopped coriander stalks or torn basil leaves) or made into a crab sandwich eaten with a view of the beach and the sea air in your nostrils.

These are my two go-to crab wines; the ones I start salivating for the minute I see crab in almost any form on the menu. Riesling also has a substantial following as the perfect crab accompaniment – 'crab and riesling together are part of the Creator's Plan,' writes Hugh Johnson in his *Pocket Wine Book* – though I tend to go for riesling only when certain other ingredients are also involved.

Here are a few suggestions for specific dishes.

crab cakes Cool, hard-edged cava bubbles are cleansing with the crunchy, fatty, crispy outsides of crab cakes.

crab cakes with chilli, lime, avocado, red onion and tomato salad Go for a bright dry or off-dry riesling from Germany, Austria, New Zealand, Chile or Australia.

Thai crab cakes Grassy young Hunter Valley semillon from Australia or the hay and toast scent of more mature Hunter semillon is good here. Otherwise, riesling. The piercing lime of riesling from Clare or Eden Valley (both Australian), a riesling from Chile, or the clean swoosh of an Austrian riesling is good with the lemongrass and ginger of Thai-flavoured crab cakes.

THAI CRAB CAKES

SERVES 2, AS A LUNCH

75ml mayonnaise
1 stick of lemongrass, finely chopped
½ teaspoon grated fresh ginger
100g white crabmeat
75g fresh breadcrumbs
2 spring onions, chopped
2 tablespoons roughly chopped basil
2 tablespoons roughly chopped fresh coriander
panko breadcrumbs, for coating
groundnut oil, for frying (*recipe continues overleaf*)

Mix together the mayonnaise, chopped lemongrass and grated ginger. Put the crabmeat, fresh breadcrumbs, spring onions, basil and coriander in a separate bowl. Stir in the mayonnaise until the mixture is bound. Divide into four, shape into patties, roll the patties in panko breadcrumbs and shallow-fry in groundnut oil, turning once, until golden and warm.

Serve with rocket or spinach salad, or steamed Asian greens and a glass of Hunter Valley semillon.

deep-fried soft-shell crab The first time I ate this was in a restaurant overlooking Sydney Harbour. On the menu there were lots of wines from the Hunter Valley, some 150 kilometres to the north. So we ordered a semillon. I think it was Tyrrell's Vat 1: an absolute classic, grassy, poised, and beautiful with the crispy, crabby food.

hot crab pots An olden but golden dish which I always find especially pleasing if there are crunchy little bits of shell in the creamy, eggy, hot, crabby pot. It is blissful with oaked chardonnay. I made this recipe when Aussie Larry Cherubino, a winemaking genius (also, an exceptionally talented tidy-upper), was coming to dinner. I thought it would work with the gleam of his Margaret River chardonnay. It did.

HOT CRAB POTS

SERVES 6

4 eggs, beaten
400ml double cream
200g brown and white crabmeat
100g Gruyère, grated
salt
butter
2 tablespoons chopped chives

Preheat the oven to 180°C/Fan 160°C/Gas 4/350°F. Mix the eggs, cream, crab and cheese together. Season to taste and divide between six buttered ramekin dishes. Cook for around 15 minutes until only just set. Sprinkle with chives and serve with really good bread, toasted.

CREAM Creamy sauces feel like cashmere blankets: luxurious and soft. Sometimes you want to pierce that softness. For instance, the classic French recipe for pork medallions cooked with cream and prunes is so unctuous, sweet and caramelized that it is excellent with the penetrating and refreshing acidity of an off-dry Vouvray. Mostly, though, creamy sauces are more likely to have me reaching for a broad white with rounded edges. Very often that white will be chardonnay, barrel-fermented or otherwise. It might also be a cloud-like grenache gris, oaked chenin blanc, or an oaked white Rioja.

CRISPS see *salty snacks*.

CRISPY DUCK PANCAKES A fruity pinot noir from New Zealand (Central Otago or Martinborough, ideally) or Chile is delicious with the meaty duck, crispy spring onion and just a smear of hoisin sauce. If you are ladling on the hoisin, though, its sweetness will disrupt the wine, so I'd switch to a fruity medium-dry riesling. The same goes for duck spring rolls, which are also very good with sparkling champagne blends – the combination of fat, sweetness, acid and crunch is very moreish.

CURRY Curry is a catch-all term that covers a broad spectrum of spicy food from all over the world. As a general guide, wine with a bit of sweetness helps to neutralize the burning effect of the chilli. Without that sugar, it can be hard to taste the wine at all. A fruity, off-dry rosé or an off-dry sparkling wine holds up well against most curried foods and this, if I'm not pouring a beer or a G&T, is what I open to drink with ready-made Indian-style curries at home.

With curry in a creamy coconut sauce, off-dry pinot gris is extremely good: gentle and softly floral. With lime-scented curries, the lime notes in a riesling play off the citrus in the food – pick an off-dry riesling to counteract the heat of the chilli. When tomatoes together with capsicum are involved, carmenère is good. With the more earthy flavours found in dishes containing lentils and with hearty tomato-and-meat-based curries, red wines with a hint of dust (such as mencía, carmenère again or a Portuguese Dão) are also good. In each case, marry the weight of the flavour with the weight of the wine – and be aware of the impact of the chilli, whose burning effect is exaggerated by the tannin and oak in red wines.

See also chilli, dhal, Indian, Thai green curry.

C

D

DEVILS ON HORSEBACK Sweet-salty prunes wrapped in bacon are great with sparkling wine.

DHAL There are many versions of this Indian staple but the earthy flavour of the lentils and some degree of spice are constants. The substantial nature of dhal is more readily matched with red than white wine. It goes especially well with those dusty, dry reds whose flavours align with the lentils: look for inexpensive reds from Turkey, the Dāo in Portugal, Lebanon, carmenère from Chile, or sangiovese or montepulciano from central Tuscany.

DILL GAME-CHANGER The distinctive aniseed and fennel taste of this herb is disruptive to many flavours, including those in some wines. Unpleasant combinations that come to mind include Rioja and dill, or Crozes-Hermitage and dill – the pungency of the herb curdles the sweet strawberry-ness of Rioja and is aggressive against the tannins of the northern Rhône.

Better to go for herbaceous white wines such as verdicchio, vermentino and vernaccia, or, where small amounts of dill are combined with creamy sauces or crème fraîche, a cool-climate chardonnay (I'm really thinking of white burgundy), which often has gentle notes of woodruff and faint tones of aniseed. My very favourite type of wine with dill, though, and in particular with dill and smoked salmon, is barrel-fermented sauvignon blanc. When it's aged in oak, sauvignon blanc begins to taste of baked grapefruits and pine and sometimes also very gently of dill. Either a straight oak-aged sauvignon or a sauvignon blanc-semillon blend will do the trick, which means that Bordeaux (and in particular the appellations of Graves and Pessac-Léognan) and Margaret River are good places to look.

Incidentally, carvone is one of the main odour compounds found in dill. It comes from the terpenoid family of chemicals and is also present in high concentration in spearmint as well as caraway. This is why Dentinox, the medicine given to soothe colicky babies, appears to smell minty when it is actually flavoured with dill. It also helps to explain the affinity between caraway seeds, rye bread and dill – all stalwarts of Scandinavian cuisine – and, indeed, that much-loved Scandinavian drink aquavit: a perfect match.

DRIED LIME see *lime*.

DUCK Pinot noir is the first grape to think of when it comes to duck. It is a winner with duck eaten any which way – with hoisin sauce; roasted; smoked; with noodles; in a salad.

With a roast duck, the first decision is whether you're looking for a light, refreshing red to slice through the fat and act like a perky vinous cranberry sauce, or a big, gruff red, as full as the duck is rich, to hunker down with.

In the case of the former, any of the following light reds are worth considering: gamay (the weight of a Beaujolais Cru might be appreciated, or a rich New Zealand gamay), nerello mascalese from Etna, Bardolino, dolcetto, bobal, mencía, an inexpensive carignan from Spain or France, the warm flow of a Cerasuolo di Vittoria from Sicily, Marcillac, and, of course, pinot noir. It's neither heavy nor light, but Fronsac – a lean and sometimes green-tasting Bordeaux appellation – also has a tannic and acidic cut that is good with duck.

If you're in search of a more cosy bear-hug of a red, pick one with a hairy chest so as to match the richness and fat with mass and tannic might. Rustic reds go well with duck: a Bergerac Rouge, Buzet, Cahors, Madiran, or a gamey Bandol from Provence will give you a bit of tannic edge. Or try a warm, smooth monastrell from Spain (the grape is known as mourvèdre in France and underpins the Bandol blend, but Spanish incarnations tend to be more fluid, more deeply fruity and liquorice-like). The autumnal notes of Barbaresco or Brunello di Montalcino go particularly well with roast duck and a tray of roasted root vegetables, from parsnips to carrots to red onions, as does the fading strawberry and autumn leaf sweetness of a maturing Rioja or Ribera del Duero. More or less any red from the northern Rhône or the Dão or Douro in Portugal would also be happy here.

Here are a few duck dishes and suggested matches.

casserole One of the hairy-chest reds listed above will meet the weight of the slow-cooked duck.

with cherry sauce Pick a bright, young pinot noir from Central Otago in New Zealand or from California for sweet fruit, or an unoaked young pinot noir from Chile or Burgundy for the taste of red berries wih a slightly sharper edge. A sangiovese or dolcetto from Italy will also taste good with duck and cherry sauce, and give you a bit more elbow.

confit de canard This speciality of south-west France is good with local and local-ish wines. Cahors, Madiran or Bergerac for a big red with grunt; Marcillac or Gaillac for a sappy light red to cut across the fat.

with mushroom risotto balls For a lighter option, pick barbera, juicy dolcetto or pinot noir. Perricone, an unusual Italian grape with a hint of forest floor and mulberryish fruit, is a good mid-weight wine. For more of a growl, try mourvèdre (known as mataro in Australia and monastrell in Spain) or syrah. Barbaresco or Barolo would also be excellent and bring out the autumnal flavours in the mushroom risotto.

à l'orange White wines go well with duck when it's in a citrus sauce. Falanghina from central Italy, which tastes of mandarins and orange blossom and has a refreshing tang, is great with both the fat of the duck and the brightness of the orange. You could also try Australian marsanne; a tangy chardonnay from Chile, South Africa or Australia; off-dry riesling; greco di tufo from Italy; off-dry pinot gris; pinot blanc; chenin blanc or a Rhône white whose almond paste flavours emphasise the exotic side of this dish.

with peas and lettuce Tender pink magrets with a tangle of braised little gem lettuce and fresh peas, perhaps cooked with crispy cubes of pancetta, suits light reds with a similarly spring-like feel. Bright pinot noir (from just about anywhere in the world), Marcillac, Beaujolais or other gamay, passetoutgrains, zweigelt, dolcetto or barbera will all act like a kind of spry, fruity sauce for the duck. Cabernet franc will emphasize the soft meatiness of the duck, while the inherent leafy taste of the grape works with the peas and lettuce. The punctuating tannin and acidity and the energy of a young left-bank claret will also work with both the meat and the green vegetables.

with plum sauce The combination of spice from cinnamon, soy, pepper, ginger, star anise and Chinese five-spice and sweet-sour plums does work with pinot noir, but it needs to be a sturdy wine, and richly fruity, so look for one from Central Otago or Martinborough in New Zealand, Sonoma in the US, or South Africa. Spanish bobal is also good with this dish. Merlot, a grape I have barely recommended in this book, comes into its own here – think of the warm embrace of a big, plush oaked merlot from Chile or the fruit rush of one from Australia. Alternatively, a fruity Argentine malbec.

with Puy lentils Head towards earthier wines. Of the heavier reds listed above, try Buzet or Bergerac for warmth; or go lighter with a Beaujolais Cru or a savoury pinot; or mid-weight with a red made with Spain's mencía (from either Bierzo or Ribeira Sacra).

ragù Duck ragù is easily made by roasting a duck, shredding the meat, then proceeding as for ordinary ragù, perhaps flavouring the sauce with rosemary or thyme or bay leaves and fresh sage. Serve it on pappardelle and eat it with a rich Valpolicella Ripasso or Rosso di Montalcino.

with redcurrant sauce The tingle of redcurrants demands a wine that can match its nervosity. The light reds suggested for peas and lettuce will work, or nero d'avola or Cerasuolo di Vittoria from Sicily.

rillettes For years I have been roasting ducks until the flesh almost melts and picking the carcass to make rillettes, using Delia Smith's recipe, found in *Delia's Winter Collection*. 'I did recently offer it as a lunch for three people with a green salad and some slightly chilled Beaujolais. Magnificent!' says Delia. Exactly so. The shiver of a sappy, minerallic Beaujolais (try a Morgon for one with more weight) is glorious with rich duck. An alternative is a softly fruity, cranberryish unoaked carignan, from southern France, Aragon in Spain (where it is known as cariñena) or Chile.

See also aligot, cassoulet, crispy duck pancakes.

DUCK SPRING ROLLS see *crispy duck pancakes.*

DUKKAH This Egyptian seasoning has found its way out of the souks of Cairo and into kitchens all over the world. There are many different variations, but essentially it is a mixture of salt, herbs, nuts and spices that have been dry-roasted and pounded. Cumin, hazelnuts, coriander and sesame often play a part, making dukkah a crunchy, dusty, exotic condiment. In small quantities with bread and oil; on vegetables; or sprinkled on dips like hummus or tzatziki, it can work with Lebanese white or rosé or indeed a white wine from elsewhere. A chardonnay with toasty oak picks up on the toastiness of the spices and adds a sunny warmth. A more neutral white refreshes: try trebbiano, with its hints of stone, apple and nuts; or a more sharply lemony pecorino. Alternatively, go for a dusty, earthy red such as a Portuguese Dão; a Lebanese blend; a rustic Italian sangiovese-based red (Chianti, Rosso di Montepulciano, Carmignano); nebbiolo; aglianico; Alain Graillot's Moroccan syrah; a Turkish or Greek red; or a red containing mourvèdre made in Provence (for instance, Bandol).

D

E

EEL (SMOKED) The principle that when matching wine to food you can either go with the texture of the dish or cut across it is beautifully demonstrated when it comes to smoked eel. Oily and strongly flavoured as well as smoky, the eel tastes good with wines that also have layers and texture. These may be provided by a touch of residual sugar: at Wild Honey in Mayfair, I once ate smoked eel with earthy beetroot purée and washed it down with an off-dry pinot gris. The thick texture of a dry white grenache, which tastes like a heavy late summer's day smells, also works well. So does the dancing texture of an off-dry riesling. At a tasting organized by Wines of Germany the cook Martin Lam, who knows a thing or two about putting food with wine, served warm smoked eel fillets on Jersey new potatoes with horseradish cream with a glittering, just-off-dry (with 5g/litre of sugar), bandbox-fresh riesling from the Mosel. This is a having-your-cake-and-eating-it kind of combination: the sugar gives the wine a fuller texture and the lithe acidity swooshes through the oil of the fish. Bone-dry riesling from Alsace also works in that cutting-across way. If drinking riesling with smoked eel and warm new potato salad, try chopping some chunks of green-skinned apple into the crème fraîche and mayonnaise mixture that binds the potatoes; the sweet-sourness of the apple fizzes pleasingly against the lime of the riesling.

The slice of ice-cold vodka is also refreshing with smoked eel and cool crème fraîche.

EGGS Eggs are not a completely natural match for wine, whatever the title of Elizabeth David's book, *An Omelette and a Glass of Wine*, might suggest. As boiled eggs, poached eggs, scrambled eggs, shakshuka, and fried eggs are breakfast items, this is probably no bad thing. The only alcohol it is acceptable to pour first thing in the morning is champagne, and by great good fortune that is a wine that works very well with almost all egg dishes. My second choice would be sparkling wine made elsewhere from chardonnay, pinot noir and pinot meunier. Cava would be the backup.

Where eggs are served as part of a lunch or salad, look at the other ingredients. The sharp acid of salad dressing is better with a simple, unoaked still white, or with the cool, hard edges of cava, than with a warm and toasty champagne.

eggs Benedict Well, maybe a glass of wine for weekend brunch ... The rounded edges and lemony glints of white burgundy go very well with the combination of eggs and buttery-vinegary hollandaise. Oaked burgundy has a rich toasty scent that fits right in with the eggs. Chablis and new-wave Australian chardonnay (look for one with lowish alcohol) are particularly successful, as their lemony edges play off the vinegar in the sauce: in fact I find it quite difficult to eat eggs Benedict without craving a cool glass of Chablis. English sparkling wine is also excellent: it is less briochey than champagne and has a brisk citrus edge that feels as if it is helping digestion. A really lovely combination.

fried eggs If the fried eggs are cooked in a tomato, onion, red pepper and spicy sausage sauce, and served with a chunk of bread as a main course, go for a wine that suits the sauce – maybe a young Rioja or barbera, or a rustic young Portuguese red based on touriga nacional. Lacy fried eggs with truffle shavings is another dinnertime classic and nothing goes better with this than nebbiolo.

oeufs en meurette A traditional Burgundian dish, in which eggs are poached in a sauce made from red wine, fried shallots and lardons. It's great with crusty bread and a glass of Bourgogne Rouge.

See also omelette, tapas, tortilla.

EMPANADAS These little savoury-stuffed pastries are a speciality of Argentina and can be made with chicken, spiced meat or sweetcorn. 'Every region of Argentina has their own style,' says Argentinian wine expert Maria Carola de la Fuente . 'In Mendoza they add olives, in Salta they add potatoes, in La Rioja, dried grapes.' With meaty empanadas, I always like to drink Argentine torrontés. This is a purely Pavlovian response, I think: this very floral white wine is what you have in Argentina, so it feels special to enjoy the two together, and reminds me of warm nights under Argentina's bright stars,

FRIED EGGS AND RIOJA

hungrily watching empanadas cook in a wood-fired stove. Otherwise, the fleshiness of a young barbera or a bonarda would be tasty and a more obvious choice with the meat.

ENCHILADAS An old Tex-Mex favourite, combining bold flavours, the endorphin-rush of chillies, and stodge. Wines that go well tend to be those that are simple, fruity, soft and safe. Don't spend too much money. With chicken enchiladas, if you want to drink white then pinot grigio, entry-level South African chenin blanc, or inexpensive chardonnay from a sunny place can all be good. Red works well with all enchiladas: try a red blend or zinfandel from California, a primitivo from southern Italy, a juicy and unoaked Chilean merlot, Argentine malbec or syrah, or a simple and unoaked monastrell or garnacha from Spain.

ESQUEIXADA This Catalan salad consists of tomatoes, shredded raw salt cod, olives, raw onion, a vinegary dressing, and sometimes also green and red bell peppers and flat-leaf parsley. If it's made using sherry vinegar (and even if it's not), the obvious choice is to drink a cold glass of fino, whose pungent iodine and sea spray scent grapples with the sting of the raw onion and cod. A glass of inexpensive, deep-coloured rosé, ideally made with the so-called workhorse grape bobal, is another good pick. A bone-dry and unobtrusive white can work here too; in Chile one producer farming vines in the stargazers' playground that is the Elqui Valley makes a white using the PX sherry grape that would be perfect here. A grassy verdejo is good too.

F

FAJITAS Wines that taste good with enchiladas also work with the unbaked version of these corn or flour tortillas stuffed with chicken or meat and eaten with salsa, soured cream, guacamole and other accompaniments. I'd also add carmenère to the list, because this grape is so good with the crispy bite of red and green peppers.

FENNEL Fennel is one of those herbaceous vegetables that can taste odd next to sweetly fruity wines. Its strong aniseed flavour (and that of its darker green, feathery fronds) needs a wine with acidic bite and a savoury personality. Anything from Italy – red or white, from sangiovese to vermentino – usually has a good chance of working with both raw and cooked fennel. Exceptions include red wines from Puglia, which are more rounded, ripe and sun-kissed. Even quite a small quantity of fennel on the plate can make it worth switching to a wine that will accommodate this tricky vegetable. Maybe you are eating roast pork with a side dish of braised fennel, in which case I'd be more likely to open a light sangiovese than a sweetly ripe pinot noir. Or perhaps a mixture of roasted root vegetables that includes a bulb or two of chopped fennel, in which case I'd say the same.

fennel gratin The tricky herbaceous quality of fennel is toned down when it is both cooked and eaten with cream. However, while chardonnay is an excellent grape with most gratins, here it's better to be more selective. Sunny, ripe, yellow, pineapple-and-melon fragranced chardonnay isn't the best with fennel. You want one that smells of woodruff and meadow grass – which leads you to Burgundy or Limoux.

fennel and orange salad (maybe with toasted pine nuts) The warm citrus flavour of orange is brilliant with whites from the south of Italy's boot, and these will also work with the fennel. Try neroli-scented falanghina; grillo from Sicily, which is reminiscent of candied peel, oranges and papaya; or the slightly tropical greco di tufo.

in salads Slivers of raw fennel in green salads, or with mozzarella and rocket, are best matched with leafy, precise white wines. Verdicchio, vermentino and vernaccia work particularly well. The damp, nettly taste of English bacchus is also good here. A grassy, smoky sauvignon blanc from the Loire can also work, as can the white pepper and grapefruit scent of a grüner veltliner from Austria.

See also fennel seeds.

FENNEL SEEDS Fennel seeds are often used with roast pork, to season sausages, and to scatter over roasted root vegetables. Their aniseed hit can be potent and is definitely a strong influence on the overall taste of a plate of food. They are more dusty and less greenly astringent than fresh fennel, but most of the wines that work for the vegetable also work for its seeds. Look for savoury rather than sweetly ripe or jammy wines. Italian reds (or whites), Austrian zweigelt, savoury pinot noir or a savoury chardonnay will do the trick.

FISH
the red wine question
'Can I drink red wine with fish?' is a question that comes up over and over again. I am never quite sure what is actually being asked here. 'May I drink red wine with fish?' 'Am I committing a social faux pas if I pour red wine with fish?' 'Will a biblical plague of locusts be unleashed on my family and all my descendants if I offend the fish with a glass of red?'

The idea that red wine with fish is transgressive appears to be a peculiarly Anglo concern that is not shared by other Europeans. The Portuguese unflinchingly pour rustic red wine with oily sardines sizzled with tomatoes and red onions. I've also enjoyed many fishy dinners in Italy with local red wines.

Spanish wine and food expert Maria José Sevilla finds the query odd too. 'We don't have prejudices about red and white wine in Spain,' she says. 'Certain ingredients make a difference to what you might drink with the fish. For instance, cod cooked pil-pil style, where the gelatin in the fish makes an emulsion with olive oil like mayonnaise, is good with red. Or if you add maybe some peppers, you cannot serve these dishes with white wine, they are too substantial.'

A better question, therefore, is: 'When might a bottle of red go on the table with a plate of fish and feel like the best and most delicious wine that could possibly be drunk with it?'

Red wine can be fabulous with fish but there is a time and a plaice for it. And before I start floundering in fish puns, I will salmon up some guidelines and examples.

As with any dish, picking wine to go with fish is simply a matter of not overpowering the food and bearing in mind the other ingredients. For instance, opening a 15% abv shiraz that has been aged for two years in toasty new oak to serve with a delicate Dover sole would just be silly. It would be nearly impossible to taste the sole through such a huge wine. As a general rule, blue (oily) fish such as sardines, trout, salmon and tuna are more robust and therefore more suited to red. But it also depends on where you are, who you are with (mood) and what else is on the plate.

a few happy fish and red wine combinations

cod wrapped in prosciutto and eaten with Puy lentils This goes well with nebbiolo or dolcetto – the nutty, earthy, meaty notes in the food chime with the dust and tannin of the wine.

Sicilian fish dishes Pasta con sarde (pasta with sardines), swordfish cooked in wine with tomatoes, stuffed squid, and all the rest can be brilliant with Cerasuolo di Vittoria, a local light red made from nero d'avola and frappato. A warm night and some ruins in your sight line are preferable, but not essential.

tomato-based fish stew With its sturdy fruitiness, this is good with Dão red from Portugal.

tuna steaks Pink in the middle, these are delicious with sappy light reds such as Sancerre Rouge, Beaujolais Cru or zweigelt from Austria.

white wine choices

Consummate fish and seafood wines include Muscadet, Douro whites (surprisingly refreshing, often made with verdelho, known in the Douro as gouveio), Vinho Verde, white wines from Provence, young Hunter Valley semillon, peachy albariño, and lemony Roussette de Savoie.

rosé wine

Almost always a good idea. Pick deeper-coloured, more tannic rosé with more assertive fish dishes.

These are only the most general of pointers. For more specific recommendations, please refer to individual entries: see *abalone, anchovies, bacalao, beurre blanc, blinis, bottarga, bouillabaisse, brill, caviar, ceviche, cod, crab, dill, eel, esqueixada, fish and chips, fish finger sandwiches with tomato ketchup, fish pie, fish soup, fritto misto and calamares fritos, Goan fish curry, gravadlax, hake, Jansson's frestelse, kedgeree, King George whiting, kippers, lobster, mackerel, monkfish, moules marinière, octopus, oysters, paella, parsley sauce, potted shrimp, prawns, red mullet, red snapper, risotto: seafood, rollmop herrings, salade niçoise, salmon, samphire, sardines, sashimi, scallops, sea bass, sea urchin, skate, sole (Dover and lemon), squid, sushi, swordfish, trout, tuna, zander.*

FISH AND CHIPS Yorkshireman Ian Kellett, who runs Hambledon Vineyard in Hampshire, has such cravings for what he calls 'proper' fish and chips – 'Haddock, skin off, and cooked in beef dripping, which fries them hotter' – that he sometimes jumps in the car and flogs up the M1 to Wakefield especially to buy them, a round trip of about 760 kilometres. That's quite a mission.

'I buy six times and put the rest in the freezer and warm them up when I want them. I have even been known to get a courier to drive from Yorkshire with them,' he once told me. 'It takes about four hours.'

Kellett is so absolutely focused on the fish and chips I'm not sure he even considers what's in his glass when he's eating them. But, as it happens, the best wine match for all that salt, vinegar, beef dripping and crunchy orange batter happens to be English sparkling wine, like the one he makes. Its vehement acidity and biting bubbles are good with salt, vinegar and fat. A young non-vintage champagne would also work, along the same lines, though I am more drawn to the cleaner swoosh of English sparkling. Personally, though, there is only one thing I would ever drink with this British institution: a pot of tea.

FISH FINGER SANDWICHES WITH TOMATO KETCHUP Fish fingers are a guilty pleasure and an inexpensive, softly fruity, safe-tasting red is perfect with slightly sweet tomato ketchup and the crunch of the breadcrumbs. Cheap supermarket wines do this job very well – you don't want a wine with intellectual aspirations. A supermarket Fitou is my tried and tested match for fish finger sandwiches (and I never thought, as I cleaned out my freezer one afternoon when I was supposed to be writing this book, that the distraction task would turn out to be actual bona fide research). I also like a very cheap, upbeat Côtes du Rhône or a Californian zinfandel or an Australian syrah-cabernet sauvignon blend. Don't spend too much money. It's best if the wine is bright and as catchy as a pop track.

FISH PIE Creamy fish pie goes well with chardonnays and fuller-flavoured whites. It doesn't mind a bit of oak either. My ultimate fish pie wine is a good, dry Loire chenin blanc, ideally an oaked Savennières or Montlouis. The acidity is refreshing against the rich dairy and there is an interplay between the smokiness of the oak and the plump pieces of smoked fish. A South African chenin would be a sunnier option, more suited to eggy fish pie than to spinach fish pie. In addition, there are all the usual white-fish suspects, such as picpoul, albariño, Muscadet and white Douro wines.

FISH SOUP One of the few soups with which a drink seems like a good idea. But there's more than one kind.

classic French fish soup The terracotta bisque of this classic, with its hot, garlicky rouille, goes beautifully with the throaty, sourdough taste of a chilled fino sherry. The oxidized style of Jura whites can also work: try a Jura chardonnay or savagnin.

lohikeitto (Finnish salmon soup) Salmon and potato soup flavoured with allspice and dill is a classic Finnish dish; a nourishing blanket of a winter supper eaten among the snowy, twilit, reindeer-stalked pine forests of the Arctic Circle. It's a creamy but robust broth, with chunks of salmon and just-disintegrating potatoes, and it goes well with a wine that also has soft, comforting curves. Try a curvaceous chardonnay, but pick one from a cool climate or with low alcohol, as the tropical flavours of very ripe chardonnay don't go well with dill. A Muscadet aged on the lees (sur lie) also has that lovely soft feeling, and Muscadet is a consummate fish wine. If the soup is very dill-heavy try an oak-aged sauvignon-semillon blend. However, I usually leave the wine alone and go for a shot of vodka or aquavit, ice cold, straight from the freezer.

FIVE-SPICE Five-spice powder is a mixture of cinnamon, fennel, star anise, cloves and ginger (or sichuan pepper and/or cardamom) – and yes, this adds to more than five. It is used in Chinese as well as other Asian cooking. Cinnamon is a spice I often describe as having a 'jagged' profile. It does not smell smooth. This is probably because cinnamon activates TRPA1, an ion channel that is thought to act as a noxious chemical sensor, and which participates in the production of pain sensations. Of course, cinnamon does not actually make you say ouch, at least not in the quantities in which it is normally used, but it is an irritant, producing a prickling sensation that adds to the pungency of this spice mix. Overly 'clean' wines don't feel right with five-spice; red or white, you want a bit of texture, a bit of rough (I don't mean that in a derogatory way), a bit of jostle. Five-spice is often used as a rub for pork, which works well with both red and white wine, or prawns, for which I'd veer towards white.

For whites, seek out fatter, aromatic varieties such as roussanne, white grenache, viognier and marsanne, all of which go well with pig, or – even better – a blend incorporating one or more of those. Judicious oak can be good, bringing its own spice to the mix. Wines from South Africa, Chile, Australia, New Zealand and the States tend to be more robust – a useful quality where five-spice is concerned.

For reds, I like the loose throatiness of South African red Rhône blends with their hints of liquorice and tar.

MILLTON VINEYARD'S CHINESE PORK BELLY
with Sichuan cucumber salad

SERVES 5–6

The Millton Vineyard is a biodynamic paradise in Gisborne, New Zealand. Annie Millton gave me this excellent recipe for pork belly rubbed with five-spice, which she likes to eat with Millton Vineyard viognier, though she says it's good with the chenin blanc too, and I've enjoyed it with South African blends of chenin blanc, viognier, chardonnay and roussanne. You need to get started in the morning of the day you want to eat it, if not the night before.

FOR THE PORK
2 cloves of garlic, peeled and finely chopped
2 tablespoons brown sugar
4 tablespoons soy sauce
100ml shaoxing wine
4 star anise, ground (or pounded to
    a grit using a pestle and mortar)
1 tablespoon five-spice
1 teaspoon white pepper
2kg pork belly, skin scored crossways
    at 2cm intervals
½ tablespoon rock salt

FOR THE SALAD
half a head of Chinese leaf, finely shredded
juice of half a lime
½ tablespoon sea salt
2 tablespoons groundnut oil
2 cloves of garlic, peeled and chopped
half a green chilli, deseeded and finely sliced
2 teaspoons sichuan pepper
1 tablespoon rice vinegar
1 teaspoon sesame oil
2 Lebanese cucumbers, peeled, halved
    lengthways and cut diagonally into
    slices (use half a normal cucumber
    if you can't find any, but deseed
    it before slicing)

In a dish big enough to fit the pork, mix the garlic, brown sugar, soy sauce, shaoxing wine, star anise, five-spice and white pepper. Put in the pork, flesh side down, and marinate, keeping the skin dry, uncovered in the fridge either overnight or for at least 3 hours before you are ready to cook it. (*Recipe continues overleaf.*)

About 1½ hours before you plan to eat, transfer the pork to a foil-lined baking tray. Cook in a preheated oven at 220°C/Fan 200°C/Gas 7/ 425°F for 30 minutes. Remove from the oven, sprinkle the skin with salt, turn the oven down to 180°C/Fan 160°C/Gas 4/350°F and cook for another 30 minutes. Now turn the oven back up to 220°C/Fan 200°C/ Gas 7/425°F and cook for another 10 minutes or so, until the skin crackles and blisters. Keep a close eye on it to make sure it doesn't burn. Remove from the oven and rest for 10–15 minutes before serving.

To make the salad, toss the Chinese leaf with the lime and salt and put in the fridge for an hour. Heat the groundnut oil in a frying pan and fry the garlic, chilli and sichuan pepper until fragrant. Set aside to cool. Combine the rice vinegar, sesame oil and chilli mixture. Toss with the Chinese leaf and cucumber in a bowl.

FOCACCIA Home-baked focaccia is a treat of a pre-dinner snack and you can customize it to go with whichever wine you're drinking. Olive Hamilton Russell of the eponymous South African winery sprinkles hers with rosemary if she's serving sauvignon blanc (rosemary is also a good bet with sangiovese) and with pine nuts or cashews for chardonnay. My old university friend and ace cook Anna Colquhoun (the Culinary Anthropologist) makes focaccia with balsamic vinegar, sweetly caramelized red onions and strawberries that is to die for (and she might have to if I'm ever going to wrestle the recipe out of her). She made it for a food and wine class we ran together and it was beautiful with moschofilero, a Greek white wine that smells of roses and lemongrass.

FOIE GRAS Foie gras, particularly if it is pan-fried and caramelized, has a lustre that is often matched with regal sweet wines such as Sauternes or Monbazillac. I prefer the lighter, more cleansing Jurançon Moelleux, a sweet wine made in the Pyrenees from gros and petit manseng, or an Alsatian Vendages Tardives. Champagne and other French or English sparkling wines also make a good accompaniment, the brisk acidity and the bubbles helping to disperse some of the mouth-coating fat. Also, clearly, champagne + foie gras is a sensational and sensationally indulgent snack. If foie gras is not being eaten by the slab but is part of a more complex dish, such as a terrine or a creamy sauce for chicken, then the curves of an oaked chardonnay or the bosomy, apricots-and-honeysuckle scent of an oaked viognier from the northern Rhône work very well.

FONDUE A great big pan roiling with melted Gruyère and Emmental, seasoned with garlic, white wine and kirsch and thickened with a spoonful of cornflour – what bliss. Even if you dip crunchy raw vegetables rather than cubes of toasted bread in it, cheese fondue is never going to make it into the nutrition sheets for cardiac care, but it is so delicious. An acerbic white wine from the Alps will give the impression of cutting through the fat in your mouth like Chemmy Alcott spraying snow on her parallel turns. My favourite is the jacquère grape from Savoie. Alternatives include picpoul from the Languedoc, grüner veltliner from Austria, a grassy sauvignon blanc from the Loire or Bordeaux, or savagnin from the Jura. A light, racy red can also work: try Marcillac, with its bloody tingle of iron, made from fer servadou in the Aveyron in France; or a frisky young Beaujolais.

FRIDGE RAID Those times when you stand hovering by the open fridge door, with an empty plate and a big appetite, prepared to eat anything and everything. Hopefully you will have a bottle of sherry tucked in there. Even if, strictly speaking, it's a bit too old and has passed into cooking sherry territory, pour yourself a glass to drink with whatever leftovers, chunks of ageing cheese and lumps of raw vegetables end up on your plate.

FRITTO MISTO AND CALAMARES FRITOS The crunch of light batter and, inside it, succulent seafood is a treat that goes well with almost any sharp dry white or white sparkling wine, from cava to prosecco to Vinho Verde to arneis. Unoaked white Rioja and floral malvasia are also good. And I love the salty-sea-spray-and-baking-sourdough riffle of a chilled glass of manzanilla sherry. Acidic red can work too.

FROGS' LEGS The primary taste of cooked frogs' legs is usually mild chicken overlaid with garlicky butter. Loire chenin blanc, Muscadet, white Côtes du Rhône or Mâcon or Saint-Véran all go well.

G

GAME see *grouse, partridge, pheasant, pigeon, rabbit, venison.*

GAMMON The salty pink meat of a roast gammon joint is beautifully complemented by the dry sweetness of ripe grenache. I'm thinking less of the pumice and herbal rasp of a southern Rhône wine (although these are good) and more of the baked-mulberry richness of an old vine grenache from Australia's Barossa or the lavish fruit of wines made from the old garnacha vines on the hillsides of Aragon in Spain (Calatayud, Cariñena and Campo de Borja are the DOs to look for). The ripe red berry taste of grenache echoes the kind of flavour explosion you have when you put Cumberland sauce with roast ham and, in fact, the three go together well. Alternatives that work in a similar vein include juicy carignan (from Chile or the Languedoc); Loire cabernet franc (Chinon, Bourgueil, St Nicolas de Bourgueil, Saumur or Saumur-Champigny) from a warm year; or ripe pinot noir from Australia, Chile or New Zealand.

White wines can also be very good with a cooked ham joint. Dry riesling from Alsace, New Zealand, Australia or Austria; white Côtes du Rhône; or Australian marsanne will emphasize the succulence of the meat.

GARLIC GAME-CHANGER Raw garlic is pungent and if you have ever thought that it also seems to taste hot, just like chilli, you are right. Like capsaicin in chilli, the allicin in raw (but not cooked) garlic activates an ion channel called TRPV1, which is used to detect thermal changes in the mouth, specifically temperatures of over 43.25°C, and this is what causes the burning sensation. Allicin also activates a second ion channel known as TRPA1, which is thought to be used to detect painfully cold (below –15°C) temperatures. So raw garlic elicits sensations of burning heat and burning cold at once. Its effect on wine is to overpower any that do not have sharp acidity or residual sugar, so with dips and dishes that are heavy in raw garlic, I always look for a mouth-cleansingly fresh wine. For instance, guacamole is good with the tingle of sauvignon blanc and aioli goes well with roussette.

Cooked garlic is much less aggressive than raw. In some heavily garlicky dishes, such as bagna cauda or garlicky pasta sauces, the garlic is still burningly pungent as it has only been heated, or partially cooked, and these still benefit from being eaten alongside a wine that has acidic bite. Thoroughly cooked garlic, whether fried or roasted, usually asserts itself in a more aromatic way; it's about fragrance, not attack, which leaves you free to choose aromatic wines that fit in with the whole dish.

GAZPACHO Fierce raw garlic, pungent onion and the sting of vinegar ensure that gazpacho is a mouthful to be reckoned with. It is a very temperamental dish, easily ruined by the use of rancid garlic, which seems to have become increasingly common and will pollute the plate with an acrid, harsh taste. Still, with good garlic – which can easily be identified by sniffing, though only once a clove has been peeled – this Andalusian dish feels more like a fresh, aromatic salad. The rich tomato base, verdancy of the green peppers, and the bite of alliums and vinegar are best matched with a sharp, cold fino or manzanilla sherry or a fuller, warmer amontillado. The sourdough-like warmth of the sherry acts as an amplifier on the tomato and its tang of sea spray underscores the crisp edges of the vegetables, while the gazpacho makes the sherry taste rounder, more fruity, less austere. A sharp white wine such as a verdejo (Spain's answer to sauvignon blanc) or one of those sauvignon blancs with a spiteful side to them can also be effective. I'm thinking of those sauvignon blancs from the Loire or from the Awatere Valley in Marlborough, New Zealand, or from South Africa that are all about the scent of citrus, grass and green tomatoes rather than nectarines, passion fruit and stewed ripe gooseberries. If you can find a wine with a barbed-wire-like tautness it will really zing against gazpacho.

MRS LEWISOHN'S GAZPACHO
(an adaptation)

SERVES 6

The best gazpacho, in my view, is made not by blending but by chopping the vegetables into very tiny pieces. My knife skills aren't that hot, so I compromise by blending but using lots of chopped vegetables as a garnish.

FOR THE SOUP
1½ cucumbers, peeled and roughly chopped
500g tomatoes, blanched, peeled
   and roughly chopped
1 green pepper, deseeded and roughly chopped
1 smallish white onion, peeled
   and roughly chopped
1 clove of garlic, peeled and chopped
125ml tomato juice
3 tablespoons good olive oil
2 tablespoons white wine vinegar
salt

TO SERVE
1 good chunk of cucumber, peeled
   and neatly diced
1 green pepper, deseeded and finely diced
2 tomatoes, finely diced
croutons
1 small bunch of flat-leaf parsley, chopped
Tabasco (optional)

Put the soup vegetables in a food processor and whizz until liquidized. You can also use a hand blender to liquidize them in a large bowl or pan, but a larger blender is easier and less likely to spatter your kitchen. Push the mixture through a sieve into a pan, bowl or large jug, discarding the pulp left in the sieve. Add the tomato juice, oil and vinegar (keep tasting, adding more if you like), stir to mix thoroughly, and season to taste. Put in the fridge for a couple of hours until chilled, then serve with small bowls of the diced vegetables, croutons and parsley for scattering on top. Add Tabasco if you think it's needed.

GINGER As anyone who loves a Moscow Mule already knows, ginger is gorgeous with lime. The two just have something special together. There is no more limey grape than riesling, and there is no more limey riesling than the stuff grown in the Eden and Clare Valleys in Australia. These wines have a rasp, a dryness, a gentle scent of lilac and a sharp cut that's like a steely blade that tastes of intense lime zest, freshly squeezed lime juice and lime blossom. They are wines to put with, say, crispy soft-shell crab fried with ginger and garlic; salad made using chicken marinated in soy, garlic and ginger; or fish cooked en papillote with ginger, lemongrass and chilli.

I sometimes find subtle hints of ginger in dry furmint, which is one reason why it tastes so good with sushi that is accompanied by thin slices of sushi ginger.

GNOCCHI With gnocchi, it's all about the sauce. See *pasta* for suggestions.

GOAN FISH CURRY The creamy coconut and mild spice of this dish from the southern coast of India go well with the aromatic florals of an off-dry pinot gris. My second choice would be a fruity, off-dry rosé, maybe from Anjou or Australia. If a more tangy, citric accompaniment is preferred, then try an off-dry riesling, perhaps from the Great Southern region in Western Australia.

See also chilli, curry.

GOOSE Goose is a fatty bird and the cut of a young claret provides a welcome contrasting edge. It's a great Christmas Day wine too.

GOUGÈRES In Burgundy, growers often serve their wines with freshly baked gougères, still warm from the oven. The smooth curves of a chilled glass of Chablis, or indeed any other chardonnay, go beautifully with the cheesy, choux-pastry balls, which are unexpectedly easy to make.

GOUGÈRES

MAKES ABOUT 20 GOUGÈRES

125ml water
50g butter
a pinch of salt
50g plain flour
a pinch of cayenne (optional)
2 eggs, beaten
75g Gruyère, grated

Preheat the oven to 220°C/Fan 200°C/Gas 7/425°F. Put the water in a pan with the butter and salt and bring to the boil. The boiling is important and you must carry on while the mixture is still very hot. Remove from the heat and add the flour and cayenne if using. Beat with a wooden spoon. Return to the heat and cook for 1–2 minutes, continuing to beat the mixture, until a film forms at the bottom of the pan. Allow to cool for a couple of minutes, then add about a third of the eggs and beat in thoroughly. Repeat until all the egg is incorporated, then add the cheese and stir until the mixture is smooth. Using two teaspoons, put walnut-sized balls of the mixture on to a sheet of baking parchment on a baking tray. Make sure to leave plenty of space between the balls as they will rise when they cook. Bake for 15– 20 minutes until golden brown, remove to a cooling tray and eat while still warm.

GOULASH The paprika and the peppers in this Hungarian stew are brilliant with carmenère, which often tastes of paprika, dust and red capsicum too. Fighty, robust Greek reds such as agiorgitiko also go well. As do reds from Portugal's Dão or, indeed, Hungarian country wines.

GRAVADLAX The thick fragrance of a dry Alsace muscat or a viognier will work with the fish and the dill. The minute you hit the sweetness of the mustard sauce, however, you run into trouble. An off-dry gewürztraminer can work here. Of course, what I'd really choose to drink is aquavit or vodka, ice cold, in shots.

GREEK SALAD Feta cheese and tomatoes have very tangy acidity and a third ingredient in Greek salad – raw onions – also delivers a sting. Pick a tangy wine to go with them. Grassy sauvignon blanc or grapefruit-pithy assyrtiko are two good options.

GROUSE The traditional answer to the question of what to drink with grouse is 'a bottle of good, old red burgundy'. This reminds me of the friend who nervously asked for advice on what to wear to a smart ball in Scotland and was told 'a long dress and your good jewels'. Devastating news for anyone who has failed either to inherit any rocks or to marry a man on a diamonds and rubies income.

Burgundy can be the same. Finding a decent bottle that is both older and ready to drink is the devil's work. You need to own it already, and, to do that, to have been in the habit of buying a case or two every year, when it is sold en primeur, for at least a decade.

Happily, I'm not sure the traditionalists are always right. The current fashion for cooking grouse is to serve it practically bleeding. With rare meat, it can be a good thing to have a prickle of tannin, a sense that is more about brightness and crunch than gentle autumn leaves. In other words, with rare grouse look for a young and not a mature wine. A sappy, young red burgundy – even a simple Bourgogne Rouge – would do the trick, as would a young, edgy claret. Save the mature burgundy for well-cooked grouse – the scent of mulching leaves and the earthy sense of place is beautiful with it.

Besides the cuisson, the level of gameyness has a huge impact on the wine. At the beginning of the season, when the birds are eaten fresh, the flavours are milder. Consider an Austrian red; or a good pinot noir from Australia (ideally from Geelong, whose wines are more savoury) or from New Zealand (Central Otago has the most weight and often a background taste of coffee or roasted fruits; Martinborough combines lift with structure).

A well-hung grouse needs a wilder red to meet the pungent flavours rising from the bird – and actually the wines I am about to suggest will go with grouse of more or less any kind. Mourvèdre can smell quite lived in and is a key grape in Bandol. Dão or Douro reds based on touriga nacional also have a pleasing element of savagery. The Languedoc is a good source of gamey reds (nose out a St Chinian or Pic St Loup) and the northern Rhône (Cornas, St Joseph,

Crozes-Hermitage) is rich with maturing syrahs that have exactly the feral, leathery pong you want. An old-fashioned Madiran, made from the tannat grape, also offers leathery austerity and firm, sinewy tannins. Nebbiolo, another mercilessly tannic grape, is a good option as well: I slightly favour Barbaresco over Barolo – it has more brightness and more of a reassuring plume of flavour to meet a well-hung grouse that is served rare. Finally, any red wine infected with a yeast strain called brettanomyces, which makes wine smell a bit horsey, is perfect with well-hung grouse. We used to believe that the niffy farmyard smell of brett was a charmingly French part of terroir. Although it's now considered a fault, it can add pleasing layers of flavour to cheaper wines. All of these wines could also very happily be drunk with a bird that is not well hung too.

G

H

HAGGIS This Scottish speciality made from sheep's heart, liver and lungs, oatmeal, suet and spices is traditionally eaten with mashed neeps and a nip of whisky. My preferred haggis whisky is Talisker 10 Year Old, a single malt from the Isle of Skye that smells like a slap of wild, brisk winter sea air with a tinge of woodsmoke in it. The piquant, peppery notes in the whisky meet the seasoning in the haggis as if they were made for each other.

Whisky aged in sherry casks has a gruff warmth and soft breadth that sidles up to the sweetness of the accompanying neeps. Try the warm spread of Macallan 10 Year Old Sherry Oak, or Kilchoman Machir Bay, which has the precise edge and peat of an Islay whisky but is also enriched with a few weeks in old oloroso butts. Japanese whiskies – the closest you get to Scotch outside Scotland – are also excellent with haggis as well as in their own right. Look for Yamazaki whiskies.

As for wine, the grape that works so well with pepper, not least because it tastes of cracked black pepper itself, is syrah. Go northern Rhône, or to cooler parts of Australia or South Africa.

HAKE Lightly fried in flour with perhaps a touch of egg, hake is gorgeous with chilled fino sherry. In Spain, the personality of hake seems to change from region to region, depending on how it is cooked, and the local wine – either red or white – is almost always the one that works the best.

HAM see *charcuterie, gammon.*

HANGOVER I drink Lucozade and endless cups of tea with a hangover. The hair of the dog cure is overrated.

HARISSA The fiery, red North African chilli-based paste is often used as a marinade or rub on chicken, quail and fish. This works well with aromatic off- or medium-dry whites such as blossom-scented pinot gris or a floaty riesling from the Mosel or Nahe. Rose harissa, in particular, is very pretty with the floral fragrance of a pinot gris.

An off-dry rosé will have a similarly soothing effect on the chilli fire of harissa. When this paste is smeared over charcoal-grilled lamb it can be pleasing to stoke harissa's heat by drinking red. A Lebanese or Portuguese blend is a good option.

HERBS GAME-CHANGER Herbs are powerful ingredients that have a huge impact on the flavour of a dish and therefore also on what wines taste good with it. There is a real potential for clash here – but also for great synergy.

See also coriander, dill, rosemary, tarragon, thyme.

HOLLANDAISE This buttery rich sauce works well with the curves and soft edges of barrel-fermented chardonnays, and also unoaked chardonnays.

H

I

ICE CREAM Cream, frozen or otherwise, is good with rich, warm-tasting spirits such as brandy and rum. Vanilla ice cream also works well with other drinks that channel Christmas flavours – nuts, spice, dried fruit and caffè mocha. And of course a vanilla ice cream base can be customized to go with just about any sweet flavour you like. There are a few ways to do this.

in Arguably the best way to mix alcohol and ice cream is to do it right from the beginning. The most obvious delicious examples are rum and raisin; Baileys; and eggy, Marsala-lashed zabaglione. Being experts in both wine and ice cream, the Italians can't resist turning practically every drink made on the peninsula into gelato, but I draw the line at gelato flavoured with nero d'avola (the red wine grape found in Sicily) and Strega (a violent yellow, bitter herbal liqueur).

over Slosh alcohol over a couple of scoops of dairy vanilla and serve it in a tall sundae glass like a boozy affogato. One wine that's good for pouring over ice cream is pedro ximénez, known as PX for obvious pronunciation-difficulty reasons. This viscous sherry is possibly the sweetest wine in the world, loading up to as much as 450g of sugar per litre. Thick, and a very dark, treacly brown, it looks and tastes like molasses might if molasses had had fat, juicy raisins liquidized into it. Ice cream and PX is one of the quickest, easiest and best-received desserts I have encountered. My granny used to go nuts for it. In fact, a slim half-bottle of PX is a very good granny stocking filler.

with – quick suggestions Stick to ice cream in the vanilla-chocolate-nuts-crème brûlée-coffee-fudge spectrum and there are many wines – most of them fortified – that will taste good in a glass beside it. Try Australian Liquer Muscat, the indulgent fortified wine that's reminiscent of demerara sugar, caramel and dried fruit; sweeter Madeiras – wines from the volcanic island between Africa and the European mainland that have such longevity they are virtually immortal (bual and malmsey are the grapes used to make sweeter styles); Marsala; tawny port; Maury (a red vin doux naturel made in the Roussillon in southern France from powdery grenache); and chocolate liqueur. My pinnacle ice cream and booze experience (to date) was at Penfolds' Magill Estate in South Australia. There for lunch, I passed on dessert, only to enrage my neighbour by eating half of hers. It was an incredibly elaborate ice cream, made with roasted almonds, chocolate, macadamia nuts, caramel and raisins that had been marinated in Penfolds' Grandfather Tawny – a rich, fortified Australian alternative to port. With it, we drank a glass of Penfolds' Great Grandfather Tawny, a more refined, intense version of the wine in the ice cream. It is easy to make an approximation of this gorgeousness using a good recipe for vanilla ice cream as a base and either an Australian fortified wine or an aged tawny port for the drinking and the raisin-soaking (this always makes me think of Roald Dahl's *Danny the Champion of the World* – do not include sleeping tablets). Claudia Roden uses a similar raisin and sweet wine combination in a favourite recipe in her book *The Food of Spain*. Also, she likes to put the booze in the ice cream as well as passing it round to drink with it.

more elaborate ideas In theory, any sweet wine could go with any ice cream, if the dessert has been put together so that the flavours reflect and complement the wine. Only remember that if your mouth is very cold you will not taste as many nuances in the wine. I once drank Tokaji, the rich, sweet golden wine from Hungary, with ice cream made with figs and orange peel stewed in sweet wine – a real hit. On another occasion an old bottle of Château d'Yquem, the famous Sauternes, was opened to go with vanilla ice cream served with slivers of fresh coconut and pineapple with Cape gooseberries and kumquats. A very clever combination.

INDIAN India makes wine but is neither a wine-drinking culture nor a wine-with-food culture.

'I learnt very quickly on arriving in France that people will stand for fifteen minutes with an aperitif, then spend three hours over dinner with wine,' Indian-born sommelier Magandeep Singh told me at a tasting of Indian wines. 'In India, the opposite. You call people for 7 p.m., they'll turn up at 8 p.m., spend three hours talking and grazing over a buffet, then rush through dinner in twenty minutes and be home asleep by midnight. Food and wine pairing is a bit lost on us, because we don't do it outside a hotel or a restaurant.'

The exploration of wine flavours with Indian food has therefore largely been left to cooks who have emigrated and set up restaurants in Britain, Australia, the US, and elsewhere, as well as Western eaters and drinkers pouring wine with food they have cooked from recipe books at home, ordered from the takeaway or are eating in a restaurant.

This means that we're always thinking about versions of real Indian cooking – adaptations and approximations, and a dilution of regionality – as we tend to have dishes originating in completely different parts of India on the table at once.

Westernization brings another shift in emphasis. The Indian wine-making company Grover Zampa tells me their off-dry viognier is very popular – the aromatics play into the spicy scents and the slight sweetness acts as a buffer against the burn of the chilli. These are the kinds of flavours I would choose with spicy dishes. However, while 70 per cent of Grover Zampa's produce is sold on the domestic market, much of it is drunk in restaurants in the big, more international, cities of Mumbai, Delhi and Bangalore. Many Indians I speak to who do enjoy drinking wine with food say they love not off-dry whites but oaked reds, the very wines I steer away from with heavily spiced dishes, as heat and spice make the tannins (from both the wood and the grape) feel tough and harsh. I had always presumed this reflected either a higher tolerance for chilli and spice, or a preference for that clash. Magandeep makes a different point: 'In India, we don't have side plates. The bread goes at the six o'clock position on the plate with the other dishes ranged around it. Every time I have a mouthful, I'm starting with the bread, or the rice, and dipping into the others. Eighty per cent of each mouthful is carbs. This has a softening effect on the spices.' In other words, when eating from the same table, an Indian's experience of the food is different from the richer hit of mostly sauce, spice and protein a Westerner might enjoy.

The world of Indian food is large and sprawling, but if you are sharing food, with several dishes on the table at once, finding a wine that tastes good with it is always going to be an art of approximation.

That's why I have written at most length about the effect of *chilli* and talked about the generic dish we call the *curry* as well as giving entries for just a few of the best-known Indian foods.

See also dhal, Goan fish curry, rogan josh, tandoori.

J

JACKET POTATO (WITH CHEESE) When the potato is cooked in bonfire embers, or in the oven without being wrapped in foil to keep the skin tender, so that it has a crisped, smoky-smelling thick jacket, try a smoky oaked St Chinian, which sometimes smells of chestnut skins. A bottle of claret is another cosy match. Ditto a cabernet sauvignon-syrah blend from Australia. If you want to posh it up, then nebbiolo, Barolo or Barbaresco is great with the buttery cheese and the smell of fire. But of course anything goes with this kind of comfort food.

JAMBON PERSILLÉ This jellied ham terrine made with pork hock and parsley and served in thick slices with bread or toast is delicious as a starter or snack. A cool, lightly oaked white burgundy is perfect.

JANSSON'S FRESTELSE Literally, Jansson's temptation – a Swedish dish that is traditionally eaten at Christmas – this is a kind of fishy dauphinoise made with potatoes, onions and 'ansjovis'. Ansjovis are sprats that have been cured in spiced brine and have a sweet, mellow, clovey taste – unfortunately, substituting Mediterranean anchovy fillets does not work. Jansson's frestelse was first cooked for me by the human gastronomic tornado that is the half-German, half-Swedish (by parentage), English-raised Joe Wadsack. Joe made it using Abba ansjovis imported from the homeland, which, despite being packaged in a tin, must be kept refrigerated. The spice mix used in these is a secret but it is said to include cinnamon, sandal-wood and ginger. An ice-cold shot of vodka (bison-grass Zubrówka, for choice) acts like a palate cleanser in between mouthfuls of this salty-sweet-spicy-oniony potato gratin, but aquavit is an even better choice as its spices play off those in the food.

'In fact,' said Joe, as we sat discussing ansjovis, 'the more I eat Jansson's frestelse, the more I think you have to drink aquavit with it.' He then proceeded to give me a rapid lesson in aquavit styles:

'Swedish aquavit – the best-known brand is O. P. Anderson – is typically very pristine and sleek and fresh, with herby dill and fennel overtones. Danish aquavit – Aalborg is the big brand – is similar but softer, not so crisp, a kind of fino to O. P. Anderson's manzanilla, and the caraway flavours are stronger. In Norway, you have Linie, which is sent out to sea in oak sherry casks. You have the unusual humidity, and the rocking motion of the boat on the waves, so it's softer still, like aged rum, and a different drink to the other two.'

A wine that is equally clean and needle-sharp – say, aligoté or the Alpine jacquère – and served at a fairly arctic temperature is a good alternative.

JERK (CHICKEN, GOAT OR PORK) Rum (with soda) is best with this hot and spicy Caribbean dish which contains thyme, fresh ginger, allspice and brown sugar. A slightly sweet beer is next best. For wine, go for an unpretentious, deep pink rosé that isn't perfectly dry.

J

K

KEBAB Home-made kebab is a favourite way of using up leftover roast lamb, but I eat these so quickly and so greedily and so messily – garlic and chilli sauce oozing out of the pitta, shredded lettuce and bits of tomato spilling all over – there is never any chance to take a sip of wine. I do know, though, that lamb kebabs in pitta are fantastic with a robust rosé (maybe one from Lebanon), or a robust red with a bit of fight in it (from Greece, Turkey, Lebanon or Portugal). Chicken kebab needs an inexpensive, neutral white.

KEDGEREE I have never got on with any wine with this mixture of smoky fish, egg and rice with cumin. Also, it's a breakfast dish. Lapsang souchong tea, whose leaves are smoked over pine wood fire, matches the intense smokiness of the fish and seems to me the only way to go.

KING GEORGE WHITING The delicate white flesh of one of Australia's finest fish, the King George whiting, is superb with young, fresh Australian riesling. The piercing lime flavours of the dry wine are gloriously refreshing in between mouthfuls of (ideally barbecued) fish on a sunny day close to a beach.

KIPPERS Smoky kippers and buttered brown bread cry out for a cup of English breakfast, lapsang souchong, or Earl Grey tea. The only alcoholic alternative is a nip of peaty Islay whisky.

L

LAMB Lamb is blessed by having a grape seemingly made precisely to go with it. That grape is cabernet sauvignon. This means that a classic match is red bordeaux, preferably one from the left bank, where cabernet sauvignon usually forms the backbone of the blend. At the high end, this might be a top growth from the commune of Pauillac in the Médoc, which you could drink with rack of Pauillac lamb conveniently raised nearby; sheep in the region, as well as wine, have protected designation of origin status from the EU. On an everyday level, stick a chop on the griddle and open the most miserly, scratchy claret you can find – anything will do, as long as there is cabernet sauvignon as well as merlot in there. When you drink and eat, a piece of magic will occur. A wine that tasted as dusty, threadbare, green and tannic as black tea is transformed, becoming riper and more succulent. It's practically a party trick and a brilliant way to make cheap wine sing.

Cabernet sauvignon does not, of course, have to mean bordeaux. There are great, slightly more rustic, versions in nearby Bergerac and in Buzet, as well as further south in the Pays d'Oc. Nor does it have to come from France. There are superb examples and blends from the Napa Valley, Argentina, South Africa, Tuscany and Australia, and that's just for starters.

Cabernet sauvignon is also far from being the only red that is absolutely gorgeous with lamb. I've lost count of the number of times I've put a butterflied leg of lamb, smeared with a mortar and pestle paste of garlic, anchovies and rosemary, in the oven and not just because it's an easy dinner. The aromatic flavour of this dish is good with so many red wines that I had to ban winemakers from recommending it in the second half of the book, otherwise that's all you'd have read about. Lamb is also fantastic with red wine from Rioja and Ribera del Duero (particularly slow-cooked lamb); Portugal; Provence, the Rhône, Madiran and the Loire (France again); Greece and the Lebanon. To get the most out of both wine and food, it's worth paying attention to how the lamb is cooked (barbecued, roasted, griddled, casseroled), for how long (seared versus slow) and what other flavours are involved. Has it been rubbed with hot spices or covered in fresh green herbs? Is it going to be eaten with bright pomegranate seeds, smoky aubergines and hummus, or with stuffed Mediterranean vegetables? Or has it been barbecued over smoky coals? There are suggestions for all of these, and more, below.

Is there any red wine that lamb doesn't go with? Well, yes, actually. At an extensive tasting of pork, beef and lamb with Argentine wines at the Gaucho Grill, I was surprised to find that lamb and malbec are the sort of bedfellows who would probably approach each other awkwardly from across the central mattress chasm, bicker over the tog rating of the duvet and end up sleeping in different rooms.

There is no need to stick with red, though. Rosé is also delicious. A glass of palest pink from Provence with new-season lamb is a real treat; the heavier and richer the accompaniments, the darker and sweeter you can afford to go with the wine. Don't rule out white wine either. Lamb stuffed with herbs, capers and olives and served with potatoes cooked Greek-style with vigorous lemon and oregano can taste great with a vibrant assyrtiko from Santorini or an oaked white bordeaux.

See also cottage (or shepherd's) pie, curry, kebab, Lancashire hot pot, moussaka, tagine.

cuts and cooking styles

barbecued The big flavours of meat cooked over smoky coals or burning wood demand wine with substance and courage. If you're picking bordeaux, go for one that's young and vital, or young-ish and more expensive (more expensive = more concentrated). Otherwise, this is a good moment to bring out a northern Rhône or a New World red: for instance, a smoky syrah from South Africa or an exuberant Barossa Shiraz. The ingredients in the marinade or rub will also determine the direction (see below).

braised shank Peasant reds with soft flavours suit the rich, melting texture of this cheaper slow-cooked cut. Reds from the

Languedoc-Roussillon – Corbières, Fitou, St Chinian – fit the bill. A Lebanese red blend or an inexpensive South African cabernet, syrah, merlot or cinsault would also be good.

cold roast The more solid texture of cold slices of meat goes well with young, fruity wines with a bit of edge (acidity) and little or no oak. Try a Côtes du Rhône; Coonawarra cabernet sauvignon; Beaujolais Cru or Villages; basic claret (perhaps a Côtes de Castillon); or a bright, focused Italian red such as barbera.

kidneys A soft, light pinot noir from Australia, or a country French pinot, will meet the soft texture of the kidney.

liver The tang of sour cherries is good with lamb's liver and this is found in young dolcetto, barbera or gamay. If lamb's liver and kidneys are being eaten together, then try the herbaceous tautness of a German pinot noir. An alternative is a strongly fla-voured red such as Chilean carmenère or South African cabernet or pinotage.

milk-fed Tender and subtle, this merits a more distinguished, older bottle, such as a mature bordeaux or burgundy, whose flavours will be complex but also much more delicate than those of a bright young wine.

pink Pinot noir or the leafy redcurrant and new-school-pencil taste of cabernet franc from the Loire is lovely with pink lamb, particu-larly if served with a tangle of peas, lettuce, baby carrots and other spring vegetables.

roast With a plain roast, you can go almost anywhere. See the list at the top of this entry for suggestions from left-bank bordeaux to Supertuscans.

slow-roast Shoulder is the cut that most often comes in for the slow-roast treatment and it is at home with Spanish reds such as Rioja or Ribera del Duero. Try them young, for the contrast between the falling-off-the-bone meat and the bright strawberry and straw flavours in the wine, or with more oak, and older, when the wine begins to mellow like autumn leaves and will melt right into the soft lamb.

with

anchovies, rosemary and garlic The Mediterranean/Italian flavours suit wines from the same place. With leg of lamb, basted or slits stuffed with this salty mixture of condiments, try Bandol or red from another part of Provence, Languedoc reds (Corbières, Faugères, St Chinian, for example), Rhône reds, north or south – both have a wild, herbaceous, sometimes almost menthol, smell that picks up on the rosemary. Central Italian wines such as Rosso di Montepulciano or Montalcino or Chianti are good too. Be extra-smart and bring in a cabernet sauvignon element by opening a Domaine de Trevallon, a red wine made in Provence from syrah and cabernet, or a Supertuscan, or a Chianti that has a small amount of cabernet bolstering the majority sangiovese in the blend (Querciabella and Fontodi are two Chianti Classico estates that use a percentage of cabernet in one of their cuvées). Italian + cabernet is a particular winner if you're putting the anchovies, rosemary and garlic in a white bean side dish – brilliant with griddled lamb steaks.

chilli/spicy rubs Try a warm, ripe hug of Australia's great syrah-cabernet blend or a bright, fruity red from Chile or South Africa.

couscous (as a side dish) With a rich, raisined couscous, try the woody, plum and tobacco flavours of a Rioja Reserva. Lamb with spicy couscous studded with pomegranate seeds can be good with cabernet sauvignon from Coonawarra in Australia, pinot noir from Central Otago in New Zealand or a roar of an Australian syrah, maybe from McLaren Vale or the Barossa. Couscous with sharper flavours, such as radish and spring onion, served with pink lamb prefers a cabernet franc or an unoaked Costières de Nîmes.

feta, lemon, capers and/or green olives The high acid and salt here need a wine that can fight back with some acidity/astringency of its own. Barbera would work, as would a Lebanese or Greek red, or a very young, keen-edged red bordeaux without too much oak on it. If the feta, lemon, capers and olives are very heavily represented either in the stuffing or accompanying salads and potatoes then you could equally well go for a young white such as an oaked white Bordeaux with its baked grapefruit, lemon pith and woodruff flavours, or a bracing assyrtiko from Santorini. Diana Henry combines many of these flavours in her glorious, Easterish recipe for Greek-influenced lamb – lamb with caper, parsley and preserved lemons stuffing which you can find in her book *Food from Plenty*.

herb crust On a simple chop, a rack of lamb, or leg, the leafy, crunchy crust calls for a cabernet of some sort – either sauvignon or franc. Head to Bordeaux, the Loire or Coonawarra in Australia.

lavender and rosemary Butterflied leg of lamb scattered with rosemary and lavender is delicious with Côtes du Rhône (Villages), either from the generic appellation or from a village that has been promoted to its own appellation – such as Gigondas, Vacqueyras, Rasteau.

Mediterranean vegetables (aubergines, tomatoes stuffed with thyme and garlic, red peppers) We're back in Provence. One of their vanishingly pale rosés would go well. Or I might be tempted north, just slightly, for a syrah from the northern Rhône or a grenache-based blend from the southern Rhône.

meze/Middle-Eastern flavours If you're eating lamb as part of a dinner with many other meze dishes, there is likely to be a lot going on: a crowd of green parsley, salty olives, tangy sumac, earthy chickpeas and spices. A wine needs growl to stand up to these boisterous flavours. Crozes-Hermitage and St Joseph from the northern Rhône do this well. Deep coloured rosés are good too. As are the more rustic, tannic reds coming out of Eastern Europe or the (much-finessed in the last few years) blends from Lebanon. A clever solution is the throaty syrah made in the heat of Morocco by Crozes-Hermitage star Alain Graillot. Or try Stellenbosch cabernet sauvignon.

mint sauce The violent vinegar and mint need a cheap, acidic bordeaux.

redcurrants and other sweet, fruity accompaniments With red berries on the plate with lamb, I veer towards bright, young reds from the Loire (cabernet franc is very good with lamb and redcurrants) or riper reds from Argentina, South Africa, Chile, New Zealand and Australia. If there's an earthy tinge – say, lentils or hummus – on the plate too, then you can take a bit more oak.

skordalia For wines to go with lamb as well as this lemon and almond mash see the *feta, lemon, capers and/or green olive* entry above.

LANCASHIRE HOT POT Any number of reds go well with this dish but I particularly like inexpensive tempranillo, from Rioja or elsewhere, as its mellow quality is good with both the lamb and the sweetness of the cooked root vegetables.

LASAGNE Lasagne to most means what the Italians call lasagne alla bolognese – pasta layered with meat ragù and béchamel sauce. There are many interpretations, from those that are light and scented with bay leaves to the cheesy, gooey Anglo versions. All go well with Italian red wine, most of which have the acidity to cut through the creamy sauce, as well as the savour to match the meat. Sangiovese is a good catch-all; pick a Chianti Rufina if you want the wine to be more refreshing. I like young (unoaked or barely oaked) nebbiolo with the less creamy, more herbaceous versions. But Italy has many other red wines that will do a good job with lasagne, from easy-drinking Biferno Rosso to nero d'avola from Sicily. Look at the entry for *ragù alla bolognese* for more ideas.

Of course, lasagne is simply the name of the type of pasta. It takes only a glance at the index of *The Silver Spoon*, the bestselling Italian cookbook, to see that there are many regional variations, including lasagne alla napoletana (made with beef, mozzarella and slices of hard-boiled eggs), lasagne with radicchio, with leeks and black truffles, with aubergine and ricotta, and so on. Add to this the number of different veggie lasagnes developed outside Italy and lasagne would probably fill a book on its own. Baked pasta dishes from lasagne to cannelloni to pasticcio are usually richer and heavier than boiled pasta dressed with a sauce, but the filling remains the best guide. Any lasagne, veggie or otherwise, made using tomatoes will usually go well with sangiovese. A radicchio lasagne demands a wine with astringency. Seafood and tarragon lasagne is good with sauvignon-semillon blends. Mushroom lasagne with almost any rich, meaty red wine. And so on.

LEMON GAME-CHANGER Lemon is an ingredient that demands attention. It's just so piercing and acidic, which can make some wines taste flat. Watch out for lemon-dressed salads, or baked dishes that include whole lemon slices: for example, one-pot chicken with chickpeas, green olives and lemons, or fish roasted with thinly sliced lemons.

If you are having a lemony salad with meat – say, steak and spinach with lemon juice and olive oil – then you can count on an Italian red wine to have enough acidity to deal with the issue. Otherwise, it is simple: look for whites that taste of lemons or other citrus fruit, as they will often have vibrant acidity. Good examples include Gavi, arneis, sauvignon blanc, riesling, verdejo and assyrtiko.

See also preserved lemon.

LEMON TART Dessert wines made from riesling have a tingle that is perfect here; look for a beerenauslese or trockenbeerenauslese from Germany.

LEMONGRASS This tropical grass with a woody base has an energizing citrus fragrance that dovetails with aromatic white wines made from riesling, sauvignon blanc (especially the pungent sauvignon from New Zealand or South Africa or Chile) and grüner veltliner. A word of warning, however. Lemongrass is often used in Thai cooking and when chilli, which prefers sweeter wines, gets involved ignore it at your peril. Still, there's such a natural affinity between those aromatic wines and lemongrass that, if cooking Thai, I often open a bottle of dry riesling or Marlborough sauvignon blanc to drink in the kitchen during the chopping and chatting part of the evening. Bone-dry Hugel riesling from Alsace – which tastes at first like just-squeezed lime juice washing over stones, then starts to swell out like peaches and clementines – is a favourite bottle to open while making a giant bowlful of 'Chicken, lime and lemongrass soup' from Tom Parker Bowles's book *Let's Eat*.

See also chilli.

LENTILS The presence of earthy, small dark green (they may not necessarily be Puy) lentils, or the little brown ones you find in Umbria, shuffles a plate of food towards a red wine. It might be a chunk of cod with pancetta and lentils, or honey-roast gammon with lentils cooked in the ham stock and mixed with chopped rosemary, garlic and a spoonful of cream, but either way red usually appeals more at this point than white. I usually go with whatever wine is suggested by the other ingredients on the plate: maybe a nerello mascalese from Sicily with the fish, perhaps an Aussie grenache with the ham. If you're looking for a wine that shares the same earthy register as the lentils, then consider mencía from Spain, Dão from Portugal or a farmhousey Chianti.

See also dhal.

LIME As with lemons, the acidity has a strong impact and, if there's lots of it, it's best to choose a wine that has decent acidity too. There is one grape that both tastes of lime and also has very vibrant acidity – riesling.

See also lime (dried), South-East Asian food.

LIME (DRIED) Dried limes are used in Middle Eastern cooking. They are intensely aromatic and the lime comes through in a very dusty and earthy, rather than in a sharp, way. They have a tendency to take over a dish, and when that happens I look to reds that remind you of soil and heat. Those from Greece, Lebanon, Turkey and Portugal often work well.

Here is an adaptation of a classic Iranian dish. I love the strong flavour of the limes in it so much that I break them up and squeeze them over the food on my plate to get even more of the dusty limeyness out. If dried limes are an alien flavour, maybe just use one the first time you make this, as the taste is quite powerful.

L

KHORESH GHEIMEH
(Lamb, dried lime and tomato casserole)

SERVES 3–4

olive oil
1 onion, peeled and chopped
3 cloves of garlic, peeled and finely chopped
500g lamb, diced
1 pinch of saffron, mixed with 2 tablespoons
    warm water
¼ teaspoon ground cinnamon
¼ teaspoon ground cumin

½ teaspoon ground coriander
1 teaspoon turmeric
1 × 400g tin tomatoes (whole)
2 tablespoons tomato purée
3 dried limes, pierced a couple of times
   with a metal skewer or corkscrew
150g split yellow peas, rinsed in cold water
500ml water
1 aubergine
plain yoghurt to serve (optional)

Put 2 tablespoons of olive oil in a small casserole dish, heat gently, add the onions and fry until they are almost soft and translucent. Add the garlic, stir and continue to cook until both garlic and onions are pale gold. Use a slotted spoon to take them out of the pan and set aside. Now brown the lamb in the same pan, turning up the heat and adding more oil if necessary. Return the onion mixture to the pan and stir in the saffron, cinnamon, cumin, coriander and turmeric. Cook for a couple of minutes, stirring. Add the tomatoes, breaking them up with the edge of the spoon as you stir, and the tomato purée. Pour some of the water into the tomato can, swirl it around and then add all the water to the pan along with the dried limes. Simmer gently, partially covered, for 45 minutes. Now stir in the split yellow peas and carry on simmering, partially covered, for 45–60 minutes. Check to make sure the casserole does not simmer dry, adding more water if necessary. While the casserole is cooking, slice the aubergine and cut into strips. Fry these in oil until they are golden and cooked, then put them on a plate, layered with kitchen roll to absorb the grease. The stew is ready when the pulses are completely cooked through and the sauce has thickened. Serve with rice studded with little chunks of cold butter, and the aubergine strips scattered on top, with a dish of yoghurt on the side if you like.

LIVER Chicken livers (served either in a spinach and bacon salad, or fried and chopped with capers on crostini) are a natural with sangiovese or Beaujolais. Seared calf's liver and bacon goes well with barbera, red bordeaux, Beaujolais, Chianti or Valpolicella Ripasso.

See also chicken: liver.

LOBSTER With hot grilled lobster, open a white burgundy – as good a bottle as you are prepared to pay for – or an oaked Bordeaux Blanc whose substance, taste of baked-citrus, and pine tree scent are perfect with the sweet lobster meat. Bordeaux Blanc is particularly good if the lobster has been grilled with lime rather than plain or lemon butter. With cold lobster mayonnaise (perhaps with freshly torn basil leaves and halved cherry tomatoes mixed in), a cool glass of chardonnay is perfect for its creamy texture. Pick one that's not too heavy: go for one from Chablis or from elsewhere in Burgundy; for one of the new-wave Australian chardonnays from the Mornington Peninsula or from other, cooler, Victorian regions; or champagne.

M

MACARONI CHEESE For a white that's refreshing against all that gooey cheese, pick picpoul or one of the citric unoaked Italian grapes (such as arneis, cortese, vermentino, slightly spiky vernaccia). But this is old-fashioned nursery food, and an old-fashioned glass of red bordeaux – youngish (for the refreshing edge), and with plenty of cabernet in it – is also satisfying.

See also cheese, pasta.

MACKEREL Choose a bracing white or red with this oily fish. Say, Gamay de Touraine or Marcillac for a red, Vinho Verde for a white.

MEATBALLS There are many different styles of meatballs, so be guided by the seasoning. With Italian flavourings – basil, Pecorino, fennel, fennel seeds – choose an Italian wine. Nero d'avola, Teroldego Rotaliano or Cerasuolo di Vittoria (a blend of frappato and nero d'avola from Sicily) is a lovely summery match with Pecorino and basil porkballs in a milky tomato sauce. With spicier cumin and coriander meatballs, pick a throatier wine, perhaps a red from Lebanon. With straightforward beef meatballs in a tomato sauce, you can very happily drink almost any cosy red.

MELON Heady, fragrant and sweet-fleshed galia and charentais melons taste of summer. Ripe halves of these, with the seeds scooped out and the hollow filled with sweet liquor, are a brasserie staple with a markedly retro vibe. In the area around La Rochelle, in western France, where pale green striped charentais melons are grown, they fill them with Pineau des Charentes, a drink made by mixing sweetly ripe, tangy fresh grape juice with the burn of eau de vie. It's a hedonistic marriage. The glow of the nectar-like Pineau is blissful with the perfumed melon and I can't imagine why we don't drink more of it. A happy alternative is port – white or, even better, tawny, which is oak-aged, so that it takes on the relaxed flavours of caramel, dried fruit and roasted hazelnuts. In both cases the port tastes better chilled.

melon with air-dried ham Often the instinct is to pour red with charcuterie, however it is served. But a fruity or aromatic white brings a juicy succulence to prosciutto, serrano or other air-dried hams, counterpointing their salty savouriness. Perfumed whites such as viognier (all heady honeysuckle and apricot skin) and muscat (grapey and floral) also play to the hedonistic qualities of the melon. These effects are enhanced if the wine is off-dry – the sweetness of the melon hides the sugar in the wine so that you barely discern it. In fact, if there's a lot of melon then you *need* a white with some sugar in it, otherwise the fruit sweetness will completely knock out the wine so that it tastes arid, like putting sand in your mouth. No need to go overboard with a super-sticky dessert wine – an off-dry or medium white or pink will do the job. Try a non-dry chenin blanc from the Loire, scented like wildflower honey and quince: Vouvray or even the cheapest white Anjou will slide beautifully up against the ham and melon. The innocent, apple blossom waltz of a kabinett-level German riesling (go for one from the Mosel or Nahe – wines from the Rheingau are often too stern and earthy for melon) is also a good option. For a little more sweetness, try a gently effervescent moscato. This style originates from the north-west of Italy where the joyful, floral, stones-and-peach-skin frippery that is Moscato d'Asti is made. This is still the best as well as the most delicate and subtle moscato. But sparkling moscato is also big in California (the mammoth E.&J. Gallo makes it) and Australia (Innocent Bystander sell their bubbly rose-coloured moscato in wine bottles, lager-sized bottles and also by the keg. Yes, it's that big).

MEZE The earthy grittiness of chickpeas; the smoky burnt aubergine dips; the tahini, the fried little balls of spinach and spicy sausages, the piles of green tabbouleh with their radish and toasty crunch; the crackle of the thin sheets of charred taboon flatbreads ... Very often with a table full of food exuding Middle Eastern flavours I will pour that 'sling it with everything' of wines – a rosé. It's not imaginative, but it works extremely well. If choosing a white wine, hold back on buttery New World chardonnay or vengeful sauvignon blanc and look instead for a less cartoon-like grape, such as a plain, stony bianco Terre di Chieti from Abruzzo in Italy or a fresh, citric roditis from Greece. For reds, sangiovese has a wonderful, gritty taste that is excellent here. Also ideal are reds from Greece, Lebanon, Morocco and Turkey and darker, heavier reds from Portugal or a brooding Languedoc blend, such as a Corbières, Fitou or St Chinian. For something a bit lighter, stick a bottle of Bardolino or Valpolicella in the fridge for twenty minutes and drink it with an edge of cold on it.

MINCE PIES The crumbling pastry and luscious dried fruit of mince pies suit the molten raisin flavour of a sweet oloroso or cream sherry. It somehow works with dry sherry too, though pick one that's robust – an amontillado or a punchy fino rather than a manzanilla. Mince pies are also gorgeous with the sweet, floral Moscato di Pantelleria, made on the island of Pantelleria, a speck of Italy that lies between Sicily and Tunisia.

MONKFISH One of the most meaty-textured of all fish, this can happily be drunk with white wine – say an oaked Rioja or an albariño – but it is often cooked as part of a casserole, or with rice, flavoured with saffron or tomatoes or artichokes, in which case a red from Rioja or Ribera del Duero is a fine accompaniment.

MOULES MARINIÈRE With a garlicky, fishy broth and the indigo shells of moules marinière (with or without cream), I am never really happy if I don't have a glass of Muscadet de Sèvre et Maine (ideally sur lie for extra texture and flavour). It's a classic combination and nothing beats it.

MOUSSAKA The heavy layers of minced lamb, béchamel sauce and aubergine are good with the prickle and tannin of agiorgitiko from Greece. Other good reds are Montepulciano d'Abruzzo or a simple sangiovese from Italy; smoky pinotage or cabernet sauvignon from South Africa; dusty carmenère from Chile; blends from Lebanon; or Bierzo from Spain. In summer, moussaka is good with rosé. Rather than choosing a subtle pink from Provence, go for a deeper-coloured wine from the Languedoc, Italy or Spain.

MUSHROOM Because mushrooms are a meaty vegetable, if you have made them the star of the dish the instinct is to reach for a red. Fragrant, earthy reds are the best bet. Pinot noir is a natural with almost any mushroom dish. Porcini and chanterelles – simultaneously both powerful and delicate – are very good with nebbiolo (Barolo or Barbaresco) from north-west Italy and sangiovese (such as a Chianti from Tuscany). For mushroom mixtures, or the juicier, more grounded flavour of flat, button and chestnut mushrooms, you can afford fleshier reds, such as a gutsy blend from the south of France, mencía from Bierzo and dusty reds from the Douro or the Dão in Portugal. Pinot noir (or, along similar lines, trousseau), Pomerol and aged Ribera del Duero or Rioja accentuate the autumnal savouriness when mushrooms are an accent to game or pork. If the dish is more concentrated, perhaps intensified with yeast extract or beef stock, then a richer wine such as a cabernet sauvignon or a pinotage from South Africa makes a sturdy, wintry accompaniment.

If you want to emphasize the umami component in the mushrooms, then certain whites will do the job even better. Oak-aged chardonnay (from Limoux, the Jura, Burgundy or elsewhere), oaked white bordeaux and oak-aged white Rioja will underscore the umami and make mushrooms taste more bosky. These are a good accompaniment to, say, garlic mushrooms on toast (with a spoonful of cream in the sauce) or chicken or pork casseroled with mushrooms in a creamy sauce.

I especially like duxelles of mushrooms with lemon thyme, spread on toast or put in vol-au-vents, with white bordeaux, Australian semillon-sauvignon or champagne. If the wine is young and vigorous serve the toasts with bright, lemon-dressed endive. If the wine is aged, and beginning to smell of mushrooms itself, keep the citrus accents gentle.

Good claret is also excellent with mushrooms on toast: an opportunity to turn a tired late-night supper into a sneaky feast.

LEMON THYME DUXELLES

SERVES 2 AS A LIGHT LUNCH OR 4 AS A STARTER

This is good over a toasted muffin for lunch, or on a small slice of sour-dough or a half slice of wholemeal toast as a starter. Serve it with leaves dressed with a lemony dressing and an oaked white bordeaux.

35g butter
2 shallots, peeled and finely chopped
2 cloves garlic, crushed or chopped
250g chestnut mushrooms, wiped and finely
   diced
1 tablespoon crème fraîche
1½ teaspoons lemon thyme leaves, chopped

Melt the butter in a medium-sized frying pan. Add the shallots and cook, stirring occasionally, for 10–15 minutes or until soft and trans-parent. Add the garlic and cook for a minute or two longer. Add the mushrooms and cook until the mushrooms release their liquid. Con-tinue to sauté gently until the moisture from the mushrooms evap-orates. Stir in the crème fraîche and herbs, heat through and serve.

See also lasagne, mushroom risotto, omelette.

MUSHROOM RISOTTO Any of the wines that go with mushrooms, from chardonnay to left-bank claret, will also work with risotto. Risotto recipes vary, though, and it's best to try to match the heavi-ness of the risotto with the heaviness of the wine. For instance, if the risotto is a very rich one, seasoned with beef stock, sherry and Bovril, don't put it with a light French pinot, give it a smoky South African one.

MUSSELS see *moules marinière.*

MUSTARD GAME-CHANGER As with chilli, cinnamon and garlic, we don't just experience mustard through the taste receptors in our mouths and smell it via the olfactory receptors in our nose, we also feel it as pain, thanks to ion channels that run through a branch of the trigeminal nerve, which is responsible for sensation in the face and also for communicating the motor commands that allow us to chew. Mustard is a kind of miracle worker when it comes to tough, hard red wines. When mustard meets red wine, it calms down the tannins. If you eat mustard with steak or roast beef, you will notice that the red you drink with it tastes even softer than it does with the beef alone. This means that a wine that tastes prickly and hard when drunk alone – a Madiran or an inexpensive green claret, for example – suddenly becomes much more approachable and delicious. It also means that a fruity, soft wine you were enjoying before you had a mouthful of mustard might now begin to taste a bit floppy and boring.

So, in short, with mustard look for wines that have a bit of poke in the form of tannin (especially) and/or acidity. Also, young wines will fare better than old. As well as sinewy Madirans and astringent young clarets, consider young sangiovese, Cahors, or peppery cool-climate syrah – any of these reds would go well with classic mustardy dishes such as lapin à la moutarde. If you're after a wine that is more refreshing, and where fighty tannin isn't involved, then try bright, young, dry wines with a good flash of acidity. Gamay is the trailblazer here for reds – Beaujolais works really well with calves' liver with a mustard sauce, for instance. For whites think about grapes such as arneis, cortese, verdicchio, vermentino, and so on – these can work really well with heavily mustardy salad dressings.

M

O

OCTOPUS Dressed with olive oil and sprinkled with paprika, Galician octopus is one of the great seafood delicacies of north-western Spain. It is at its best when washed down with the salty-apricot taste of a glass of albariño, but a chenin blanc (or chenin blanc blend) from South Africa is also fruitily satisfying.

OLIVES Gin and tonic goes well with olives. So does a vodka martini. And a glass of chilled manzanilla or fino sherry is near perfect with a small plate of them. If olives are part of a dish, then the salt and astringency will tilt you towards more savoury wines. Black olives tend to be rich, green ones more acidic and sour. Sangiovese, for instance, has no problem with black olives. Nor do most of the reds from the south of France (from Bandol to Corbières to Fitou) or from the Rhône. Green olives tend to demand a bit of acidity in a wine. Again, sangiovese can offer this, as can many white wines.

OMELETTE

plain or cheese The regal toastiness of Bollinger, a champagne that is matured in oak and majors on the pinot noir grape, is a real treat with the rich yellow of a Burford Brown omelette with or without gooey strands of melted cheese. Cava is a good second choice. The softness of a Lugana or Soave (especially one of the richer, more nuts and savoury-custard types of Soave) or albariño, or a lighter chardonnay, either unwooded or with some but not too much oak, melds with the dairy but gives a fresh backdrop too.

aux fines herbes A light red, even one verging on the under-ripe, makes a sappy complement to the green herbs. Try a gamay from Touraine. For a white, try a pinot blanc from Alsace.

with bacon The floral perfume of a pinot gris mingles well with smoky bacon and just-cooked egg.

with mushrooms A chardonnay would be good here – this is a grape that works well with both eggs and fungi. Limoux makes wines that have just the right weight. Otherwise, a humble white burgundy, perhaps a Bourgogne Blanc, Mâcon or nutty Montagny.

See also tortilla.

ONIONS, STUFFED The flavours and in particular the herbs in the stuffing will determine what wine goes best, but with a creamy stuffing I like a high-acid wine which could be red (think nebbiolo or sangiovese) as well as white.

STUFFED ONIONS

SERVES 4 AS A SIDE OR STARTER

The finest stuffed onions I've eaten were part of a lunch served at Trattoria della Posta in Monforte d'Alba in Piemonte in Italy. Creamy and rich, with a spoonful of rabbit terrine on the side, they were perfectly accompanied by a glass of nebbiolo. I usually make baked onions as part of a small-plates dinner because they can be done in advance but feel quite special as part of a spread with tagliata of veal or steak, spicy sausages, potatoes diced and roasted in olive oil, rocket dressed with olive oil and lemon, and a big tomato salad.

4 large white onions
25g butter
2 tablespoons olive oil
2 cloves garlic, peeled and chopped
2 sprigs fresh rosemary, leaves picked
    and chopped
50g fresh breadcrumbs
125ml double cream
100g Parmesan, finely grated
pinch of grated nutmeg
4 slices of pancetta

Preheat the oven to 200°C/Fan 180°C/Gas 6/400°F. Cut a small slice off the base of each onion, so that they can stand up without wobbling over. Discard the base. Peel the onions and boil them in a large pan of hot water for about fifteen minutes. When the onions are cool enough to handle, cut off the tops and put to one side – don't throw them away. You now need to scoop the middle out of each onion without destroying the outer layer. I find the easiest way to do this is to pull out the central layers and then slice a thick piece off the bottom of each these to put back inside the shell and act as a base to stop the filling falling out. Finely chop the onion middles. Melt the butter with the olive oil in a large frying pan and sauté the chopped onion until it is soft and translucent. Add the garlic and fry one or two minutes more. Stir in the rosemary, breadcrumbs, double cream, Parmesan and nutmeg. Remove from the heat. Place the onion shells, bottom down, on a baking tray and wrap a slice of pancetta around each one. Fill with the onion and rosemary mixture, piling it up, and balance the onion tops on top of the mounds of filling. Cook for 25 minutes.

ONION TART A barely set savoury custard mixed with soft, tangled long strands of golden onion in a crunchy, cheesy pastry is one kind of onion tart. Onion tarte tatin, all caramelized allium and rich base, is another. Both of these are beautifully offset by a not-quite-dry pinot gris from Alsace. Alsatian pinot gris is not a fashionable style. Fragrant and feminine and roiling with criss-crossing undercurrents, these wines are the anti-aperitif. They don't come at you like a gleaming blade or a piercing shot of cold citrus, and in this case that's a good thing. Pinot gris melds gently with the sweetly caramelized onions, and it has an ample texture that sits comfortably with the cream and the eggs. Other whites that work well include aromatic Côtes du Rhône, Alsatian muscat or glossy Jurançon (with both kinds of tart) or a simple French viognier or Alsatian riesling (with the eggy version).

What I really love to drink with onion tart, though, is red wine made from nebbiolo (the Barolo grape). I love the sensation of nebbiolo's tannin and acid cutting through the richness. The wine comes in like coal dust with pinking shears, nibbling away at the dairy, creating a pleasing contrast. Nebbiolo loves a bit of eggs, cream and cheese; and eggs, cream and cheese love nebbiolo too – they take a wine that, tasted alone, might appear thin and hard and mean, and they plump it out, rounding its edges. The firm backbone of both Irouléguy and Madiran also works well with a creamy onion tart. Because I like drinking sappy, light-bodied wines in cold weather – a bracing reminder of the new shoots of spring – I'd also pour a glass of Marcillac with a nice, hot slice of onion tart to eat beside the fire on a cold winter night.

ONION TART

SERVES 4–6

FOR THE PASTRY
175g plain flour
100g cold butter
salt
50g Gruyère cheese, finely grated
1 egg yolk, beaten with 2 tablespoons
    ice-cold water

FOR THE FILLING
50g butter
2 tablespoons olive oil
775g white onions, peeled and finely sliced
3 sprigs of thyme, leaves removed from stems
2 eggs
1 egg yolk
150ml single cream
salt and pepper

To make the pastry, sieve the flour into a large bowl. Use a knife to cut the butter into small rough cubes and rub into the flour with your fingertips. Keep going until the mixture resembles fine breadcrumbs. Stir in a pinch of salt and the cheese. Add the egg yolk and water and mix with a knife and then with your hands until it's bound. Wrap the dough in cling film and pop it in the fridge to rest. For the filling, put the butter and the olive oil in a large, heavy pan and heat gently until the butter has melted. Add the onions and cook gently for 20–30 minutes, stirring occasionally, until they are soft and just beginning to colour. Heat the oven to 200°C/Fan 180°C/Gas 6/400°F. On a floured surface, roll out the pastry and use it to line a greased deep 20cm or shallow 23cm flan dish. Cover the pastry with a circle of greaseproof paper weighted down with baking beans. Wrap in a damp tea towel and refrigerate until the oven is hot enough before baking blind for 15 minutes. Remove the paper and beans and cook for 5 more minutes to dry the pastry out. Meanwhile, sprinkle the thyme over the cooked onions, stir in the eggs, egg yolk and cream, and season generously. Pour the eggy onion mixture into the pastry case and cook for 15–20 minutes, until the filling is just cooked – it will still seem slightly wobbly. Serve with a salad of bitter leaves.

ORANGES Some dishes rely heavily on the flavour of oranges. For instance, Ottolenghi's 'Saffron, orange and chicken herb salad', which uses syrup made from a whole boiled orange (I found the recipe online); fennel and orange salad; or clementine pork steaks. With these I often open a pinot blanc or a falanghina. Both are refreshing whites that have a faint taste of oranges and orange blossom that plays to the taste of the food.

OSSO BUCO Reds from Piemonte are the obvious choice – nebbiolo, barbera and dolcetto. But a sturdy white from the Rhône can also be very good, as can a lighter or older Chianti.

OYSTERS I think every oyster-slurper has his or her own favourite raw oyster wine. You can go sharp and piquant, with manzanilla sherry, English sparkling wine, Vinho Verde, bacchus, Sancerre, or non-vintage champagne. Or slightly gentler, with picpoul or Muscadet. Or gentler still, and more succulent, with Chablis. If you are eating the oysters with shallots and red vinegar, be sure to go for one of the sharper wines. A pint of porter is, of course, another traditional accompaniment.

O

P

PAELLA With this Spanish rice dish red wine is just as good as white. Or rosé for that matter. But paella is a hugely movable feast. *The Oxford Companion to Food* reports that the traditional ingredients for the authentic Valencian dish are 'rice, chicken, rabbit or lean pork, green beans, fresh butter beans, tomato, olive oil, paprika, saffron, snails (or, a curious alternative, fresh green rosemary), water and salt'. The wine to drink with this (and with vegetarian versions) would be a local red, though the following would work equally well: an inexpensive Côtes du Rhône, a simple tempranillo from elsewhere in Spain, a young cabernet franc from the Loire, a young Bierzo, or a more internationally styled red from Somontano. Many incarnations of paella exist. Made with chicken, artichokes and oloroso, it's good with white Rioja, verdejo or sherry. With pork, chorizo and spinach, then more or less any red Rioja or Ribera del Duero suits the sweet chorizo. With artichokes, monkfish, fat prawns and saffron, try a young Rioja Crianza or other young tempranillo without too much oak; a mellow (older) Rioja Reserva; or an older (older because it will be softer and gentler than a brash, youthful wine) Ribera del Duero. Adapt the wine choice to the star ingredients in the dish.

PAPRIKA Smoky, earthy paprika is made from dried and ground chilli peppers and gives a soft warmth and a rustic dustiness to the food it seasons. Often found in Hungarian and Spanish cooking (chorizo is full of it), this dusty component can trip up elegant or thoughtful wines, so look for something hearty. When paprika is prominent in an ingredient list, Spanish wines can be a good option. Albariño and white Rioja (oaked or unoaked) have fragrance and acidity but also a hidden power that can handle the spice of the paprika, whether it's sprinkled over a cold octopus carpaccio or dressing a piece of hake served with olive oil and boiled potatoes. Where paprika, in particular smoked paprika, is added to a more meaty dish, or present in the form of chorizo added to a chicken or chickpea stew, a Bierzo, red Rioja, Ribera del Duero or Ribeira Sacra would make a suitably robust partner. It's no surprise that Hungarian reds are good with paprika too. The grape blaufrankisch (also known as kékfrankos) has a spicy, dried-tomato taste also found in paprika. The Austrian red grape zweigelt (a cross between blaufrankisch and St Laurent) is an easy, lightish-bodied, cherryish grape that goes well in a sluicing-down-a-hearty-stew kind of a way. Chilean carmenère, which is rugged in texture and smells of black tea leaves, roasted red peppers and dried tomato, is another excellent partner.

See also goulash.

PARSLEY SAUCE White sauce with curly parsley is an old-fashioned but delicious accompaniment to poached white fish such as haddock or cod, and usually eaten with boiled potatoes. It suits an equally plain white wine. An inexpensive cool-climate chardonnay is perfect with the slightly damp taste of the parsley. Try an unoaked Bourgogne Blanc or Mâcon.

PARTRIDGE An excellent option with this game bird is a generous pinot noir – 'I had partridge with Pommard last night. Finesse, class, ahhhh,' said Sebastian Payne of the Wine Society when I saw him at a recent tasting. Other good ideas include Rioja (especially graciano-rich Rioja) and juicy rustic reds that aren't too tannic, maybe a wine from the Languedoc, or a Montepulciano d'Abruzzo or a country syrah.

PASTA Italy is the first place to look. Italian wines, both red and white, usually have good acidity that fits well with the angular feel of pasta made tangy with concentrated tomatoes, salty with Parmesan, anchovies or olives, or hot with garlic. Their refreshing bite also cuts cleanly through olive oil and cheese. If I were to give just one pasta-wine-picking guideline, it would be to drink red Italian with any sauce that incorporates cooked tomato and white Italian with 'white' (non-tomato) or raw tomato sauces. But I can immediately, of course, think of about a dozen exceptions.

For pasta dishes that have been anglicized or Americanized the world opens up more readily. I'm thinking of macaroni cheese, so unctuous and rich it will rejoice in an acerbic white from any mountainside; or intense, almost barbecue-like meatballs with pasta that seem more at home in a burger bar than in a trattoria and will go well with a smooth, ripe red from California, South Africa or Chile.

Contemporary recipes that take inspiration from Italian flavours but play them into a lighter, more nuanced expression also suit wines from beyond the Italian peninsula. For example, a particularly clean and refined version of linguine al granchio brought home in a doggy bag from Trattoria Nuraghe in Tufnell Park in north London was delicious with a Japanese white wine made with the koshu grape.

But even if you stick to Italy, picking a grape from a country with over 3,000 registered varieties (even the extremely thorough *Wine Grapes* by Jancis Robinson, Julia Harding and José Vouillamoz deals with only the most important 377, from abbuoto to vuillermin) can be quite an adventure.

pasta dishes and suggested wines

amatriciana and arrabiata (the hotter version) Suits a basic red with some guts from Tuscany, Emilia-Romagna or Umbria.

broccoli and garlic orecchiette Pinot grigio is cleansing against the garlic and bitter broccoli. For a better class of pinot grigio, look to the pristine wines made in Friuli, in the north-east of Italy, on the mountainous border with Slovenia.

cacio e pepe A classic Roman dish, just peppercorns, spaghetti and Pecorino Romano, so in theory it would be blasphemous to have anything but a wine from Lazio. Frascati is the obvious choice. Good alternatives include Vernaccia di San Gimignano and verdicchio.

crab linguine A white with a slightly creamy texture but a cool, calm profile offsets the crabmeat. Chardonnay is good but it needs to be the right sort of chardonnay: a white from a humble burgundy appellation (one of the Mâcons or a Bourgogne Blanc), Chablis or a linear chardonnay from northern Italy or Australia. Soave would also do it, but I prefer Lugana. This northern Italian white is a camel cashmere cardigan among wines – never coveted but has a quiet sophistication that brings a dinner (or an outfit) together. Timorasso, a white grape from Piemonte, revived only recently after nearly dying out, is used to make gloriously textured wines that are nutty and aromatic and play against the brown as well as the white crabmeat. If you want to go Spanish, head for an apricotty albariño, which is light and fragrant; or try a more clean, neutral wine such as a white from the Marche region of Italy; or go for a squeeze of citrus with pecorino or Gavi. When cream is involved (as in my recipe below) I prefer the slightly heavier, more closely textured options of chardonnay or Lugana.

CRAB LINGUINE

SERVES 2

You can also use spaghetti for this crab dish. The secret is the mixture of gentle white and full brown meat.

2 tablespoons olive oil
2 shallots, chopped
1 clove of garlic, chopped
175g linguine
½–1 red chilli, depending on heat
    preferences, finely chopped
3 tablespoons full-fat crème fraîche
100g white and brown crabmeat
3 tablespoons flat-leaf parsley, chopped

Heat the olive oil in a small pan. Add the shallots and fry, stirring, for 5 minutes. Add the garlic and continue to fry until soft and golden. Bring a large pan of salted water to the boil and add the pasta. Add the chilli to the onion mixture, fry for a couple more minutes, then turn off the heat. When the pasta is almost al dente, add 2–3 tablespoons of its cooking water to the shallot mixture and stir in the crème fraîche and the crabmeat over a gentle heat. Drain the pasta as soon as it is al dente and mix it with the hot crab mixture. Divide between two serving dishes and sprinkle with chopped parsley.

garlic, oil, chili and parsley For a red, a light Bardolino or Valpolicella. For white, any of the crisp, herbaceous Italian whites – verdicchio, vermentino, vernaccia and so on.

pea and spring onions The spring vegetables need a bright white such as vermentino, arneis, pecorino or young Hunter Valley semillon.

pomodoro crudo Simple raw tomato sauce works well with a crisp, unoaked white wine. Vermentino, verdicchio, pecorino, soave ... Also good is a light sauvignon blanc, not too shrieky – say, a basic unoaked white bordeaux or a bottle from the Pays d'Oc.

prosciutto and radicchio Dry-fry some prosciutto until it's crispy, stir shredded, wilted radicchio into a garlic and cream sauce and you have a superb winter dinner. One problem: radicchio is so bitter it will nuke almost any wine. As ever, Italy to the rescue: they make wines that go with their food. For red, try dolcetto, barbera or a young nebbiolo. For white, verdicchio. I also enjoy two Spanish reds, Bierzo and Ribeira Sacra, with this.

puttanesca This full-flavoured, olive, anchovy and cooked tomato sauce (*puttana* translates as whore) is a southern Italian dish, though no one can agree on exactly where it's from. It is attracted to the almost lasciviously fruity reds made in the heat of Puglia – for example, Salice Salentino and Brindisi.

salsiccia More or less any Italian red tastes great with sausage pasta.

con sarde This Sicilian dish made with raisins, pine nuts, sardines and chopped fennel tops sounds strange on paper but is delicious in practice. For a white, fiano works. For red, frappato.

vongole My brain tells me I ought to drink white with this salty clam pasta, but for some reason I always want a glass of nervy Valpolicella. My white choices, if I ever drank them, would be simple and unoaked so as not to interfere with the fish and salt – pinot grigio, albariño, Muscadet, picpoul, Frascati, verdicchio.

See also bottarga, carbonara, lasagne, macaroni cheese, meatballs, pesto, ragù alla bolognese, ravioli, truffles.

PÂTÉ For any kind of pâté, rustic reds from Spain, Italy, Portugal and France have my heart.

PEACHES The best way to have peach with wine is to slice it into a simple but delicious glass of cold white wine (Côtes du Rhône or vermentino for choice) and eat it in the bath. With the door locked. I discovered this piece of food and wine heaven as an au pair in

Florence, charged with the care of three-year-old twins, and relished every second of getaway.

If raw peach is a prominent ingredient – in, say, a salad or on crostini – remember that it brings sweetly juicy acidity that may require you to ramp up the acidity and/or the sugar in the wine. For instance, I make a salad using peaches, marinated in lime juice, olive oil and salt, with mozzarella or burrata and rocket. It's great with just off-dry riesling or a very ripe Marlborough sauvignon which itself tastes of nectarines. Chenin blanc is a good grape to consider when peaches are involved in savoury dishes too.

PEAS AND PEA SHOOTS Peas have a fresh, green taste that is redolent of spring. I like them with bright, unoaked white wines that share the same vibe. For example, Gavi, vermentino, verdicchio, vernaccia, young Hunter Valley semillon, assyrtiko, roditis, gros and petit manseng, white wines from Crete, piercing dry young Loire chenin blanc, sauvignon blanc.

Sauvignon blanc from Chile and New Zealand has a luminous quality that is particularly suited to freshly podded peas, snow peas and mangetout, while the sinewy taste of pea shoots is mirrored in the sauvignon blancs from the Awatere Valley in Marlborough.

Any of these wines would be perfect with a salad made from acidic feta cheese, fresh peas and pea shoots, dressed with olive oil and grated lemon zest.

See broad beans for a recipe for a 'Broad bean, pea shoot, asparagus and ricotta bowl'. (p. 44)

P

PENNE see *pasta.*

PEPPERCORNS Syrah grown in a cool climate, and in particular syrah from the Rhône Valley, often has the earthy, floral fragrance of freshly cracked black peppercorns. This helps to make it a beautiful match for steak with a peppercorn crust or steak served with a green peppercorn sauce. I also like tannic young red bordeaux, or Beaujolais Cru, with green peppercorn sauce – the wine has a vigour (from acidity and astringency) that fits well with the bite of the peppercorn. Or, to put it another way, both of them pep you up.

STEAK WITH FRESHLY CRACKED BLACK PEPPERCORNS

SERVES 4

Until I made this for the first time, I was a black peppercorn peasant who paid no attention to the type of pepper I was buying and certainly not to how long it had been languishing in the cupboard. Now I appreciate the crackling, floral, dizzying smell of freshly smashed peppercorns so much I pay as much attention to them as some do to their coffee. I eat this with a fiery salad of watercress or rocket and spinach. An inexpensive syrah from South Africa or France works beautifully.

2 beef stock cubes
3 teaspoons Dijon mustard
4 pieces of fillet steak, weighing about 175g each
4 tablespoons top-quality black peppercorns
olive oil, for frying

Crumble or squash the stock cubes in a small dish and use the back of a teaspoon to mix in the mustard until you have a thick paste. Rub the paste into both sides of each steak. Smash the peppercorns using a mortar and pestle until they are lightly crushed but not powdered. Transfer the smashed peppercorns to a plate and dip both sides of each of the steaks in so that they are coated with pepper. When you are ready to eat, heat a little oil in a frying pan and cook the steaks to your preferred cuisson. If you want to make a sauce, once the steaks are removed to plates, use some of the drinking wine to deglaze the pan, bringing it to a brisk bubble and scraping the meaty, peppery gubbins off the bottom of the pan as you do so.

PESTO This garlicky, basil and pine nut sauce originates in Liguria, where the local white grape is the herbaceous and green-tasting vermentino. It's a perfect match. Alternatives are vernaccia and verdicchio. But watch out: wine tasters are wary of pine nuts because of a phenomenon that has been called 'pine mouth'.

See also pine nuts.

PHEASANT If the bird is in a casserole, claret or Madiran or Bergerac. If it's roast, then red burgundy will help bring some succulence to the dry meat.

PICNICS These occasions are more about mood than food. Pink fizz is a sheer delight – find a good cava rosado or hunt out something more obscure, such as the Rosé Frizant made by Mas de Daumas Gassac in France. Everyone is always pleased to see a chilled bottle of fine Sancerre (or Pouilly-Fumé from the opposite side of the river) at a picnic. Or go with a light red such as dolcetto, a good Loire cabernet franc or a Beaujolais Cru, which as well as capturing the sappy promise of spring will feel like the right thing to be drinking when you're sitting on the grass and have the damp, sweet smell of turf up your nose. By chance, all of those reds happen to go extremely well with a spread of different picnic foods. So-called 'natural' or 'low-intervention' wines are another good option at picnics. They often have an atmosphere and sense of the outdoors that just works. Finally, I have never seen anyone complain if you arrive at a picnic with a bottle of champagne.

PIEROGI These small, half-moon-shaped Polish dumplings can be made with a variety of fillings and may be served boiled, or boiled and then fried in butter and onions. I asked Polish wine writer Wojciech Bońkowski for his recommendations.

pierogi z kapustą i grzybami: pickled cabbage mixed with forest mushrooms The sour tang of the pickled cabbage is not great with heavy reds. Bońkowski suggests pinot noir for a red, or 'a rustic white wine – chenin blanc, for example'. Zweigelt from Austria would be an interesting match here.

pierogi z mięsem Bońkowski says, 'The traditional ground veal filling is often spiced with marjoram and peppercorn. This is a good dish to match with light- and medium-bodied red wines; look for acid rather than oak.' I suggest unoaked barbera, Bardolino, zweigelt or an unoaked, cool-climate syrah.

ruskie: cottage cheese and potatoes Bońkowski says, 'These are often served plain boiled with no sauce, and go well with a dry or off-dry riesling, or with unaromatic dry white wines such as sylvaner, Soave, or a light furmint.'

PIGEON Lodovico Antinori, the septuagenarian scion of Tuscany's most famous and powerful wine family, likes to drink one of his own Supertuscans with pigeon. 'Colombaccio sui crostini – pigeon casseroled and then served on croutons – is good with our Insoglio del Cinghiale, which is made from syrah, cabernet franc, merlot, cabernet sauvignon and petit verdot. Pigeons taste much better in Italy because, when they fly to us, they're in the wild, they eat acorns. You know for sure because when you shoot one you can always find seven or eight acorns in their stomach. In England they eat cabbage.' A Supertuscan – a red wine made in Tuscany using bordeaux grapes – is an excellent choice with this wild bird: structured but also spicy and rich and generous. Pigeon served pink and bloody is also good with the tang of Chinon or Bourgueil from the Loire.

PINE NUTS Eating pine nuts can trigger an effect known as 'pine mouth', a mysterious condition that temporarily alters your sense of taste, leaving an unpleasant astringent or metallic taste in your mouth. I've never experienced it, but those who have report that the sensation may kick in straight away, more usually begins twelve to forty-eight hours later and may persist for as long as three weeks.

The cause of this effect is unknown. Research conducted by the FDA (America's Food and Drug Administration) found that sufferers of pine mouth did not notice any unusual flavours in the pine nuts, and had usually eaten the pine nuts raw (frequently in pesto or in a salad), though whether that reflects a higher preference among Americans for eating raw rather than cooked pine nuts, or relates more directly to the pine mouth effect is not known. Other researchers have pinned the blame on certain batches of *Pinus armandii* imported from China, which are shorter and plumper than the slim European versions.

If you have pine mouth, I'm afraid wine will not taste good. If not, what wine you pick will depend more on the overall dish than on the presence or otherwise of pine nuts.

See also courgette flowers (stuffed and fried), pesto.

PISSALADIÈRE One could happily drink rosé from Provence all day long with this niçoise pizza topped with caramelized onions, salty anchovies, olives and garlic. Provence rosé now also comes in bubbly form – delicious and decadent. Lebanese rosé, which often also includes a bit of silky cinsault in the blend, is a more emphatic, equally delicious partner. A simple inky red is also pleasing: for instance, a Provence red or a country syrah with a bit of bite.

PIZZA On the one hand, I want to say, 'Pizza is street food, it is sofa food, it is fresh out of the wood-burning stove and eat it in the garden, casual, happy food. Please, eat it with anything.' On the other, there's a Paulie Gualtieri from *The Sopranos* inside me, twitching away, moments from picking up a dangerously heavy glass ashtray and saying, 'I know I said anything, but why did you have to go and drink something that wasn't Eye-talian?'

Look, I spent a year living in Italy and, as a result, am pre-programmed to favour Italian reds with pizza. To be fair, they are particularly successful because, as a general rule, Italian reds have a bite that meets the bite of the tomato and the heat of any spicy cured meat. But while I was writing this book I got a Facebook message from lovely Emily O'Hare, an Italian wine expert and former River Café sommelier now living in Florence. She was canvassing opinions on what wine to drink with pizza – because all the Italians she knows drink beer. Figurati!

My go-to at home pizza reds are sangiovese or Montepulciano d'Abruzzo or a particular wine a friend has christened 'The Mighty Biferno' (its real name is Biferno Rosso, and it's made in Molise from aglianico, montepulciano and trebbiano). I also like wines from Puglia. Ole Udsen is an expert on southern Italian food and wine who goes for something more unusual: 'Pizza is traditionally paired with the young, lightly sweet and sparkling Peninsola Sorrentina Gragnano red wine from the Sorrento coast (if not with beer). Otherwise, much depends on the topping in terms of wine choice. I would generally go for a light, sappy red wine.'

Beyond Italy, cabernet-carmenère blends from Chile are chunky and pleasing with pizza as well. Lebanese reds or rosés work with slightly burnt wood-fired pizzas eaten outside. Any of the inexpensive, rustic, unoaked, swill-it-back reds you find in France, Spain, South Africa ... everywhere will work, provided the wine you pick is not too sweet with the topping. I have reservations about tempranillo with anything but a chorizo pizza. I'd steer clear of South African pinotage unless you have a strong meat like biltong on the pizza. You get the idea. Pizza is one of those foods that most suits what you most feel like drinking (as already mentioned, for many Italians this is not actually wine but beer). The one wine–pizza combination that would really fox me, in a toothpaste and orange juice kind of way, is top burgundy. I'd have a little drinking session, then an eating session, then drink a bit more. They just don't bring out the best in each other, like friends you wish you'd invited round on separate evenings. Though both are fabulous.

There are just a couple of pizzas that might tempt me to open certain types of wine. With anchovies and olives on pizza, Venetian reds – a light Valpolicella or Bardolino – have a cool edge that is good. With the sweet flavours of spicy salami and pepperoni mixed with caramelized onion and red and orange peppers, I love the sweet flow of a riper red from the south – examples include Salice Salentino, Copertino and Brindisi, and grapes to look for are primitivo and negroamaro.

PLUM AND ALMOND TART The sweet taste of cooked plums (or prunes) with ground almond frangipane, and slivers of toasted almonds calls for Armagnac.

PORK Pork is at least as happy with white wine as it is with red. Actually, I'll go further and say that a pork chop or joint of roast pork with crackling is even more succulent and tasty with white: try riesling, chenin blanc, chardonnay (especially white burgundy), Australian marsanne, white Rhône blends (from the actual Rhône, or from the US, South Africa or Australia), viognier, godello or fiano. If you're after a red, then pinot noir (from anywhere), tempranillo (perhaps Ribera del Duero or Rioja), an Etna red, cinsault, carignan and the hard to pronounce xinomavro (from Greece) are all pretty good too.

When shoulder of pork is slow-roasted and unctuous, then I veer towards the red wines in that list, and in particular the mellow wines from Rioja. With slow-roast shoulder of pork, I also like the juicy quality of good natural red wines such as those made from syrah and pinotage at Lammershoek in South Africa, or the gamay and syrah of Hervé Souhaut in France.

with apple sauce or caramelized apples or apple pommes bou-langère With a generous helping of sweet apples alongside the pork, an off-dry riesling or off-dry chenin blanc (say, a Montlouis or Vouvray) from the Loire really sings with the fruit. Alternatively, if the fruit isn't over-sweet, try dry versions of those grapes. The lusciousness of the apple also goes well with hedonistic viognier; with the orchard taste of chenin-based blends from South Africa; with white Rioja; and with white Rhône blends (incorporating some of roussanne, marsanne, viognier, bourboulenc, grenache blanc) from anywhere in the world.

with apricot or other stone fruit stuffing Albariño, chenin blanc, white Rhône blends, and riesling all celebrate the juicy sweetness of the fruit.

with bay leaves, garlic, anchovies and sage, slow-cooked in white wine and served with chard This is a Stevie Parle recipe that I fished off the internet (it appeared in the *Daily Telegraph* in 2011). It's gorgeously savoury and tastes good with dry rosé (don't limit yourself to Provence, think also of the fuller, slightly tannic but still-dry rosatos from northern Italy). Slightly astringent whites work well with the savoury herbs – say, verdicchio and vernaccia. Godello and good verdejo offer a glossier approach. White burgundy, with its undertones of woodruff and toast, is superb. I also enjoy this dish with red: ideally an unoaked or barely oaked nebbiolo.

(pork loin) with calvados cream An old-school match with this creamy, appley sauce is an off-dry or medium-dry riesling. But cider also goes really well and is probably my favourite here. Just close your eyes and think of the Seventies. Perhaps even get things going with a Kir or Kir Royal first.

(belly of pork) with cinnamon, star anise, five-spice, ginger and cloves Pork belly cooked with Asian spices is fantastic with the leaping florals of viognier, as well as with blends incorporating roussanne, marsanne, viognier, clairette and grenache blanc (and chenin blanc if the wine is from South Africa).

with fennel seeds White burgundy often has a faintly aniseed tinge that works well with fennel seeds. Italian whites go well too, as does the prickle of sangiovese if you're after a red.

stir-fried with lime and cashew nuts Dry riesling has the limey zing to go with this.

with prunes and cream Pork medallions cooked with sweet prunes in a thick double cream sauce are brought to life by the ripe pear sweetness and cleansing acidity of a medium-sweet Vouvray.

with quince Chenin blanc mirrors the floral-orchard taste of quince and is lovely here in combination with pork, and perhaps also roast parsnips in maple syrup. If there's a lot of sweetness on the plate, go for an off- or medium-dry wine (the Loire has plenty to offer, from Vouvray to Montlouis to Savennières). Otherwise try a dry chenin blanc from South Africa or one of the Loire appellations, or one of the wines suggested as a match with apple sauce.

with roasted root vegetables I tend to opt for the reds listed in the introduction to this entry when there's an autumnal tray of roasted onions, parsnips, carrots, pumpkins, turnips and beetroots on the table.

See also barbecues, Cajun, cassoulet, charcuterie, five-spice, gammon, jerk, meatballs, pork pie, pulled pork, rillettes, sausages, suckling pig.

PORK PIE I can't help feeling that pork pies are beer more than wine territory – a pint of Black Sheep Best, perhaps? But a simple red would also be good, maybe the sour cherry-burst of a rustic bobal from Spain.

POTTED SHRIMP Teeny little shrimps with lots of butter – chardonnay or albariño, please.

PRAWNS There are so many seaside wines to choose from, from Vinho Verde (whose alertness is great with garlic prawns) to rosé, delicate Cassis, sauvignon blanc from San Antonio in Chile or peachy albariño, a classic seafood white that brings out the best in succulent pink prawns.

With buttery, fried prawns or prawn mayonnaise, then choose chardonnay (from Burgundy or elsewhere, Chablis is the classic; Mâcon also has a good balance of curves and edge).

prawn cocktail in Marie Rose sauce mixed with halved cherry tomatoes and shredded lettuce A good pick is Coteaux du Giennois, a sauvignon blanc from the Loire that has a softer, lemon-meringue pie edge compared to some of the sauvignon made in neighbouring appellations. Alternatively, Sancerre or Reuilly for a grassy, herbaceous cut.

PRAWN COCKTAIL

SERVES 1

A classic dish that became part of my repertoire when a friend who lives alone came to stay and made it for us. Prawn cocktail is so quick to make. It works well with a glass of Chablis, Bourgogne Blanc or Mornington Peninsula chardonnay. Away from chardonnay you could go Lugana, or if you want to cut across the creaminess with a squeeze of lemon try Gavi or pinot grigio. This is a light dinner I often make just for me but it's obviously very simple to scale up.

1 little gem lettuce, shredded
½ avocado, peeled and cut into chunks
120g cooked prawns
2 heaped tablespoons mayonnaise
1 teaspoon tomato ketchup
splash Tabasco
splash Lea & Perrins
salt
squeeze fresh lemon juice

Put the lettuce and avocado in a small bowl and mix together. Place the prawns on top. Mix the mayonnaise and ketchup in a small bowl and season to taste with the Tabasco, Lea & Perrins, salt and lemon juice. Spoon the sauce over the prawns.

prawns fried with garlic and a generous squeeze of lemon Try rosé, inexpensive fizz (I like the teeny bubbles and alka seltzer taste of txakoli from the Basque country) or a refreshing dry white, perhaps with a lemony-flavoured edge such as pecorino or Gavi di Gavi from Italy, young Australian semillon, or assyrtiko from Greece. An old favourite is Torres Viña Esmeralda from Spain – a floral blend of muscat and gewürztraminer that sings of holidays and summer time off.

with Thai flavours (lemongrass, chilli, ginger and so on) Look to luminous sauvignon blanc from Marlborough, or to the piercing lime of New World riesling – maybe a glittering, pure riesling from Washington State; a clear-edged riesling from Chile; the lime rind and lilac scent of an Eden or Clare riesling from Australia; or the tangerine and lime fragrance of riesling from Australia's Great Southern region. Consider increasing the sweetness of the wine to balance the heat as the *chilli* is ramped up; there are some gorgeous non-dry rieslings made in Marlborough, New Zealand.

PRESERVED LEMON <u>**GAME-CHANGER**</u> The pithy taste of preserved lemon is powerful and acerbic, far more so than the bright tang of a fresh lemon, and just a small amount of it can alter the balance of a dish. You could try any of the lemony wines mentioned in the lemon section, but I particularly like assyrtiko from Santorini, which is grown in volcanic soil. It has some weight, and you can almost taste the black lava that the roots of the vines have grown in, as well as feel a kind of voltage charge. Gavi di Gavi (as opposed to the lighter Gavi) is also good as it often has a thick taste of lemon and grapefruit rind. Don't be afraid of oaked whites either – the baked grapefruit flavours in oaked sauvignon blanc and oaked assyrtiko really resonate with preserved lemon.

PULLED PORK Xinomavro (it's pronounced zeeno-mavro) from Greece is an unorthodox wine to drink with the sweet fruitiness of pulled pork with a barbecue sauce, but it tastes really good. This red grape is reminiscent of nebbiolo, if nebbiolo also tasted of squashily ripe wild strawberries, and the combination of warmth with astringency is gorgeous with a mouthful of sweet burger bun, coleslaw and pork. The slack, ripe warmth of Californian zinfandel also goes down well with pulled pork, as does the brightness of cheaper Chilean pinot noir. Red or white Rhône blends made outside the Rhône (in California or South Africa) have the easy-going exuberance and ripeness to work too. Alternatively, a bottle of cheap American beer is just great.

PUMPKIN AND SQUASH Pumpkins and squashes are chameleons, on the one hand very rich, their orange flesh almost sweet; on the other surprisingly watery.

richer pumpkin and squash dishes, perhaps roasted and spiced Roasting gourds has a concentrating effect on flavour; it brings out a sunny, sweet opulence. To play into this, choose a fleshy, bold wine – white or red – such as an oaked chardonnay or a juicy merlot, perhaps from Chile, or a full-throttle zinfandel or primitivo from the US or Puglia. All of these will work with pumpkin that is pimped with spices (for example, cumin, cayenne, star anise) and chilli flakes too (including with spiced pumpkin soup, with the caveat that soup and wine – liquid against sloshy liquid – are not really ideal together). A luscious pinot noir, perhaps from California or Chile, can also have the same effect and is particularly sumptuous when the pumpkin is being served with roasted duck.

If you want to savoury things up a bit, then pick a leaner red, with tighter tannins. This might mean choosing a more sappy pinot noir, a mencía from Spain or Italian reds such as nebbiolo from Piemonte or sangiovese from central Tuscany, whose tannins reign in the splurgey flavours. Actually, the sangiovese can bring the best of both worlds as it can be rich and warming as well as prickly and tannic. These Italian reds are especially good when pumpkin is roasted with pancetta, sage, garlic or thyme.

See also ravioli (and other filled pasta), risotto.

P

Q

QUAIL If the quail is coated in sage and salt, roasted until it's crispy, and served with spinach leaves and a garlicky dressing, then I like Brunello or Rosso di Montalcino or nebbiolo. If the bird is simply seasoned and roasted without herbs, then mencía, claret and pinot noir all make fine accompaniments.

Q

R

RABBIT If simply braised (and perhaps eaten with cheesy noodles) this lean white meat bounds along with a light to medium-bodied red wine such as one made from cabernet franc (from anywhere in the world; in France look to the Loire appellations of Chinon, Saumur, Saumur-Champigny, Bourgueil and St Nicolas de Bourgueil); gamay (Beaujolais); a light and rustic sangiovese (try Chianti Rufina); or one of the lighter South African pinot noirs. Other good options include Marcillac (with its tang of iron); a taut Irouléguy; or a fuller-bodied rosé such as Tavel. A nutty chardonnay from the Jura would also work well.

with broad beans and pancetta in a creamy casserole, served with mashed potatoes This was the first dinner I ever cooked for an (ex-) boyfriend who was horrified to be fed bunny, ate it politely at the time, and refused ever to touch it again. The cosseting cream and mash make a rounded white a good pick. I like gently oaked chardonnay or aromatic viognier or a blend of viognier/roussanne/marsanne (from the Rhône, California or South Africa).

with mustard sauce (and bacon) Any of the light reds at the start of the entry will work, but heavier wines are better and tannic wines go well with the mustard. Try a richer sangiovese-based red from Tuscany (a Chianti Classico, Carmignano or a Rosso di Montepulciano); an aglianico or nebbiolo from Italy, a hairy red from Provence; the fresh edges of a young bordeaux from the Médoc; or a smoky cabernet sauvignon blend from South Africa that will underscore the smokiness of the bacon.

ragù on pappardelle An Italian red with some astringency – say nebbiolo, aglianico or Sagrantino di Montefalco.

stew (with the cream) and served with cheesy noodles A bracing riesling from Alsace is good against the rich dairy; for reds try a sappy, light Marcillac or a simple, grainy sangiovese.

stew (without the cream) Many winemakers, from Italy (sangiovese) to Australia (syrah), vengefully tell me they love to eat rabbit stew with their wines. Hop to it!

RACLETTE This cheesy Alpine speciality needs a refreshing wine. Think of head-out-of-ski-lift mountain whites such as chasselas, or Savoie whites like jacquère. Northern Italian whites and reds are also good – think pinot grigio, ribolla gialla, Gavi, arneis, Refosco, schiava, and lagrein. Also needle-sharp whites like aligoté or Gaillac Perlé, or bracing reds like Marcillac.

RADICCHIO The dramatic carmine and white-veined leaves of the radicchio are bitter as well as beautiful. The more the radicchio is cooked, the more this bitterness is minimized. Particularly watch out, therefore, for the shock of raw radicchio leaves. They are really horrid with sweetly fruity, oaky white wines; lean, herbaceous whites (such as vermentino, arneis or vernaccia) are a better counterpoint.

Italian reds – from just about anywhere in the country – hold up to radicchio's astringency better than most. With a radicchio salad, I like the fine balance of a nebbiolo (especially a more rustic nebbiolo from Ghemme or Valtellina). Other Italian reds I'd be tempted to open include barbera or dolcetto also from northern Italy, or a relatively raw young sangiovese, perhaps from Chianti Rufina.

Radicchio that has been braised or chargrilled goes well with the Italian reds above but also with Bierzo from Spain and zweigelt (it's a cross of St Laurent and blaufrankisch), a kind of light-bodied, Austrian alternative to pinot noir. The bitter-sweetness of blackened radicchio that has been dressed with sticky, dark balsamic vinegar is mirrored by a sweet-sour, cherry-and-dust scented Valpolicella.

See also risotto.

RAGÙ ALLA BOLOGNESE (WITH PASTA) There are many, many versions of this meat and tomato pasta sauce but the original takes its name from the city of Bologna in Emilia-Romagna, where it is often washed down with a glass of dry red Lambrusco (yes, dry, you read that correctly). This sparkling wine, often a deep violet colour with a slightly earthy smell, has recently experienced a fashion renaissance in the bars and restaurants of east London. It is best served by the tumbler and makes a great casual accompaniment to a bowl of penne con ragù.

In Piemonte in northern Italy, where they serve ragù with tajarin, a sort of hand-cut tagliolini made with a lot of eggs and whose edges seem very soft in your mouth, they like to eat it with barbera. Something about the combination gives both the wine and the food a very silky feel. If you visit the village of Barbaresco, go to the Trattoria Antica Torre. The restaurant is named for the medieval tower next to it, which was built a thousand years ago to defend the village against the Saracens, and it is famed locally for its excellent, egg-rich home-made tajarin. Order this and a bottle of Bruno Rocca barbera.

Other good options for ragù are central Italian reds such as Chianti, Rosso di Montalcino or Montepulciano d'Abruzzo. A generic sangiovese (the Chianti grape, with its classic, crenellated feel and sour cherries and dust notes) or a softer, fruitier red such as a Salice Salentino from Italy's heel offer more budget options. Such a simple plate of food can also be a good occasion to showcase a fabulous Italian red: a good Brunello di Montalcino, perhaps.

Of the non-Italian reds, a cabernet sauvignon-carmenère blend from Chile is a really good choice.

RATATOUILLE The laid-back aromatics of this Provençal vegetable stew relax into red wines that also smell of herbs and sun. Whether eating ratatouille as a main course on its own with slices of crusty baguette or dauphinoise potatoes, or putting it with merguez sausages, roasted leg of lamb or lamb casserole, wines I'd look to include Chianti, Bandol, Palette (and other reds from Provence), St Chinian, agiorghitiko from Nemea in Greece, Vacqueyras, Gigondas, Douro reds and the peppery depth of the syrahs from the northern Rhône. A friend who insists on making ratatouille without the courgettes, which results in a richer and more unctuous aubergine and tomato stew, reports that it goes extremely well with the warm embrace of Australian shiraz. Finally, on a summer's evening the wine it's always hard to avoid opening with ratatouille is palest pink rosé from Provence.

RAVIOLI (AND OTHER FILLED PASTA) Mostly I go with the same types of wines that I'd drink when the sauce was on the outside rather than the inside of the pasta. However, filled pasta is usually (though not always) fresh and that sometimes makes a difference: the softer texture feels completely different in your mouth to the flick-flack of spaghetti cooked very al dente. Plus, there are a few fillings that you don't find as sauces.

pumpkin With butter melted on to it and Parmesan grated on top, a verdicchio or vermentino will provide a punctuating textural contrast, while a clean (oaked or lightly oaked) chardonnay or the luscious flavour of an upmarket Soave will play into the curves. I more often serve pumpkin pasta with just-brown butter and fried sage leaves and then I'm chardonnay or Soave all the way for whites, but also like the herbal cut of a light red such as an unoaked or barely oaked Chianti Rufina.

ricotta and spinach For a white with a lemon tinge go for Gavi. More herbal but still citrusy options include vernaccia, verdicchio and vermentino. To go gently with the softness of the pasta, pick a Soave.

RED MULLET Red mullet is one of those fish that is particularly comfortable with red wine but happily moves from red to white depending on what you put with it. At The River Café in London I once ate red mullet with tomatoes and black olives, which was perfect with a Valpolicella – Ca' Fiui from a producer called Corte Sant'Alda. With fennel and olive oil, red mullet is good with a red from Etna or a nero d'avola. It also works with pinot noir as well as with the subtle aromatics and warmer feel of Rhône whites and fresh rolle/vermentino from Provence/Italy.

RED PEPPER The intense paprika-like fruitiness of red peppers that have been thoroughly cooked in a casserole or a hot oven has a natural affinity with dusty Chilean carmenère but it also goes well with bold reds from South Africa (in particular Rhône blends and tobacco-scented cabernet sauvignon); cabernet sauvignon from Chile; and also some of the more exuberant Spanish reds from Rioja, Ribera del Duero and Navarra. The leafy taste of crunchy raw red peppers is good with rosé made from cabernet sauvignon and also rosé from Navarra in Spain. It also goes well with the freshly podded pea and grassy taste of sauvignon blanc from Robertson or Darling in South Africa, and with the sweet snow pea taste of sauvignon blanc from Chile. Red peppers that have been partly blackened on a grill (perhaps as part of a kebab), barbecue or griddle often strike a halfway mark between the sweet power of cooked peppers and the more acidic brightness of raw and I like them with both groups of wines, as well as with bright reds such as gamay (the Beaujolais grape) and barbera.

red pepper filo Roasted red pepper filo is good with any of the wines listed above. Pick the wines that are better with raw red peppers if the filo is made with acidic ingredients such as feta.

stuffed peppers If they are loaded with rice, courgettes, fresh tomatoes, olives, thyme and garlic (and lamb), then head to Provence, the Rhône or the Languedoc (white, red or pink, it doesn't matter), or to the Rhône blends of South Africa. With the more tangy flavours of feta and oregano, I look for a more bracingly assertive, acidic wine such as sauvignon blanc, a Greek island wine (the pithy grapefruit and lemon flavours of assyrtiko are perfect) or pecorino for whites or barbera for a red. The aromatics of xinomavro from Greece, which smells like dried thyme with ripe wild strawberries, are also good here. If the peppers are stuffed with fat-grained rice enriched with stock and flavoured with an onion and pepper soffritto, tomato purée, and perhaps some saffron, then try the mellow smoothness of tempranillo – say, a Rioja Crianza.

RED SNAPPER The sweet, firm flesh of this tropical fish is often cooked with fragrant herbs and spices. I've eaten it baked en papillote with lemongrass and fresh coriander, barbecued with lime and chilli, and grilled and served with cumin and fresh coriander potatoes. With all of these dinners I'd pick similar wines – lithe whites with a lift of lime, lemon or bergamot zest that also carry the scent of lemongrass, starfruit, or nectarines. Riesling (from South Africa, New Zealand, Chile, Washington State in the US, or Australia – say Eden Valley, Clare Valley, Great Southern or Tasmania) will play into the green lime; sauvignon blanc from Adelaide Hills in Australia has an understated taste of Meyer lemon and starfruit that underscores the succulence of the fish flesh; sauvignon blanc from Leyda in Chile will bring in a vibrant taste of crunchy snow peas and green capsicum; a young semillon from Australia will lift it with a meadowgrass and citrus flavour; and an oaked semillon-sauvignon blanc from Margaret River brings a waxy texture with hints of lemon, papaya and toast. For a wine with cool clarity and a hint of orange, try pinot blanc from north-east Italy or Alsace. If the fish is cooked with heavier spices

R

and/or more chilli (for instance, with jerk seasoning), then seek out a wine with more sweetness, perhaps a riesling from Germany or one of New Zealand's sweeter offerings. In all cases, as so often, another good choice is rosé.

RILLETTES With goose or pork rillettes on a baguette with cornichons, the wine I really love to drink is a Cornas or St Joseph. Those black northern Rhône syrahs taste granitic and gravelly, like having your bare feet on pebbles; then you get the milky white softness of the bread; then the chippy, argumentative wine; then the cold creamy butter; then the vinegary cornichons; then the proud, stony wine again. It is pure bliss. That is the really gorgeous match. Failing that, a simple French red, what used to be called vin de pays, or its equivalent from Italy, will do.

RISOTTO The wine I pick to go with risotto very much depends on what ingredients have been added to it. The classic risotto is the almost naked Milanese (made with shallots, chicken stock and saffron). A traditional match would be a local red – barbera, say, or a light nebbiolo or dolcetto – and I like these because they have an earthy savour that showcases the delicate powdery taste of the rice. Milanese also goes well with limpid Soave, Frascati, Lugana or a light, cherryish Valpolicella, all of which have a transparency that allows you to taste the rice. With an absolutely plain risotto (no saffron), the controlled, teasing style of a dry Pfalz riesling or a subtle pinot bianco is refreshing. With more complicated risottos, as with any other plate of food, the richer the ingredients, the richer the wine can be. I prefer not to drown the rice, though: it deserves to be the star of the dish, not an invisible flavour-carrier. Here are a few ideas.

asparagus The cool geometry of grüner veltliner from Austria and the pithy lemon of arneis from Italy are favourites, but any wine that is good with asparagus would naturally be splendid.

chicken Invigorating light reds are good with a brothy chicken risotto: say, the transparency of Valpolicella, or a summery, chilled Beaujolais Cru. For whites, Lugana and Soave are subtle options. This is also an opportunity to get out the chardonnay, which will go especially well with a more dairy-rich chicken risotto, into which you've perhaps stirred some crème fraîche and gone particularly heavy on the butter and cheese; try a Mâcon for a chardonnay with a cool, crisp cut, or a grander white burgundy for indulgence. Limoux chardonnay is underrated and perfect here too.

fresh tomato A grassy Loire sauvignon blanc with a raw tomato risotto makes for a lovely outdoor summer's evening dinner. A very precise pinot grigio from the Collio or Colli Orientali region of Italy, or a lemony white from Crete, will also play into the fresh edges of the tomato. You could use lemon thyme in the risotto too. With raw tomato and oregano, a herb that has warmth, I'd be tempted to try the more opulent, spicy greco di tufo from Campania in Italy.

mushroom This has its own entry, as it's such a popular dish.

peas (risi e bisi) A Venetian classic that really does go well with the local wines (Lugana and Soave) as well as with pinot grigio. I also love risi e bisi with that rare creature, Beaujolais Blanc, a very gentle and refreshing chardonnay.

primavera (with peas, broad beans, and all things fresh and green) If there's asparagus in the dish, go with asparagus choices. Otherwise pick any crisp, clean white, from pinot grigio or verdicchio to Soave or an unoaked viognier.

pumpkin The glow of roasted pumpkin risotto is delicious with oaked chardonnay from almost anywhere in the world or with a white Rhône. If the pumpkin has not been roasted it will be more subtle in taste; squash and pumpkin often taste surprisingly aqueous in a risotto, like a dawn tribute to the lagoon of Venice. Try the soft but rice-grainy texture with round-edged, gently nutty Italian whites such as posh Soave. A very light, unoaked chardonnay, such as a Bourgogne Blanc, also matches the delicacy of this type of risotto, and, again, it has no corners so doesn't jab at the silkiness of the squash. Prosecco is a good alternative.

radicchio and pancetta The bitterness of the radicchio and the salty-meaty bacon is most delicious with a red: barbera, nebbiolo, sangiovese and dolcetto will all do you proud. As will a Valpolicella Ripasso. A touriga nacional from Portugal is a more inky, heavy partner. País from Chile also works well.

red wine with chestnut mushrooms and sausages Any of the reds that go well with a radicchio and pancetta risotto will also work here. Alternatively, pick a Beaujolais Cru, a Spanish red made from mencía, or a light, cool-climate pinot noir (stern German pinot works well here) to be refreshing against the risotto stodge or a rustic syrah for heartiness. Take care not to use a sweet wine when you are cooking this; you'll ruin the risotto. I speak from bitter experience here. Many cheap red wines do contain sugar and it sticks out even more on the plate than it does in the glass.

seafood There are many different versions of fish and seafood risotto. The best I have eaten were all in the lagoon city of Venice, where the plate of rice and stock is often very liquid. A glass of limpid prosecco makes a fine accompaniment but it must not be one of those cheap, commercial wines that taste of boiled sweets. Instead look for a cool, crisp prosecco that tastes of stones, hard pears, and winter mornings, and has been made with care by a small-scale producer. Other Venetian white wines that work well include Bianco di Custoza and Soave. I also like the earthy taste of Crémant du Jura (a sparkling wine made in eastern France from chardonnay) and the clean lightness of Crémant d'Alsace. Otherwise, find a relatively transparent white wine that does not have obtrusive fruit. Muscadet, picpoul, trebbiano, or pinot grigio are all ideal.

with truffles I feel cheated if I don't have nebbiolo, in one of its many forms, with truffles.

ROCKET Rocket is such a bitter leaf that it makes gentle, sweet or plump wines wilt. Oaked chardonnay or jammy shiraz or sweetly ripe pinot noir are not the answer. Bite – in the form of tannin or acidity – helps. Earthiness does too. Try a citrusy white with a simple, dressed rocket salad; vibrant oaked sauvignon blanc with a rocket and cured ham salad or a rocket and blue cheese and pear salad; sangiovese or nebbiolo with tagliata and rocket dressed in lemon and olive oil; mencía with fig, rocket and ham. And so on.

ROGAN JOSH This aromatic, tomato-based dish is often made with lamb and goes brilliantly well with the rugged capsicum scent of Chilean carmenère. Melvin D'Souza of Soul Tree wines says that with rogan josh he likes to drink his own shiraz-cabernet, a smooth-fruited red made from grapes grown in India that's aged in oak barrels.

ROLLMOP HERRINGS Herrings that have been gutted, boned and rolled (sometimes round pickled cucumber) and preserved in vinegar or a mixture of vinegar and wine that might have been flavoured with dill or other herbs and spices are pungently flavoured. They are at their best not with wine but with a cold shot of vodka or aquavit.

ROQUEFORT, PEAR AND ENDIVE SALAD The spice of the blue cheese and juiciness of the pears needs a succulent white with good acidity. A glossy dry Jurançon, made from gros and petit manseng, with a tang of white grapefruit and taste of sunflower seeds will do it, as will an oaked sauvignon blanc. With blue cheese, bitter leaves and the sweetness of the pears I particularly enjoy the tangy, floral notes of oaked sauvignon and semillon blends such as those made in Bordeaux and in Margaret River in Australia.

ROSEMARY Rosemary's heady fragrance sends you first to the Mediterranean, where the blue-flowered herb grows wild in the garrigue. The pumice-dry reds from the southern Rhône (Vacqueyras, Châteauneuf-du-Pape, Gigondas, Sablet and Cairanne, as well as the more generic Côtes du Rhône blends), which smell like a dry, stony hillside on a hot day, are made for rosemary. The herbal reds of Provence (including Bandol) also complement rosemary's soaring scent. Chianti reds from Montepulciano and Brunello di Montalcino play well with this herb's pungency, particularly when meat is involved. For instance, these Tuscan reds are good with rosemary focaccia but really shine with braised rabbit with rosemary potatoes; rosemary and juniper-rich wild boar stew or ragù; or lamb roasted with rosemary and eaten with white beans with rosemary and garlic. Rioja can also work well with rosemary, but its youthful strawberry taste isn't quite such a natural fit as the earthier grenache-based wines of France, so I tend to choose a slightly older Rioja that has begun to melt and mellow and take on autumnal flavours. The eucalyptal notes of shiraz from McLaren Vale in Australia and the earthy base notes of shiraz from Heathcote, Australia, also resonate with rosemary.

R

S

SAFFRON Saffron is a subtly powerful spice with notes of hay and iodine that gently yet firmly tilt the flavour of a whole dish. It doesn't have an obvious wine partner but it never fails to make an impact. In a vegetable, chicken or seafood paella or other rice dish, for instance, saffron's steady presence can open the door to serving a substantial red rather than the more obvious white: think of monkfish and artichoke saffron rice with Spanish tempranillo; or one-pot chicken cooked with rice, olives, chickpeas, cumin and saffron eaten with a feral Bandol. Conversely, with saffron-scented side dishes such as raisin and pine nut couscous, I often open a floral white wine such as viognier, or a white Rhône blend, even when they are being eaten with red meat such as grilled or tagined lamb. Viognier has an *Arabian Nights* charm that dances seductively around calm saffron.

Perhaps a general principle is that, where rosé and white are concerned, quietly forceful wines tend to work well with saffron. Examples include rosé from Provence (it's subtle, but with understated power and a spicy sandalwood tone); orange wines (made from white grapes, but with extended skin contact giving them tannin and hold and a pale amber hue); Douro white blends; and Rhône blends (floral and almond-blossom-scented).

With fishy dinners containing saffron, such as bouillabaisse or barbecued sea bass with a saffron aioli, manzanilla sherry has a salty, bready edge that zings against the spice.

SALADE NIÇOISE The sight of the runny egg yolks, tuna, black olives, anchovies and green beans of this salad from the Côte d'Azur instantly evokes in me the desire to drink the pale pink rosés of holidays in Provence. It might be a Pavlovian match but it's one I stick by: rosé ought to be mandatory with niçoise salad. As a backup, perhaps consider a white from Bandol or elsewhere in Provence, or the herbaceous riff of a vermentino from Corsica.

SALADS Watch out for the dressing. The acidity of a lemon and olive oil emulsion or of vinaigrette can make low-acid, oaky wines taste quite odd. Dressings that are high in mustard, raw garlic or salt can also have a distorting effect on the perceived flavour of a wine. Of course none of this matters if you are just eating a small side salad, or if (like me) you heap the salad on to an empty plate as a palate cleanser after the main course, but if the salad is a big, or the main part of a meal, then it might be worth choosing a wine that will still work. To balance the effects of raw garlic, lemon juice, vinegar or mustard in a dressing, look for a wine that is high in acid.

A few other powerful ingredients in a salad (or its dressing) that are worth taking into consideration include blue cheese, goat's cheese or goat's curd, bitter leaves (see below), chilli, herbs and anything sweet (for instance, sugar, maple syrup or honey in the dressing or sweet fruit in the salad itself – also see below).

bitter leaves and radish sprouts Chicory, watercress, rocket, radicchio and fiery radish sprouts need reds that have some astringency or a red or white with refreshing bite. Italian wines are an easy solution. Arneis, vermentino, verdicchio, vernaccia, and cortese are vibrant whites that will do the job. Nebbiolo, dolcetto, sangiovese, sagrantino, montepulciano and sometimes nero d'avola work for the red team.

crunchy Thai salads It doesn't really matter what vegetables – crunchy carrots, snake beans and so forth – are in the salad because it's the sweet-sour-heat of the palm sugar, lime juice, green papaya and chilli and also the coriander and mint that drive the flavour. The happiest match here is medium-dry riesling. Its aromatics play beautifully with the vibrancy of the herbs and lime, its acidity works well with the pungency of the citrus, and its sweetness has a calming effect on the heat of the chilli. Off-dry pinot gris is another option.

sweet dressings and salads containing other sweet ingredients, such as quince cooked in syrup, or sweetly ripe fruit, such as pears or peaches It's best to balance the sweetness in the salad with sweetness in the wine. This might be as subtle as choosing a just off-dry, juicy rosé or chenin blanc from the Loire to drink with a salad containing sweet figs, quince or juicy pears. If the sweetness is very noticeable – for instance, if the salad is coated in a honeyed or

maple syrup-rich dressing – then a medium-dry wine (try a riesling from Germany or New Zealand) will feel more comfortable
than one that is bone dry.

See also aubergine, avocado, chili, chorizo, duck, esqueixada, fennel:
in salads, Greek salad, liver, peaches, radicchio, rocket, Roquefort,
pear and endive salad, salade niçoise, Thai beef salad, Waldorf salad,
watercress.

SALMON The classic salmon dinner is a pale pink poached fillet
with a big pile of buttery new potatoes and hollandaise sauce, and the
roundness and gloss of a chardonnay goes beautifully. Chardonnay's
curves perfectly cushion and cosset the salmon, emphasizing the
soft luxury of the hollandaise. Pick anything from the scale, from a
richer wine, all toasty, barrel-aged and fat, to the taut, matchstick-
scented new-wave Australian chardies with their refreshing flashes
of lemon, to a Chablis, to the limpid, apple-blossom crispness of a
young, unoaked Mâcon.

Simple, fine ingredients are the best way to enjoy more serious bottles. I can hardly think of a more exquisite dinner than a piece of wild
salmon with a heap of Jersey Royals scattered with fresh herbs and
a good white burgundy. Among other wines that are beautiful with
salmon with potatoes and/or a plain salad are whites from Provence
and the Rhône and pale rosé.

If the salmon is fried rather than poached, then try godello or an
Australian semillon whose grass and hay and lemon flavours buzz
against the crispy, fatty skin.

As the texture of chardonnay works well whenever creamy sauces,
eggs and butter are involved, it's also a good pick when salmon is
served with poached eggs, spinach and hollandaise; richly buttery
rösti; mayonnaise; or as salmon en croute. Chenin blanc, from South
Africa or the Loire, is a fine alternative as it combines vibrant citrus,
which acts like a squeeze of lemon, with curves.

Different accompaniments might send you to different places.
For instance, I sometimes make a hot potato salad, maybe mixed
with cucumber or wild garlic or dressed with dill vinaigrette. These
are punchy ingredients: aniseedy dill, wild garlic or the heat of a
mustardy-vinegary dressing demand a wine with at least a bit of

elbow. The woodruff flavours found in some burgundies can still dovetail beautifully here, but I veer towards one with a youthful kick, the better to cope with the vinegar of the dressing. A more refreshing, herbaceous acidic white, such as verdicchio, vermentino, or grüner veltliner, will pick up on the aniseedy notes in the dill, while a Loire sauvignon blanc or a Bordeaux Blanc (oaked or unoaked) will provide a grassy backdrop. These wines are also good ones to pick for salmon with asparagus.

As salmon is quite meaty it can also be delicious with light, tensile reds. Pinot noir seems to underscore the pinkness and sleek muscularity of the fish. If you are chargrilling salmon on a barbecue or griddle pan, so that the skin is crispy and black, those fuller flavours make red wine a very stylish option, be it a Bierzo from Spain, a nerello mascalese from Etna, a gamay, a cabernet franc from the Loire, or a lighter (say 11.5–12.5% abv) syrah such as the textured wines made by Craig Hawkins in Swartland, South Africa; or the low-intervention wines made by Hervé Souhaut in the Ardèche, France. With nutty lentils as a side dish, definitely go red, and ideally a red that is more earthy than fruity – say, to a pinot noir from Germany or one from the excellent Puy de Dôme co-operative in France, or a Bardolino from northern Italy.

Side dishes of salads containing hot, peppery radish sprouts or mustardy micro-herbs and Ottolenghi-style salads or soy, chilli and coriander marinades provide more excuses to head towards light reds – gamay (the Beaujolais grape) is a good choice here. Put the red in the fridge for 20–30 minutes and the chill will give it more definition and a bit of cut.

blackened salmon with miso aubergine My top choice would be champagne, but steer away from harsh zero dosage wines, and other styles that are dagger-like in their directness, as these will cut into the beautiful silky texture of the food and rip it to shreds. Fruitier champagnes like Canard-Duchêne would be lovely with that glutinous sweetness. Sake is clearly an option too, or try a medium-dry Vouvray.

fishcakes With clouds of potato and Anglo ingredients, try chardonnay or chenin blanc. With Thai flavours – lemongrass, chilli, ginger – aromatic riesling, semillon, and sauvignon blanc really sing.

hot-smoked salmon and horseradish The heat of the horseradish and the smoky fish are perfect with an aged Australian semillon. These wines begin to taste like toast as they mature – you'd swear they had seen the inside of a barrel even when they've lived in stainless steel.

scrambled egg and smoked salmon This feels like a breakfast dish to me, so it's too early for anything but sparkling wine, which happily goes very well.

smoked salmon Zesty, citrusy wines such as sauvignon blanc from Sancerre to Marlborough or Gavi from Italy or grüner veltliner from Austria act like a squeeze of citrus over the smoked fish. I prefer fuller versions, where some of the wine has been enriched by time in a barrel, as this meets the oily texture of the fish. With buttery bread (and the butter does make the salmon taste better – fat is such an effective flavour-enhancer), the roundness of Chablis (or another white burgundy or chardonnay from elsewhere) is appealing and, of course, Chablis also has a dash of lemony zip. A favourite choice with the richness of smoked salmon is chenin blanc from the Loire. Go for anything from Vouvray to Savennières to a Saumur blanc. Dry, off-dry or even medium, these wines have a winning combination of texture and acid that brings succulence to the fish. The smokiness of the fish is also well matched by the toasty edge of crisper whites that have been fermented in oak barrels – sauvignon-semillon blends from Bordeaux, Margaret River, and elsewhere have a smoky taste of hot grapefruit that spritzes and hums with the citrus squeezed on the fish and the salmon's own smokiness. Likewise, the peaty-bonfire-iodine smell of Islay whisky, reminiscent of sea and land at once, brings out the smoky-savoury salmon flavours. Maybe water it down, one part water to three parts whisky. If the salmon is on rye bread, the strong caraway scent of a tot of ice-cold rye vodka or aquavit draws out the savoury, aromatic smokiness of both bread and fish.

tartare of salmon For raw salmon, move away from buttery chardonnay. The cool, sinewy flesh is good with bracing wines with cut, such as sauvignon blanc, chiselled grüner veltliner and chenin blanc, though there is one caveat. High-acid wines can also change the texture of the fish, 'cooking' it like ceviche in your mouth. For tartare served with pickled cucumber, I like greener-tasting herbaceous wines (such as verdicchio or vernaccia) or a wine with some sweetness – for instance, a chilly medium-dry Vouvray, reminiscent of stewed apples and wild honey. Pinot gris from Alsace is another interesting, textured choice, while the clean cut of a pinot grigio or other white (say, ribolla gialla) from Collio or Colli Orientali in north-east Italy brings cool precision and calm.

teriyaki The brightness of a young, unoaked new world pinot noir plays well with the sticky ginger and soy flavours. Sake, koshu or a fino or manzanilla sherry would also work and seem to boost the umami flavours in the sauce.

See also gravadlax.

SALSA VERDE Look for a wine with bite to stand up to the piquancy of the sauce. If the salsa verde is to go with white fish, then white wines that will do the job include Loire sauvignon blanc, Spanish verdejo, arneis, Gavi, assyrtiko and young dry Loire chenin blanc. Salsa verde seems to like oak, so you could look for an oaked assyrtiko or white bordeaux. These oaked white wines also hit the spot if the salsa verde is to be eaten with lamb and lots of salads, ideally outside on a hot evening. With lamb, however, you may already be thinking about red bordeaux and that's a very good idea. Vinegary salsa verde and lamb have a miraculously redeeming effect on clarets that are green and tannic, which makes this the perfect opportunity to open a bottle of more astringent young claret, or perhaps a Fronsac.

SALT Food that is very salty, whether because it's rich in anchovies, salted capers or brined olives, or simply because it's been very highly seasoned, needs a wine, red or white, with good acidity. This is because salt reduces our perception of acidity, so a wine that's rounded and low in acid from the start can taste flabby and flat. There are loads of wines with good acidity, from champagne to sauvignon blanc to riesling. Reds from northern and central Italy can usually be relied on to have a good spine of acidity too.

SALTIMBOCCA ALLA ROMANA With this classic dish of veal escalopes wrapped in sage leaves and prosciutto, fried in butter and drizzled with a sauce made by deglazing the pan with Marsala, try the prickle of a nebbiolo from Valtellina or the Langhe; the savour of a lagrein from the Südtirol; a dusty dry red Lambrusco; a leathery Montepulciano d'Abruzzo; or a Chianti Rufina. For whites, Frascati would be the local match, but I also like the seltzer, just-floral taste of sparkling chasselas from Switzerland – if you can find one.

SALTY SNACKS I'm happy to say that one of the very best vinous accompaniments to crisps and other salty snacks is champagne. Seriously. Champagne has high acidity, which is good with salt. English sparkling wine, too. And most other dry sparkling whites. Sauvignon blanc is also perfect with lovely vinegar as well as salt and fat.

SAMPHIRE A breezy Vinho Verde is good with salty samphire. Douro whites and Muscadet work too – both are classic fish wines and samphire is almost always served with fish. Nettley-tasting English bacchus also has an affinity for this slightly damp-tasting sea vegetable.

SARDINES Cooked with red onion and chunks of tomato on a beach barbecue or under a fierce grill until the skin blisters, golden and crunchy and black, sardines scream to be washed down with a glass of rosé. I wouldn't pick a pale, almost invisible rosé, but one with more guts and colour. Try Spanish rosado, from Rioja or Navarra, or one made with bobal from the unglamorously named region of Utiel-Requeña. Alternatively, a rosé from the Dão or Douro in Portugal or a Lebanese or Chilean rosé with some cinsault in the blend. This oily fish is also fantastic with red wine. With the sweet red onions and smell of basil, a young, inky inexpensive Ribera del Duero (not too much American oak) might not be the first wine you'd think of but it is a great match. Alternatively, a sangiovese di Toscana; the bright and slightly smoky smell of an unoaked pinot noir from Chile or South Africa; a cheap nerello mascalese, frappato, or Cerasuolo di Vittoria from Sicily; a red from Portugal's Dão. Intensely bright, lemony whites also work to sluice the mouth in between forkfuls – for instance, Roussette de Savoie.

SASHIMI The very best matches I've found with raw fish, served Japanese-style, with daikon, wasabi and a soy-based dipping sauce on the side, are unoaked white wines made from the koshu grape; fino or manzanilla sherry; sake; and champagne or English or other sparkling wine made from a combination of chardonnay, pinot noir and pinot meunier and fermented by the traditional method. With leaner fish, the precision and keen edges of grüner veltliner from Austria can also be wonderfully refreshing. Fattier fish such as the richer parts of tuna meld better with the softness of koshu and sake.

See also sushi.

SAUSAGES Isn't every red wine good with sausages? From tough tannat to light dolcetto to Barossa shiraz, it's hard to think of one that's not and so picking a wine becomes more about scene-setting. Here are a few combinations that I enjoy.

On a cold winter's night I love a chilled, juicy, granitic Beaujolais to rinse down mouthfuls of buttery mash, onion gravy and bangers. Solid Chilean reds are cosy and comforting, but rather than the usual cabernet sauvignon, carmenère or syrah, why not open a bottle of a less mainstream grape, such as país or carignan?

In summer, outside with a plate of salads, give me the redcurrant-leaf scent of a chilled Bourgueil or Chinon. Garlicky sausages or sausages cooked on the barbecue or eaten with ratatouille are beautiful with herbal Bandol, which will recall the heat of a Provençal summer even if the sun's not shining. They go similarly well with the thunder of a Lebanese red. With barbecue-blackened sausages I also have a weakness for Australian syrah-cabernet sauvignon blends.

The dried figs, and the scent of wild hillsides covered in tinder-dry herbs that you find in Languedoc reds such as St Chinian, or the wild, flaring fire of a Côtes du Roussillon seem to suit late summer or autumn evenings when the nights are closing in. If there's a Tuscan vibe – maybe herby-garlic-fennel sausages, and a dinner that begins with crostini and follows up with potatoes cooked in rosemary and olive oil or a borlotti bean salad – then how about a hearty Rosso di Montalcino, a Chianti or a Supertuscan?

With sausages on the menu you can go in any direction. And, obviously, while a simple dinner is always a good opportunity to bring out a bottle of good wine, sausages and mash are also fantastic with beer. A pint of London Pride would be ideal.

SCALLOPS There is an intrinsic sweetness to scallops which makes them a natural with chardonnay (I'm thinking expensive white burgundy), particularly if they have been fried so that the edges brown and caramelize. Tweak the wine according to the accompaniment. For instance, with pea purée pick a younger, fresher chardonnay, and with woody parsnip purée or with scallops with chorizo choose a richer, oaked chardonnay.

Other wines that are generally good with seared scallops include ageing white bordeaux and also champagne. Also surprisingly good: a shot of frozen Cognac.

For scallops with fresher-tasting ingredients, such as pea purée, pea shoots, micro-herbs, lime, or coriander, sauvignon blanc can work very well. I prefer to pick a riper sauvignon blanc that tastes of nectarines and has a heavier, softer feel in your mouth and usually look for wines from Marlborough, New Zealand; the Adelaide Hills or Margaret River in Australia; or Chile. These sauvignon blancs often also have a luminous quality that suits the plate of food.

With scallops with beurre blanc, an off-dry riesling, say Dönnhoff can be just right as the zing and sweetness of the wine play against the vinegar in the beurre blanc. With scallops with chorizo or wrapped in bacon or prosciutto, it's hard to beat champagne; a sparkling wine elsewhere made from the champagne grapes (chardonnay, pinot noir and pinot meunier); or cava. Oaked white Rioja works too. With carpaccio, that sweetness still survives, and the tender, white translucent slices of scallop have an almost meadow-flower mood that goes well with colombard-ugni blanc blends from south-west France or with Spanish muscat.

SEA BASS A delicate fish that suits whites with either elegant finesse or a light touch. If served plain, then try Rhône whites; pinot bianco (weissburgunder) from either north-east Italy (or Germany); or a fine pinot grigio such as one from Friuli-Venezia Giulia in north-east Italy, or a pinot grigio ramato, which is made by leaving the grape juice on the skins so that the wine is coppery pink in colour, a rosé, and has a faint taste of dried acai berries. If introducing sharper flavours on to the plate, then perhaps up the ante. Sea bass served with roasted baby vine tomatoes is good with a precise pinot grigio too, but the cool green notes and barbed-wire feel of sauvignon blanc

S

from Awatere in New Zealand will boost the bright intensity of the tomatoes. With lemongrass, lime and ginger sea bass, try the streak of a young, limey riesling from Clare or Eden Valley in Australia or Martinborough in New Zealand. If chilli is involved, you could also try an off-dry riesling.

SEA URCHIN The intense seawater and iodine taste can be very good with sharply aromatic, floral wines. I have vivid memories of a plate of sea urchin pasta, eaten on a broiling evening at a pavement café in Palermo with a glass of dry zibibbo (muscat) made by Sicilian producer Marco de Bartoli.

SHEPHERD'S PIE see *cottage pie.*

SKATE A pungent and closely textured, meaty fish, skate goes well with stony dry riesling from Alsace, saline Muscadet and also sauvignon blanc blends from Bordeaux. The classic dish of skate with capers and brown butter sauce works well with Vernaccia di San Gimignano; verdicchio; or pinot blanc from Alsace.

SKORDALIA This Greek purée of potatoes and almonds is very garlicky so I usually put it with a fierce white wine such as assyrtiko from Santorini, whose pithy citrus and high-voltage energy fire back at the garlic. Gavi from Italy would be a good lemony alternative.

SLAW Home-made slaw – a world apart from the tired, pre-prepped stuff you buy in a little plastic box – is crunchy and hearty with a sweet-and-sour vibe. It will kill a subtle wine, but it's unlikely that a delicate dinner is planned if coleslaw is in the mix. Coleslaw is more often eaten with highly flavoured food, such as pulled pork, barbecued meat or vegetable kebabs, strong marinades, burgers or cold roast gammon. Everything else on the plate will probably be leading the wine choice here, but with the bite of raw onion and the peppery heat of the mustard in the dressing, perhaps veer towards a wine with more acidity and/or more tannin or just one with a bit of punch. For example, I'd pick a riesling rather than a Chablis; an awkward, young red rather than a fine old bordeaux. Mustard has the magical quality of calming down a difficult wine, so slaw will actually make an imperfect, tannic, green red taste more expensive – a good time to uncork a difficult, young claret – though don't do this if there's chilli or heavily flavoured sauces in the rest of the meal.

made with chipotle and paprika The smoky, fruity warmth of chipotle is good with the high-alcohol-burn and cough-mixture-scent of American zinfandel. It's also good with ripe Chilean, Australian and Argentine reds and upfront wines that have a ton of oak. The charred vanilla and sweet strawberry taste of young, modern Ribera del Duero fits right in here, especially if you're eating the slaw with pulled pork.

SNAILS The squeamish might be tempted to choose a wine big enough to obliterate any hint of mollusc. In reality, the sauce, generally vibrating with garlic, tends to do that for you. In Alsace I once ate snail pizza, which was a bit of a shock as I had presumed those smooth-looking grey-brown chunks nestled among the melted cheese were actually mushrooms. The pizza was washed down with sparkling pinot blanc. It was fine, though I won't recommend it as a match that will make your toes tingle. Escargots are good with almost any young French red. They can work with the lightness of young Chinon or Saumur from the Loire; with entry-level red burgundy such as Mâcon Rouge; with a simple Corbières or Fitou; or indeed with any wine of indeterminate origin (but from somewhere in France), of the type that is sold in a brasserie by the carafe or from a petrol-type pump at which you fill your own bottle/saucepan/bathtub.

SOLE (DOVER AND LEMON) A good white burgundy is a beautiful accompaniment for Dover or lemon sole, either grilled or fried with butter.

SOUFFLÉ With cheese soufflé, try a chardonnay, served not too cold; a red burgundy; a mature claret; or a nebbiolo (especially good if truffles are involved). With the prickly pungency of a blue cheese soufflé, how about the precision of a ribolla gialla from north-east Italy, a minerallic greco di tufo from southern Italy, or the texture and florality of a malvasia from Istria in Croatia?

SOUP Soup is tricky with wine. Liquid + liquid just do not go brilliantly together. However, one wine that does taste very good with many kinds of soup, from gazpacho to mulligatawny to fish soup, is dry sherry. Fino (slightly punchier and more yeasty) or manzanilla (finer and more delicate) provides an edge that garlicky soups can rest against, and has a savoury, umami-like richness that works well with stock. Sherry also acts as a flavour-intensifier for tomato-based soups, in the same way that a slug of amontillado improves a Bloody Mary. Either serve the sherry on the side in a glass or add it to the soup. Both fino and manzanilla need to be poured chilled and from a freshly opened bottle.

See also fish soup, gazpacho.

SOUTH-EAST ASIAN FOOD This area encompasses Thailand, Vietnam, Singapore, Cambodia, Indonesia and Malaysia among others. It might seem peculiar to lump the cuisines of such a vast area together but in contemporary kitchens the ideas and ingredients behind them have been reinterpreted, cross-pollinated and redeveloped. In most places where a large choice of wines is available you're likely to be eating a version of the originals, not the real thing. These foods are often shared, too, with several dishes placed on the table at once, and there is a common thread in terms of the sorts of wines that drink well with the ingredients often found here.

Now that disclaimer's done, a quick look at the ingredients likely to feature.

Chilli is the first one. Unless the aim is to ramp up the jangle and discomfort factor, wines with low tannin, no oak and a touch of sweetness are best.

The sharpness of lime juice, tamarind, green papaya and green mango calls for wines with good acidity.

Flavours such as Thai basil, lemongrass, mint, lime leaves, fish sauce and galangal or ginger demand wines that have a seamless brightness. Don't hamper them with the dust, incense and jagged texture of, say, a Chianti, or the farmyardy brett of some Old World red wines.

Wines that work here are ones that have 'Good acidity, natural fruit sweetness, and either a light touch with oak or no oak at all,' advises

Sam Christie. He is a former sommelier and now managing director of his own four restaurants, including Longrain Melbourne, which serves beautiful South-East Asian food and has an excellent wine list.

Christie says that wines that work with the food at Longrain include 'really crisp Austrian and Australian riesling. I love that acidity and pristine river stone taste. We have a lot of pinot noir too, both Australian and New Zealand but also French. Once again I'm looking for cleansing acidity and no clumsy overtones. Often rosé goes well with the more spicy food – sweeter Spanish or Australian styles work best as you're looking for a bit of residual sugar to wrap up and meld with the spice.

'In terms of specific dishes, look for synergy with the herbs. Fresh green peppercorns are particularly tricky – make that a nightmare – with wine. Coriander and lemongrass work well with herbal styles of riesling, chenin blanc or sauvignon blanc but not so well with chardonnay. Mint can go quite surprisingly well with red wine, as long as the red is soft and juicy. Grüner veltliner from Austria is good with Thai basil and lemongrass too. Viognier is good with herbs but not with chilli. Pinot blanc, semillon and new-wave taut, lean Australian chardonnay are also worth a try.'

You're really looking here not for a wine that is a perfect 'match' but one that gets in the way of the food as little as possible, and isn't nuked itself by what's on your plate. Once chilli gets involved, you really need a bit of sweetness in the wine. If chilli is minimal, then besides Christie's recommendations, I would also consider Adelaide Hills sauvignon blanc, pinot gris, albariño, unoaked Australian semillon, sekt and nerello mascalese.

VIETNAMESE NOODLE SALAD

SERVES 2

You can add chicken to this to make a more substantial meal; use leftover roast chicken or poach a chicken breast, shred it and add it to the finished salad. The sweet-sour-hot dressing works very well with an off- or medium-dry white wine that has good acidity. A lime-scented riesling is the obvious choice, but a young Loire chenin blanc is also good.

FOR THE DRESSING
4 tablespoons lime juice
1 tablespoon rice vinegar
2 tablespoons Thai fish sauce
1 tablespoon vegetable oil
half a red chilli, deseeded and finely chopped
2 teaspoons demerara sugar

FOR THE SALAD
2 medium carrots, shredded if you have
    the patience and grated if you do not
half a head of Chinese leaf, shredded
4 tablespoons fresh coriander leaves
    and fine stalks, finely sliced
4 tablespoons mint leaves, finely sliced
1 shallot, peeled, halved and finely sliced
2 spring onions, finely sliced
2 tablespoons roasted peanuts, chopped
100g rice noodles

To make the dressing, combine the ingredients in a small bowl and whisk together with a fork. Cook the rice noodles according to the instructions on the packet. While the noodles are cooking, put the other salad ingredients in a large bowl and mix them together. When the noodles are cooked, drain them well, refresh under cold water, drain again and mix them into the salad with the dressing.

SPAGHETTI see *pasta*.

SQUASH see *pumpkin*.

SQUID In its simplest form, grilled or griddled and dressed with lemon, garlic and olive oil, squid will go very happily with almost any rosé or bright, young, unoaked white wine. A few examples: South African sauvignon blanc brings a grassy freshness, Gavi di Gavi from northern Italy underscores the lemon, young semillon from Australia adds zip and vibrancy, albariño brings a tickle of apricot stone and marine salinity, and so on.

cool cucumber, cumin and squid salad There's a recipe for this in *Leith's Cookery Bible*. It's very good with a neutral dry white, such as a Terre di Chieti from Italy or a picpoul from France.

grilled with lime and chilli Riesling is superb with lime and the joyful clarity of a dry or off-dry wine from Australia, Chile, Washington State or South Africa really hits the spot.

salt and pepper squid (and salt and chilli squid) I've only ever eaten this nose-ticklingly aromatic snack, lunch or starter in restaurants, but Nigella writes that it is 'unexpectedly easy to shop for as well as easy to cook'. Her recipe is on her website, nigella.com. If you want wine, pick a dry white with a snap of acidity, perhaps also with bubbles to slice through the crunchy batter. Cava will do it. Pink fizz is good too; sparkling gamay made in Touraine in the Loire has a delicious bracing freshness, though any dry fizz will do the job. But I'd be making a saketini by shaking two parts of ice-cold Tanqueray Ten gin with one part of chilled daiginjo sake and ice, and straining the mixture into a cocktail glass.

squid ink risotto Emily O'Hare, an Italian wine expert and former wine buyer and head sommelier at The River Café, has the best advice here: 'Soave is just heaven with it and is exactly what I had when I ate it at the caff. I mean a straightforward Soave, nothing flashy-fruity, as it's such a subtle dish, all about texture and that squiddy flavour and colour. You don't want the distraction of anything too up itself. Otherwise, possibly a Ligurian pigato, or one of those Cinque Terre whites – they've way improved.' Another serious foodie friend – Joe Wadsack – remembers once enjoying a softly floral white Graves with squid ink risotto – an unusual non-Italian match.

stewed with chorizo and red peppers The paprika and the peppers lend themselves more to red than to white wines. Try a soft-cornered Spanish red, either one made from tempranillo or one from Navarra.

STILTON The traditional match with this blue veined cheese is port. I've never been entirely convinced by the combination of tannin which puts up a vigorous fight against strong blue cheese but it's such a festive pairing that I'm slowly coming round to the idea. The sweetness certainly helps. The classic choice would be an LBV, or a vintage port with some age on it but the mellow sweetness of a tawny makes for a gentler combination. Blue cheese kills delicate mature claret but it can go very well with an older cabernet sauvignon from Australia or Napa – the brighter fruit and age-softened tannins hold up well against the mould. In the depths of winter a glass of oloroso sherry is also good. My favourite match of all was suggested to me by the wine and food expert Fiona Beckett whose website matching-foodandwine.com is a superb resource. Beckett points out that a nip of sloe gin is delicious with Stilton.

STRAWBERRIES

hold the cream One of my life's perfect lunches was eaten on a chilly June day in the Loire, in the garden of septuagenarian (and totally not looking it) winemaker Paul Filliatreau. We drank his Saumur Champigny, made from cabernet franc, tasting of leafy summer berries, with lamb barbecued over burning vine trunks, but the *pièce de résistance* was the pudding: a huge bowl of strawberries with Saumur Champigny poured over them. Red wine – cabernet, to be precise – and strawberries is one of those quirky and unexpected marriages. It works with cabernet franc from the Loire or cabernet sauvignon from Bordeaux and not much else. The strawberries need to be good (wild and other outdoor-grown strawberries flourish; big, watery Dutch greenhouse strawberries flounder) and the wine is better if it has noticeable tannin and not too much overt oak. Fragrant Margaux is particularly fine with strawberries. Ice-cold rosé (from almost anywhere) is also good to drink with, as well as to pour over, strawberries. Pick dry Provençal rosé for berries that have not been sprinkled with sugar, darker and sweeter coloured rosé for those that have.

As for white wines, for sheer razzmatazz champagne is hard to beat; demi-sec champagne is not fashionable, but it is sybaritic. For lazy summer afternoons and early evenings, a glass of moscato is an inexpensive alternative. This effervescent, sweetish wine smells of blossom and peaches, a heady combination with the sweet, fragrant strawberries. Moscato has recently enjoyed a nightclub renaissance thanks to its appearance in hip-hop tracks (fans include Lil' Kim and Kanye West). The original and best version is Moscato d'Asti from Piemonte in Italy; but moscato is made elsewhere too. Soundtrack optional.

and cream Cream transforms the strawberries into a full-blown dessert. I tend to prefer puddings without wine but many disagree, and a properly sweet wine such as Jurançon moelleux or a floral Muscat de Beaumes de Venise will hit the spot. Grand Marnier and strawberries is also a match made in heaven – add the Grand Marnier to the cream, or drink it separately and enjoy the fusion of the intense orange with Cognac and red fruit.

STROGANOFF If you want to do this properly, go for Balkan refosco or kékfrankos from Hungary. Ideally you want a red that is rustic and prickly and tastes like it's drunk out of chalices. Greece and Turkey are good places to look for wines that still have prickle and an air of the untame.

SUCKLING PIG While ordinary roast pork can be rather dry, the meat of roast suckling pig is tender and juicy. It goes well with all the whites suggested for roast pork, but a red is my favourite match, and because the meat is succulent, you can afford the savoury tannins of a serious wine, from the Douro, say, or from Bordeaux. Rioja and Ribera del Duero are both excellent too. Says Ferran Centelles, a Spaniard and former sommelier at El Bulli: 'Tempranillo Crianza and suckling pig is a classical match, but I also love suckling pig with the intensity and power of a Médoc wine, especially if it is slightly aged.'

See also pork.

SUSHI It's normal to eat several different types of sushi at once, so the wine choice is necessarily quite general. Sake very obviously works beautifully and Western palates usually prefer the lighter daiginjo style, which is drunk chilled. The Japanese grape koshu, like a cross between pinot grigio and sauvignon blanc, with subtle flavours of starfruit, is brilliant here. It's a wine that tastes almost invisible when drunk on its own, but swells and blossoms with food. Look for chiselled, calm wines such as dry furmint (which often has hints of sushi ginger and Japanese pears), pinot blanc from Germany

S

or north-east Italy, albariño, pale rosé, grüner veltliner, Loire sauvignon blanc (Menetou Salon and Reuilly are particularly good), aligoté, Pfalz or Rheingau dry riesling, verdicchio, rosé champagne and English sparkling wine. Pinot gris is more floral and softer but also good with the rice element. Red can work too – think German pinot noir or gamay.

SWORDFISH The robust white flesh of swordfish is among the most meaty of fish. With lemon garlic sauce or the anise flavours (fenugreek, aniseed, fennel tops or Pernod) with which swordfish goes so well, try oaked sauvignon blanc-semillon blends and oaked assyrtiko, which also have tinges of fennel and baked-lemon flavours. Powerful yet fresh Douro whites are good here too, as is South African semillon and oaked white Rioja. If you are treating swordfish like a steak and serving it with, say, Café de Paris butter or mixed peppercorn butter, then think more steaky on the wine too, with a young and unoaked red such as Côtes du Rhône, or garnacha from Calatayud in Spain. Plain swordfish dressed with just a squeeze of lemon and a slick of olive oil also suits red wine, but go for a little more tartness with young gamay or Marcillac.

S

T

TAGINE The combination of heat, spice and fruit is a difficult one for wine. Provided that the chilli is not too hot and the spice not too strong, with lighter, chicken, vegetarian or pork-based tagine, then aromatic viognier, which smells of honeysuckle and apricots, has a suitably Scheherazade air to it. With heavier meats, I like the warm spice of Lebanese reds or the fading splendour of an old Gran Reserva Rioja or silky Montsant. All too often what I actually end up opening, however, is rosé: dry and pale for a low-chilli tagine, deeper and sweeter the more spice-heat there is.

TANDOORI With tandoori you retain the juiciness and succulence of the meat or fish and this becomes the core that goes with the wine, unlike with a wet curry, where the sauce almost overwhelms other flavours. Tandoori monkfish or sea bass is great with dry muscat, if you can find a good one. There are an awful lot of cheap perfume horrors around but I've had a few excellent ones from Spain, with a hint of orange blossom woven into the florals and with which the lightness of the wine dances around the spice. Dry furmint is a good alternative. Tandoori prawns are beautiful with an aromatic gewürztraminer. Tandoori chicken works well with a very bright but not too oaky chardonnay from South Africa, Australia or Chile. The warmth found in the wine glows with the heat but is limpid enough for the spice. Succulent tandoori lamb is good with red, but as tannins have the effect of concentrating the dried spices, go for one that's smooth: for example, an inexpensive Mediterranean pinot noir or a blend from the Midi. A Turkish red can also work, though the spices might taste more aggressive.

TAPAS A glass of manzanilla, fino, tempranillo or cava is the classic accompaniment to the different flavours on a table loaded with tapas. But go with your mood.

TARRAGON This herb has a powerful, slightly aniseed taste. It's best friends with semillon (in particular, with barrel-fermented semillon), which makes a white bordeaux a good bet with, say, roast chicken with tarragon butter under the skin. In such simple dishes tarragon also works well with the woodruff taste of young, oaked white burgundy. In salads where tarragon is added as a raw herb, it's usually better to stick with the vibrant tang of a sauvignon-semillon blend. With tarragon mustard (in a hot dog) I like the herbal vigour of a young German pinot noir.

Aged syrah – say, a mature Cornas or Hermitage or older Heathcote syrah from Australia – can also be superb with tarragon.

See also beef: béarnaise.

TARTE TATIN Caramelized orchard fruit in a buttery pastry – tarte tatin is one of the few desserts that really plays up to a dessert wine. The obvious choice is a beerenauslese or trockenbeerenauslese riesling whose own luscious apple-strudel flavours mirror those of the tart. Sweet Loire chenin blanc, and the saffron and crystallized fruit flavours of Sauternes, as well as other sweet sauvignon-semillon blends (Monbazillac, Loupiac and so on) are good too. The golden-brown sugar in the tart underscores the honeyed flavours of the wines.

THAI BEEF SALAD Steak seared so that it's pink in the middle and smokily charred on the edge; the scent of torn Thai basil, mint and coriander leaves curling up your nostrils; threads of crunchy raw shallots; the grit of the rice powder; and the sour lime of the dressing ... eating Thai beef salad is a very fragrant, and intense, experience. And I haven't mentioned the chilli. See *chilli*.

A hot version of this will nuke wine. My favourite match for a very mild Thai beef salad is Marlborough pinot noir, silky and perfumed. Failing that, a young pinot noir from elsewhere in New Zealand, or from Australia or from Chile. You could also try one of the soft, lusciously fruity old-vine carignans coming out of Chile; the white pepper and soft mulberry of a cinsault from South Africa; a brambly, unoaked Fitou or Minervois or Costières de Nîmes; the cranberry and tea flavours of an unoaked Chilean carmenère; or the warm pom-pom of strawberry that is a simple and unoaked Spanish garnacha. Put the bottle in the fridge for 20–30 minutes and drink it slightly chilled to give it a refreshing edge against the herbs and lime.

THAI GREEN CURRY The piercing, almost luminous, quality of a sauvignon blanc from Marlborough, New Zealand, plays off the fresh lime, the burst of the pea aubergines and the crunch of the snake beans but fares less well up against chilli. I often open a bottle to drink as an aperitif, or while cooking, as it anticipates the dinner beautifully. With the food, an off-dry wine is better. Non-dry riesling from Australia, Chile or New Zealand (first choice) or Germany (second choice) will counteract the chilli heat and float along with the aromatic coriander and lime. A pretty pinot gris or Chilean gewürztraminer with an edge of sweetness is a good choice too and its gentle florality will cosy up to the coconut milk.

THANKSGIVING You can expect there to be a turkey on the Thanksgiving table. Depending on family and cultural traditions, there might also be sage, sausages, chestnuts, cranberries, sweet potatoes, bacon, apples, raisins, mashed potatoes, corn on the cob, cornbread, homity and squash. The overall effect is one of sweet abundance, with sweetness coming not just from the dried and fresh fruit or the sweet cure of fatty bacon, but also from the corn and sweet potatoes. For a white, go for more ample styles of chardonnay in which you can taste sun, butter and oak. For reds, a luscious and supple pinot noir (perhaps from Sonoma) will harmonize all those flavours; and the fruity roar of a zinfandel wraps the whole feast in fruity warmth. Cinsault and carignan (particularly natural styles of these wines) also work well. Randall Grahm, whose winery in Santa Cruz makes superb Californian wines using Rhône grape varieties, tweeted, 'Just a reminder: virtually every Bonny Doon wine seems to go very well with turkey.' Indeed they do: the aromatic qualities of most Rhône-style blends, both red and white, from the Rhône itself and elsewhere, mesh beautifully with the many flavours on the plate.

As the original point of Thanksgiving was to give thanks for the blessing of the harvest there is good reason to drink native wines, but looking further afield, a Beaujolais Cru will act as a pert counterpoint in much the same manner as the cranberry sauce. More alternative suggestions: an Etna red for its flow and light-bodied refreshment; a trousseau or poulsard from the Jura for its elegance; a chenin blanc (or chenin-roussanne-marsanne blend) from Swartland, South Africa, for the scent of warm orchard fruit and texture that go particularly well with mashed sweet potato and corn.

See also Christmas dinner, turkey.

THYME Woody and aromatic, thyme is not a tricky herb with wine but it does have a tendency to make commercial (fruity and slightly sweet) reds and whites taste trivial and embarrassingly simple. Thyme has a special affinity with pinot noir. It also suits those Mediterranean red wines, from Collioure to Bandol to Cannonau di Sardegna, that seem to smell of sun-baked slopes covered with dried scrub and herbs.

TOFU Not exactly abundant in flavour itself, wines that go well will be those that take their cue from the other elements of the dish. Tofu is often used as a substitute for chicken, or another meat, in which case look up that dish and use those guidelines.

TOMATOES The cool zing and green aromatics of sauvignon blanc really pick up on the refreshing bite of tomatoes (especially raw ones). It's quite a special match, though of course not the only grape that tastes good with a tomato. The main point about tomatoes is that they are super-acidic, which changes the balance of a plate of food and can make a low-acid wine taste flabby and dull, so it's best to look for one with a bit of nip. Here are a few of my favourite tomato and wine experiences.

fresh tomato salad, pan con tomate, insalata tricolore If I were in Barcelona, I'd hope to be sitting on the waterfront with an open bottle of Torres Viña Sol, a quintessential slug-it-back holiday wine made from cava grapes. Cava would also do very nicely. With a lunch or outdoor dinner of warm roast chicken and a big plate of sliced tomatoes sprinkled with freshly chopped chives or basil, or with an insalata tricolore (tomatoes, mozzarella and basil), I'd look to meet the cool green herbs with a grassy Loire sauvignon; a South African sauvignon blanc; one from the Awatere in New Zealand; a generic Touraine sauvignon; a Coteaux du Giennois; or a Sancerre or one of its satellites (Pouilly-Fumé, Quincy, Reuilly, Menetou Salon). Herbaceous Italian wines – vermentino, verdicchio – do well here too. As does young Loire chenin. For red wines, think Bardolino, Beaujolais (or gamay from elsewhere), or just a young red with low alcohol (say, 12% abv), which indicates that the grapes were likely to have been picked with plenty of acidity in them.

oven-dried tomatoes Halves of tomatoes dried slowly in the oven at a low temperature until the flavour intensifies to a piercing burst can take richer, more demanding wines. Consider ripe sauvignon blanc from New Zealand that tastes of nectarine and passion fruit; the warm gooseberries and white currant of a Chilean sauvignon; the broad, pink grapefruit-tinged fumés from California; or a more premium Loire sauvignon with a bit of barrel-fermentation. Look at the other ingredients too; all of these wines go particularly well with dried tomatoes in, say, a salad of peaches, mozzarella and rocket. Chenin blanc and also carricante from the slopes of Mount Etna in Sicily can also be good alternatives, depending on the dish. For instance, chenin blanc is good with a combination of oven-dried tomatoes and goat's cheese. Carricante works well as a palate cleanser with very savoury dishes, such as pasta with oven-dried tomatoes, garlic and olives or oven-dried tomatoes with fried white fish and capers.

salsa cruda For a raw tomato pasta sauce, perhaps with flat-leaf parsley chopped in, as well as fried courgettes and Parmesan gratings, I pick watery, inexpensive French sauvignon blanc, whose grassiness will mesh with the chlorophyll without overwhelming the delicate sauce. The wines mentioned in the entry for *fresh tomato salad, pan con tomate, insalata tricolore* above will also work here.

tomato gratin In her (sadly out of print) book *Modern British Food*, Sybil Kapoor has a recipe for tomato gratin – tomatoes cooked in cream with a cheesy topping – that is the very definition of heavenly summer eating with cold roast beef or chicken. The creamy sauce absorbs much of the acidity, so I pick pinot noir with beef and with chicken, light chardonnay – a Mâcon or one of Australia's twangy, low-alcohol new chardonnays.

tomato tart Layers of thinly sliced tomatoes, laid on a puff pastry base, garnished with capers, olives and anchovies (for those who like them), then gently baked in a slow oven is really a version of pissaladière. The following recipe was first made for me by my friend Stephen, on a villa holiday in Provence during which a copy of F. Scott Fitzgerald's *Tender is the Night* was making an increasingly factor 30-smeared round of the sunloungers by the pool, hence 'Dick Diver's Tart'. This is a much-repeated recipe in my house. I often make it to cut into tiny squares as a pre-dinner G&T or V&T snack, but everyone always eats so much that the main course becomes almost superfluous. The wine needs to be savoury with all those salty-vinegary additions. White (or pink) wine from Provence or Loire sauvignon blanc or Gavi or arneis or one of the Italian V-grapes mentioned under *fresh tomato salad, pan con tomate, insalata tricolore* is just delicious.

DICK DIVER'S TOMATO TART

SERVES 3–4 AS A MAIN OR 6 AS A STARTER

350g ready-made puff pastry
3–4 tablespoons passata (if you like you can fry
    some garlic in olive oil until golden, then cook
    a larger quantity of passata gently with the
    oil until the flavour is infused, and use this
    garlicky passata to spread on the tart)
1.5kg medium-sized tomatoes, washed and
    evenly sliced (about 5mm thick)
a handful of capers (optional)
a handful of black olives (optional)
salt and freshly ground black pepper
1 tablespoon olive oil
fresh basil (optional)

Heat the oven to 200°C/Fan 180°C/Gas 6/400°F. Roll the puff pastry out into either a 30cm circle or a rectangle, roughly 20 × 35cm. Spread a very thin layer of passata over the pastry, then lay the tomatoes on top, in circles or lines, according to whether you are making a round or rectangular tart, so that they overlap. They will shrink a lot when cooked so ensure that there is a good amount of overlap. You need to overlap both the slices in each row and the rows themselves. Scatter with capers and black olives if using. Season. Drizzle with the olive oil. Bake for 25–30 minutes, keeping an eye on the tart to make sure it doesn't begin to burn, then turn the oven down to 150°c/Fan 140°c/Gas 2/300°F and cook very slowly for about 45 more minutes or longer if required. The tomatoes need to dry out and the base to become crisp. Take out of the oven, scatter with fresh, torn basil leaves (if using) and that's it.

Well done, as Stephen would say.

tomatoes in cooked sauces The acidity is the reason nippy Italian reds are so good with pasta sauces. Cooked tomato sauces are richer than raw ones and so they can take heavier wines.

TORTILLA Sparkling wine is often a winner with eggs, and cava or champagne or a sparkling pinot-chardonnay from elsewhere in the world is a very cheery way to wash down a deep, runny-centred tortilla. Sherry – manzanilla or fino for choice – is also a good option.

tortilla española (with potatoes fried in olive oil) Any of the above sparkling wines go nicely with this. The earthy potatoes make red wine appealing too. A young, unoaked Navarra or a bright Rioja Crianza feels casual and hearty. A Spanish friend once cooked the best, most melting tortilla española I have ever eaten. She served it with home-made chips fried in a gigantic Le Creuset and a green salad. Her husband opened a cru Bourgeois – it was Château les Ormes de Pez. So, a left-bank claret and a Spanish omelette. Unorthodox but brilliant. It was a clever way of turning a humble tortilla into a highly prized Saturday dinner with friends. I was curious to know what Spaniard Ferran Centelles, who was the sommelier at El Bulli from 2000 to 2011 and specializes in matching wines to high-end food might like to drink with tortilla, so I asked him. He said, 'Eggs are always difficult to pair. However, if you use onions and potatoes and really cook them well the tortilla will be easier to match. I love to eat the tortilla with a sort of oaky rosé wine produced in Navarra, but a delicate rosé from Provence is also a great match.'

See also omelette, tapas.

TRIFLE If it's a sherry trifle, then sherry is what you must drink with it – ideally the same stuff that has been used to make it, which in our house is always cream. Cream sherry is a throwback, but so is our family trifle. Made with bright layers of pink packet blancmange and wobbly yellow Bird's Custard, it is a thing of beauty that no one else seems to understand. 'As natural as a nuclear reactor,' said the last person I tried to feed it to. But we love it, and we love it with the rich raisin taste of cream sherry too.

With more delicate fruit trifles, perhaps made with fresh custard and fresh summer berries, ratafia champenois is delicious. This is quite rare, because champagne grapes command such a premium when they're made into fizz. It's made by mixing fresh grape juice with alcohol, so has a sweetly grapey taste. The Ratafia de Champagne from Dumangin is particularly good – it's aged in solera (in barrels) and smells very gently of dried figs and spices, and buttery, sugar-crusted Madeira cakes baking in the oven, as well as having a luscious melon sweetness and kick of spirit.

TROUT This delicate river fish shies away from wines that are too fierce. Fresh trout is lovely with Austrian grüner veltliner, with the cool hedgerow flavours of English bacchus, with dry furmint, or with simpler, unoaked burgundy such as Mâcon or Bourgogne Blanc. Hot smoked trout is good with refined, non-shouty riesling from Austria, or from Pfalz or Rheinhessen in Germany.

TRUFFLES The scent of truffles is both captivating and giddying. At least it is to some of us; 25–50 per cent of the population (depending on which study you read) can't smell them properly or, in a few cases, at all. I pity those people. For others, like me, the smell of a truffle is so intoxicating that even the thought of one is enough to bring on heart palpitations and a kind of meerkatty alertness.

The specific cause of all the olfactory excitement has been the centre of much debate. Around fifty volatile odour-carrying components have been identified for the black Périgord truffle, *Tuber melanosporum*, and more than 200 across all species of truffles, a number that keeps on going up as increasingly sensitive instruments for identifying the volatiles become available.

Back in 1981, three German researchers published a paper

reporting that truffles contain a steroid, androstenone, that has a musky smell and is a main component of boar pheromones. As well as being found in boar saliva and truffles, androstenone also occurs in the armpit sweat of men, in bacon and, unexpectedly, in celery. The scientists speculated, not unreasonably, that this must be the smell that attracts wild pigs to nuzzle and paw at the ground until they have unearthed a dirty, smelly tuber, and which causes humans to sigh in contentment. However, later students of truffles demonstrated that it does not appear to be androstenone that draws boars and dogs to buried scent caches but another compound present in truffles – dimethyl sulphide (DMS), which has been described as 'the smell of the sea' or, less attractively, when present in higher concentrations, 'the smell of rotting cabbage'.

What effect does androstenone have on humans? Women find it more appealing during ovulation, according to one study, so perhaps appreciation of truffles also changes through the female cycle. My own never flags. Indeed, it is so intense that for a moment I seriously considered acting on a friend's suggestion to organize the world's first wine and truffle matching championship – 'Just think how many you will get to eat, and what fine wines!' – before I realized that he was teasing me. A small part of me still wonders if it might be possible to pull this off. The realistic side says otherwise.

Magnificent with truffles at most times: nebbiolo, in all its guises; vintage champagne; white burgundy; Pomerol.

white truffles The three best ways to eat white truffle, in my opinion, are shaved on to thin strands of eggy pasta with butter, shaved on to a fried egg, or in fonduta. White truffles are of course also used to flavour risottos and puréed squash. They are shaved on to carpaccio of beef with rocket, and also on to tartare of beef or veal, and all manner of other foods. In all these cases, the dried rose and sandalwood scent of nebbiolo (Barolo or Barbaresco or one from Valtellina, Ghemme or a simple Langhe nebbiolo) is the best possible wine to be drinking. The fragrance is heavenly. Also, with dairy-rich, creamy, eggy dishes, nebbiolo's fine, sinewy tannins offer a bit of a workout in between those dizzying mouthfuls of fat and fragrance. You will have invested heavily in the truffle so it's worth making a bit of effort with the wine. Either young or old is fine, but don't open a super-grand bottle that is also young, as it's likely to be so oaky, and so powerful, that it's not pleasant to drink and drowns out the truffle. Failing nebbiolo, seek out another wine from Alba, such as barbera.

There is also a synergy between white truffles shaved on to seafood/fish and vintage champagne.

black Périgord truffles Mature Pomerol has a soft, sumptuous texture, and it smells gently fungal, which resonates with, say, black truffles stuffed under the skin of a roasted chicken. A maturing red burgundy would also be good here. The luxe of white burgundy is also gorgeous with black truffles with chicken, as well as black truffles when they are put with seafood.

At a Noble Rot lunch at The Clove Club in east London, I once ate carpaccio of scallops with black truffles, sudachi (a Japanese fruit with a citrus twang) and hazelnuts with a glass of young Jacques Carillon Puligny-Montrachet. The wine was the perfect counterpoint for the sweetness of the scallops, the crunch of the nuts and the scallop shavings together with the subtle burst of citrus. It was a genius plate of food with a genius wine beside it.

other truffles: English summer truffles, Australian truffles, black Istrian truffles Milder in flavour, these truffles need a more subtle wine. Rosé champagne is perfect, as I discovered after going truffle hunting at a secret location in the south of England with the cook and restaurateur Roger Jones and his Manchester United-loving son Richard, who was then eleven and as good a truffle hunter as any Périgord pig. He said he could feel them through the soles of his trainers. Once we'd unearthed a few dirty truffles from among the roots of the trees, Roger whipped out a little camping stove; fried some turbot; sliced subtle, nutty and freshly unearthed English summer truffles over them; and opened a bottle of rosé Gosset. Both food and wine were delicate, elegant and blissful. White champagne works too, as does white burgundy, as long as it's not too heavy. In Istria, Croatia, local truffles are a speciality that goes with the fragrant, floral, textured local white wine made from malvasia. The Istrian version of the summer truffle is glorious with filled pasta, foraged wild asparagus and a carafe of local wine.

TUNA Of all fish, tuna is the most likely candidate for eating with red wine, so much so that I can't actually remember the last time I ate cooked tuna with white. Seared so that it's brown on the outside and a translucent stained-glass window pink in the middle, it is lovely with chilled light or medium-bodied reds, such as Beaujolais; Cerasuolo di Vittoria; Etna reds from Sicily; zweigelt from Austria; crunchy pinot noir from Chile, Burgundy, Germany or Austria; cabernet franc; Bierzo; dolcetto; Valpolicella; Bardolino; lagrein and so on. If you are cooking it with a crushed-peppercorn crust, then consider a lighter cool-climate syrah, such as a young St Joseph that has been sparingly oaked.

carpaccio of tuna Drizzled with olive oil and scattered with slices of spring onion, carpaccio of tuna is excellent with a lemony white such as cortese, assyrtiko, or a lemony sauvignon blanc. I once ate this dish with a fantastic sauvignon made by Sevilen in Turkey.

TURKEY A juicy or aromatic wine, whether red or white, helps to combat turkey's tendency to dryness. Dolcetto, Beaujolais, pinot noir, unoaked Spanish garnacha, grillo and falanghina are all happy contenders, while the soft aroma of pinot gris brings a succulence to the meat. What you're eating with it makes all the difference.

See also Boxing Day leftovers, Christmas dinner, Thanksgiving, turkey sandwiches.

TURKEY SANDWICHES A festive favourite, often eaten in an over-indulgent stupor while surrounded by scrunched-up wrapping paper and relatives. Crack open a bottle of dry, red Lambrusco, a superb and underestimated sparkling wine from the Emilia-Romagna region of Italy. It's sparkling, slightly earthy and dusty and often tastes of cranberries, which makes it perfect if sausage-meat stuffing, cranberry and bread sauce are also involved in the sandwich-making.

See also Boxing Day leftovers, Christmas dinner, Thanksgiving, turkey.

V

VEAL A versatile meat that can go with both red and white wines, though I more often pick a red. The perky acidity and fine delineation of north-western Italian wines made from nebbiolo, dolcetto and barbera are always a good bet, or, in the same vein, a sangiovese. I also like the reds from the Italo-Alpine region of Alto Adige made from lagrein or teroldego, or a chilled Valpolicella from the Veneto. With veal chop or roast, simply cooked with no sauce, besides the wines mentioned above, try the frisson of claret (a lighter, inexpensive wine, or one from the left bank; not St Emilion); a Marcillac; or a simple, young pinot noir. The earthy tones of mencía (from Bierzo or Ribeira Sacra in Spain) also work well, as do older, fine red wines from Brunello to Rioja to burgundy, that have mellowed with age. The accompaniments make quite a difference, however.

with braised fennel or with sage, rocket and white bean salad Those edgy reds with good acidity go well with tricky fennel: sangiovese, frappato, nebbiolo, gamay, or at a pinch barbera. For whites try a more complex Gavi, oaked white burgundy, white bordeaux or greco di tufo.

with creamy sauces With a richer, creamy sauce, either stick with one of those Italian reds mentioned above, which have the acidity to cut through the fat, cleansing the mouth between forkfuls, or pick a richer, heavier wine from Bordeaux to match the weight of the food.

escalope, fried in butter with a squeeze of lemon A white wine would be just as good as a red, perhaps a fuller-flavoured Gavi di Gavi or a Chablis.

meatballs made with pine nuts and Pecorino A northern Italian red or a richer Italian white, such as fiano or greco di tufo.

veal parmigiana Brought to the US from Italy and enriched over the generations, this dish has become an Italian-American classic. Its layers of cheese, tomatoes and veal escalopes are heavy and

V

comforting. Choose sangiovese, frappato or dolcetto to cut through the clag or a rich primitivo or zinfandel to roll with it.

veal Milanese see *wiener schnitzel*; also *osso buco, saltimbocca alla romana, vitello tonnato.*

VENISON This meat has forceful flavours that can take (and sometimes demand) big red wines.

rare steak or loin Here, however, pinot noir can be a good choice. A plumper wine from New Zealand or Oregon will bring juice and ease in a similar way to a dollop of redcurrant jelly on the plate. This is also a good pick if the venison is served with sweet red cabbage or a rich jus. The compressed red fruit flavours of a youthful Châteauneuf-du-Pape or grenache-based Côtes du Rhône also make a good counterpoint to pink venison. With more savoury accompaniments, such as mushrooms, you could try a stern German pinot noir, or a mature burgundy. An oaky barbera, Montepulciano d'Abruzzo or even a younger, fruitier St Joseph, or young Australian shiraz, works well here too.

venison burgers with redcurrant jelly With these, play into the sweet fruit with an Australian, North American or New Zealand pinot noir, a Beaujolais Cru, a juicy young unoaked or barely oaked syrah from pretty much anywhere in the world, or a fruity carignan.

venison casserole or braised venison When slow-cooked with herbs and, possibly, bacon and juniper, the feral scent of venison is at its most pervasively intense. It's time to call on the big boys: try a gamey syrah, old or young, from the northern Rhône (Cornas, Côte Rôtie, Crozes-Hermitage, Hermitage or St Joseph); an earthy or eucalyptal Aussie shiraz (perhaps from Heathcote or McLaren Vale respectively); a savage touriga nacional from Portugal; a herbal oaked carignan; a St Chinian; or the smoky flare of a Côtes du Roussillon. Mourvèdre is an especially good match as this grape has a gamey flavour, which makes red Bandol another good option. Venison casserole also likes a bit of brett – the yeast that can make a wine taste of old leather horse saddles, or stables – so if you have a bretty wine (maybe a Bandol or a claret or a Rhône), then bring it out now. Wine aside, the bitter flavours of a dark beer can be utterly superb with the dark, dense flavours and meaty perfume of venison casserole. Look for either rich, smooth, malty, fairly

V

strong old-school brown ales or fresh, fragrant, thymey, hoppy black beers with acidity and a bitter-chocolate finish. Try Fullers 1845, Beavertown Black Betty or Yeastie Boys Pot Kettle Black.

VINEGAR GAME-CHANGER Vinegar demands a wine that is high in acidity so as to match its bite. Bear this in mind if you're picking a wine to drink alongside a vinegary salad dressing or have a very lot of pickles on the plate. Sauvignon blanc, riesling and chenin blanc are all whites that are naturally high in acidity. Italian reds often have good acidity; acidity is one of the reasons why nebbiolo and sangiovese are often considered 'good food wines'. Champagne and English sparkling wine also have plenty of bite and will go well with fish and chips regardless of how much vinegar they are doused in.

VITELLO TONNATO Pick the clean bite of verdicchio, a vermentino or a lemony Gavi or arneis if you like white wine; a sangiovese rosato for a pink with a prickle of tannin; or a Provençal rosé that tastes more of herbs than it does of strawberries. My favourite wine to drink is actually red: a chilled Valpolicella or lighter nebbiolo or, failing that, a dolcetto or barbera.

V

W

WALDORF SALAD The cold crunch of green apple, the brisk bite of celery and the cold slap of mayonnaise go very well with a fresh, unoaked Saint-Véran from the Mâconnais in Burgundy. However, it's not often anyone eats Waldorf salad without a plate crammed with so many other foods (quiche, slices of ham, pork pie, pickles, rice salads – all those classic Seventies buffet staples), so the choice of wine isn't too important, though I'd happily drink a Saint-Véran with all of that as well.

WALNUTS If you were sitting by a fire, cracking open walnuts, with a glass beside you, you might want that glass to contain a rare, old Madeira. Madeira is a wine that is almost immortal: it still tastes good when it is not just decades but more than a century old, and it has flavours of dried fruit and nuts, all of which make it a perfect, meditative combination with walnuts.

Otherwise, it's unusual for walnuts to play an insistent enough part on the plate to steer the wine choice. This is partly because walnuts are friendly to most white wines. Crisp, fresh, fruity whites provide a similar pleasing contrast to that found between apple and walnut in a Waldorf salad. More complex, oaked whites, perhaps with extended skin contact, which gives them texture and tannins, from dry to sweet like those rich old Madeiras, draw out the more complex flavours, as dried figs and raisins do with most nuts.

There are times, though, when walnuts, along with other ingredients, haul a plate of food in a very savoury direction: for instance, Diana Henry's recipe for 'Jerusalem artichokes and chicken with anchovy, walnut and parsley relish' (found in *A Bird in the Hand*). In these cases, good matches are savoury red wines such as those made from mencía (for example, Bierzo or Ribeira Sacra) or blends from the Dão in Portugal.

WASABI Much commercially available 'wasabi' contains only a small proportion of the real stuff, consisting mainly of horseradish and a pale green-coloured mustard. It can still produce explosive effects, however. I once put a whole teaspoonful in my mouth, presuming it was guacamole (I was in South Africa and not a Japanese restaurant, so perhaps the mistake is understandable). A few seconds later, a burning in my nose and a kind of electric slicing at the front of my head, similar to what you might expect to feel if you dived into a pool of iced water, alerted me to the error. Wasabi activates the trigeminal nerve, which carries pain sensations in the mouth. Its pungency can be tricky with wine. The best advice is to go easy on the wasabi if you want to be able to taste the wine too, but with small amounts then zesty whites such as grüner veltliner are good.

WATERCRESS This cool, peppery leaf suits the chilly, damp nettles-and-hawthorn taste of English bacchus – a good option for a white to go with watercress salad with trout. I often eat watercress in a salad with papaya (have you noticed they share a similar flavour?) and also feta, in which case a white with good acidity is key. Bacchus can certainly supply that, but I like a white with a bit more gloss – a dry Jurançon or a white St Mont is ideal. Watercress salad with steak would make me look for a red that is prickly or leafy rather than mellow – sangiovese or peppery syrah or cabernet franc or claret in place of warm Rioja or mellifluous merlot.

WIENER SCHNITZEL The crispy, fried-breadcrumb crust around this veal escalope demands a white wine with some edge. A refreshing grüner veltliner or dry riesling is the obvious choice for this Austrian dish. A measured sauvignon blanc, such as a Reuilly from the Loire, or a sauvignon blanc from Australia's Adelaide Hills, is good too, as are the precise and clipped wines of northern Italy: Gavi or arneis will act like a squeeze of lemon, while friulano and ribolla gialla are more aromatic.

W

Z

ZANDER When it has been pan-fried and served with simple flavours, this lake and river fish also known as the pike-perch is good with dry white chenin blanc from the Loire, riesling from Alsace, or dry Jurançon. In the Loire it is sometimes cooked in red wine, in which case choose a Loire red to drink with it.

Wine portraits

Here is a quick introduction to twelve of the best-known grapes.

WHITE

CHARDONNAY Chardonnay is a chameleon grape that may be lean or rich, plain or voluptuously complex, and makes some of the world's greatest sparkling (hello, blanc de blancs champagne) as well as still wines. It's a grape that is very responsive not just to the soil and climate of the place in which it's planted but also to the decisions of the winemaker. At one extreme, chardonnay can taste almost neutral, like plain sheets of paper with the gentlest tinge of lemon. At the other, in sunny, warm places if the grapes are left to get very ripe and then fermented in brand new, toasty oak barrels, the wine turns a deep yellow and might taste buttery and fat with a twang of pineapple cubes, tropical fruit, vanilla and wood spice.

Chardonnay reaches its pinnacle in Burgundy in France, where alterations in the geology create huge taste differences not just from one subregion to another but from one village to another, and from one vineyard to the next. Chablis tastes of damp limestone and lemons; Montagny is nutty, reminiscent of hazelnuts; and the finest wines such as Puligny-Montrachet have great majesty and detail, sometimes also an astonishing heavy perfume with notes of wood-ruff and dried meadow flowers.

Chardonnay is widely planted and makes superb wines elsewhere, too, notably in New Zealand, Oregon and California in the US, and in cooler sites in Australia. Back in France, Limoux, in the foothills of the Pyrenees, is a good place to look for finely structured yet inexpensive bottles.

CHENIN BLANC To my mind chenin blanc is hugely underrated: an incredibly versatile grape, capable of making superb still wines at a range of different sweetness levels. It has a piercing acidity that can bring a thrilling edge to its dry wines and a refreshing quality to those that are intoxicatingly sweet. Its wines can be drunk while they are vibrant and young and aged for many years. It is also responsible for some very attractive sparkling wines.

Chenin blanc excels in two places: the Loire Valley in France and South Africa. It's in the Loire that you find the most keen-edged wines. In places like Vouvray, Savennières and Montlouis the wines have a luminous clarity and a scything acidity gleams through them. Quince is the grape's hallmark flavour and it is very evident here: floral with a hint of apples and pears and a touch of honey that becomes more evident in older as well as in sweeter wines.

In South Africa, chenin blanc has become the country's signature white grape, covering almost a fifth of all vineyards. It is planted in abundance for mass-market wines but there is also a drive to preserve the pockets of decades-old, gnarled vines as well as to make complex and textured wines that reflect the terroir. South African chenin is typically rounder and more beeswaxy, often tasting of riper fruits like honeydew melon, glazed pears or Sharon fruit, with the golden glow of an autumn sun.

Food? With young, dry wines try prawn cocktail, fried salmon filet or a crab sandwich. Off-dry wines are good with hot and salty noodles, fish pie, or roast pork with spices or apple sauce.

RIESLING A lithe, thrillingly acidic white grape, riesling is held in the highest esteem by the winerati. And yet (at least for now), it is stubbornly unfashionable in a broader sense. Usually made without oak, it comes in a vast range of sweetness styles: it can be austerely dry, displaying a laser-like focus and precision; intensely sweet (like the trockenbeerenausleses of Germany, which are made from individually selected, botrytis-shrivelled late-picked berries); or anything in between.

Lime is a dominant flavour and this might translate as the spry fragrance of fresh lime zest; a more honeyed, mellow taste like shreds of lime peel in marmalade; the floral scent of lime blossom; the vital sting of just-squeezed lime juice and sometimes all of these at once. As riesling ages the aromatics mutate and a petrol-like smell often described as 'kerosene' or 'paraffin' comes in. Chemically, this is a modified version of naphthalene, says Harold McGee in *Nose Dive: A*

Field Guide to the World's Smells, which might not sound very appealing but is much admired.

Modern palates often seek out brisk, dry (or only-just-off-dry) rieslings from Alsace, Austria, Australia and even Chile and these can be superbly refreshing. It's not well enough acknowledged that riesling with just a tinge of sweetness is an important weapon in the food matcher's arsenal. The luminous, waltzing kabinetts from the Mosel, Nahe or elsewhere in Germany are brilliant when there's a touch of chilli heat or the sweetness of fruit in a savoury dish. They also marry well with certain meats, making pork or ham taste more succulent.

SAUVIGNON BLANC The maligned grape of the moment, sauvignon blanc is reviled in some quarters for the very qualities that have made it so popular. Pungently aromatic, especially when grown in Marlborough in New Zealand, savvy b can deliver a piercing hit of elderflower, cut grass, citrus, blackcurrant leaf and gooseberry that to some is shrill, to others divine. Even its detractors, though, can usually agree to appreciate the more mineral and savoury sauvignon blancs made in the Loire Valley in France, which include Sancerre and Pouilly Fumé across the river.

The classic plate of food with Sancerre is crottin de Chavignol (a local goat cheese) toasted on baguette and served with dressed lettuce – so good I can't have one without thinking of the other. Sauvignon blanc has bite. It loves tomato dishes, asparagus and tabbouleh. The more green-tasting wines, the ones that smell of green tomatoes and river rocks, are, unsurprisingly, particularly good with raw tomatoes and with the sharp acidity of feta cheese. The more fruity wines, which tend to smell like nectarines and mango, like Thai flavours, though beware of chilli. (And see page 56 for why.)

In Bordeaux and in Margaret River in Australia, among other places, sauvignon blanc is blended with semillon and sometimes aged in oak to make wines that are redolent of baked grapefruit and dried lemon peel and often have a tang of dill or the scent of pine forest. The best of these wines age beautifully; the lemon fades and gentle edges of mushrooms appear. Younger sauvignon-semillon blends are good with smoked salmon and, especially when oak is involved, with creamy sauces involving tarragon.

VIOGNIER Fragrant in a way that's reminiscent of peaches, honeysuckle, and jasmine tumbling over the rugged wall of a hillside in Provence, viognier can be captivating. The email and photograph I received from a friend, John, one cold winter evening is typical of the response to a good bottle. 'This wine was incredible. Where can I buy another one to share with Claire?' I couldn't find an identical wine and directed him to an essay by Jay McInerney who describes a similar phenomenon, of friends keen to remember the name of this grape ahead of a romantic dinner.

Viognier reaches its heady pinnacle in the small appellation of Condrieu, close to Lyon in France (Domaine Georges Vernay is a good place to start). Good, often simpler, viognier is also made elsewhere, in particular in southern France, in Chile and in Australia. In the southern Rhône, viognier is often blended with other white grapes such as clairette and grenache blanc, which is appreciated for the aromatic qualities it brings to the mix. Viognier is best drunk young while the dance of florals is still fresh. The grape doesn't have tons of acidity which can lead it to feel flabby or oily in the mouth. The better wines avoid this sensation, harnessing the soft, hedonistic side of the grape but doing so with a light touch.

Viognier goes well with the white/pink meat of crab, langoustine and lobster; it accentuates the succulence of pork or chicken dishes with a fruity element, for instance coronation chicken, curried chicken with peaches, pulled pork, or peach and noodle salad. It's also good with eggy quiche and with cooked onion-based dishes such as caramelized onion tart.

RED

CABERNET SAUVIGNON The world's most widely planted wine grape, cabernet sauvignon is grown across the globe, from Australia to Uruguay. It is capable of making architectural wines as beautifully structured as the Pantheon or the Colosseum and which, in the best cases, can age and improve for many decades. It's cabernet sauvignon that provides the spine of some of the world's finest and most traded wines, but unlike pinot noir, which soars alone, cabernet sauvignon is at its best when it is blended. Bordeaux is cabernet sauvignon's spiritual home. Here, in combination with some or all of merlot, cabernet franc, petit verdot and malbec it makes fragrant Margaux, imposing Pauillac and thousands of clarets from other sub-regions of this vast wine region.

The telltale scent of cabernet sauvignon is a waft of blackcurrant or cassis. The former recalls the fruit; the latter the deeper, softer scent of the liqueur. As cabernet-based wine matures you might also smell cedar, pencil shavings, graphite, dried tobacco, old leather or cigar box. These wines have a measured feel, a reassuring dignity and the grace of their proportions is at least as important as the flavours you find in there. Good cabernet sauvignon is also grown in Bergerac in France; California in the US; Coonawarra and Margaret River in Australia; Tuscany in Italy where it's used in Supertuscans; and in South Africa where it's sometimes blended with pinotage and other grapes to make a Cape take on a Bordeaux blend.

It is most easily matched with meat. Steak and burgers are the obvious choice; but it also complements robust dishes like chilli con carne and cottage pie, while lamb and cabernet are particularly good together. Cabernet sauvignon also goes very well with beetroot.

MALBEC Malbec is a little like Janus, the two-headed god. In the region around the ancient fortress city of Cahors in south-west France, this grape has traditionally made wines so savoury, dense, dark, and tannic that in their youth they are as impenetrable as a medieval keep. In time – we're talking decades – those black wines mellow into a drink that's reminiscent of a mature claret, more rustic and brambly and much less expensive.

The other face of malbec looks forward, not back. It's piercingly aromatic, exuberant, and bouncy. It smells of violets, blueberries, mulberries and earth and tastes of liquorice, chocolate and an abundance of black, juicy berries. It is meant to be drunk young, capturing the bright intensity of the fresh fruit, and it's a style that Argentina has both popularised and made its own.

Argentinian malbec has become such a go-to choice in pubs and restaurants, that it is now a non-negotiable element of many wine lists. But nothing stays the same for long, and these two polarized styles are shifting as many winemakers in Argentina seek to make less oaky, less ripe and more finessed terroir wines and some of those in France look to emulate the success of those young, bright wines of South America.

Foodwise, beef is very much the big thing: try a burger or steak served with humita (a creamy-textured side made from ground corn) perhaps with a palm heart salad. Malbec is also good with pasta Bolognese, lamb with mint, pulled pork with spicy sauce, Toulouse sausages, cassoulet, and magret de canard. Vegetarian options need to be hearty: try a rich pulse stew, say butter beans with sage and squash or chickpeas and roasted red peppers.

MERLOT Of all grapes merlot is the one that gets the least credit when it shines. That's because it has a soft fleshiness that makes it brilliant in blends, so the producer or region ends up stealing the glory. Merlot is the predominant grape in St Emilion and in Pomerol where it is entirely responsible for the cult wine Le Pin. Merlot is indispensable in all red Bordeaux blends, as well as in similar styles made around the world, whether that's in California, Tuscany, Chile or Stellenbosch. Yet wine labelled simply 'merlot' has become associated with a vinous lowest common denominator: wine slurry that is smooth and fruity but undistinguished. This is, after all, the wine famously so reviled by wine snob Miles in *Sideways* that sales plummeted after the film's release.

Despite the bad rep, merlot does make some very good cheap wines. Its wine often has the vivid taste of damsons or stewed plums. It can also have a fresh, leafy scent. In warmer climates it might taste richer, brambly and slightly chocolatey. Add in oak and you get a dense and spicy drink.

As for food, if you have one of those cheaper, brighter, unoaked merlots it will bring out the succulence of roast gammon or the fruit of lamb and redcurrant burgers. More dense or oaked wines are good with cottage pie, enchiladas, chilli con carne (made with a square of plain chocolate), barbecue sauce and heavy meat marinades. With a good St Emilion try rib of beef with slow-roasted carrots. If the wine is mature then gentler flavours like veal chop with dauphinoise are good. Roasted root veg mixes also work well.

PINOT NOIR Pinot noir is the only grape I know that makes people cry when they drink it. I mean that in the sense of being profoundly moved by the wine, not in the sense of drinking too much and crying about everything else. Of all grapes it has the keenest ability to capture a sense of place, an imprint of the land in which it's grown. In the words of Aubert de Villaine, proprietor of the fabled Domaine de la Romanée Conti in Burgundy, 'Pinot noir does not exist. It's a ghost.' The very best is sublimely effortless, treading so lightly you experience it as a seamlessly fluent, graceful song of a wine with the place in which it was made hovering around the rim of the glass.

Burgundy is where pinot noir reaches its finest and most dreamlike expression, though the best wines command steep prices and are made in such small quantities that securing an allocation demands planning and big spending. Finding a truly magical pinot noir also requires persistence; this is a capricious grape. That said, pinot noir does also make excellent bright, juicy inexpensive wines that taste of cherries and sometimes also have a whiff of dried herbs, lavender or roasted red fruit or raspberries. Beyond Burgundy, look to New Zealand, South Africa, Germany, Oregon, California, Australia and, for the cheaper options, to Chile.

Pinot noir is the ultimate food red. It even tastes incredible with potatoes, and I never thought there'd be a wine match for the humble spud.

SANGIOVESE 'For me a good sangiovese is like sniffing the back of the neck of someone you really, really like.' So says Emily O'Hare, a wine consultant and former River Café sommelier who now lives in Siena. She is talking about the very particular, savoury fragrance of Italy's most widely planted red variety, a grape that at its best has edge, perfume and a certain delicacy.

Sangiovese forms the backbone of Chianti and Chianti Classico, in which it is sometimes seasoned with grapes that might be local (colorino and canaiolo, for instance) or international (merlot, cabernet sauvignon). And it is the only grape in the richer, denser magisterial wine from southern Tuscany, Brunello di Montalcino, and its more affordable sibling, Rosso di Montalcino. You'll also find sangiovese growing in Corsica where it's known as nielluccio and there's a little in Australia, too – here the fruitiness shines out more.

Sangiovese is rarely smooth. Rather, it feels crenellated, thanks to its grainy tannins. It has the sweet-sourness of fresh cherries and, apart from warm skin, it can smell of church incense, dried herbs, earth, roses and violets and truffle. It also has a mouthwatering acidity, which makes it truly a wine for the table: think of a grainy mouthful of chickpea soup followed by a prickly sip of sangiovese, or a forkful of fatty slow-roast joint of pork rubbed with fennel and garlic swooshed back with a refreshing gulp of Chianti Classico.

In Tuscany they like to eat wild boar with sangiovese. That's not just a food match but a dish of revenge served piping hot: wild boars are a nuisance to grape growers because they rampage through the vineyards eating grapes.

SYRAH Syrah is both powerful and perfumed. It might smell of black peppercorns, violets, baked raspberries, blackberries, liquorice, tobacco, and even eucalyptus. It can be intensely, richly fruity: think of a warm Barossa shiraz, a vinous cuddle of a wine, all mulberries and raspberry jelly. It can also be blood-stirringly savage with a feral, gamey edge, like the northern Rhône syrahs: Cornas, Hermitage, Côte Rôtie, St Joseph and Crozes Hermitage.

This red grape also has two linguistic identities: syrah and shiraz. It was once the case that Europeans talked about syrah while the New World grew shiraz. Now it's often labelled to reflect the winemaker's ambition for the wine he has put in the bottle. Those who have their sights on refined perfume, stony minerality, a kind of meatiness, a hint of wild undergrowth and perhaps also inscrutability tend to refer to their wine as syrah. Those (often working in warmer climates) who favour riper grapes, higher alcohols and a great unleasing of booming fruit are more likely to call it shiraz.

Another hallmark of syrah – especially of syrah grown in a cooler climate – is the tickle of just-crushed black peppercorns. This isn't an olfactory illusion. The aroma molecule rotundone is found both in wines made from syrah and in peppercorns. The presence of rotundone helps to explain why syrah goes so well with food that has a lot of black pepper in it: peppery sausages or steak with a black pepper crust.

Syrah is also good with mildly spiced meat curries (but not the very creamy sort), black lentil dhal, game, spicy veggie burgers, beef short ribs marinated in five-spice and hoisin sauce, beef and black olive stew or duck breast with plum sauce and sesame noodles. Pick a more plush, more jammy wine for sweeter, more fruity food.

TEMPRANILLO Young tempranillo tastes of bright red fruit with a bit of a crunch and a lick of russet – fresh redcurrants and strawberries with a suggestion of tomato and tobacco. Add in some more oak and age and you get more savoury flavours – cedar wood, dried herbs, more tobacco, old saddles, nutmeg, cloves, spice, mulching leaves, coconut, vanilla and strawberry pie.

This grape is the star of Spain's two best-known reds: Ribera del Duero and Rioja. In Ribera del Duero tinto fino, as the local strain of tempranillo is called, is usually bottled neat and only sometimes blended with a little cabernet, merlot, and/or malbec. Here it makes wines that are particularly dark-fruited and firm and often also generously oaked. Rioja, confusingly, may be made from 100 per cent tempranillo but does not actually have to contain any tempranillo at all. In practice, though, tempranillo does form the base of most Rioja either in pure form or as the anchor in a tempranillo-based blend also featuring one or more of garnacha tinta, graciano and mazuelo.

Wherever tempranillo is grown, the impact of the oak is keenly felt. American oak brings a sweet vanilla perfume and sometimes also a suggestion of coconut. French oak is more savoury. As tinta roriz, tempranillo is also used in Portugal, notably in the Douro Valley where it forms part of the blend in table wines as well as in port.

Particularly attractive about tempranillo is its capacity to be mellow – a quality that makes it a very good partner to slow-cooked meats or roasted root vegetables.

Quick look matches

Favourite matches

Some of the food and wine combinations that have stayed with me.

sea urchin spaghetti and zibibbo	Thai beef salad and Marlborough pinot noir
vitello tonnato and Langhe Nebbiolo	octopus, waxy potato and paprika salad and albariño
soft shell crab and Hunter Valley semillon	sliced peach in a glass of pinot grigio
salade niçoise and rosé from Provence	chicken with morilles and vin jaune
	fish pie and savennières
	lamb with a herb crust and left-bank bordeaux
	fried egg with white truffles and nebbiolo
	slow-cooked lamb shoulder and Rioja Reserva

Sofa snacks

For all those evenings when you are pouring a glass while picking at food and cracking on with a few chores – or chatting to friends.

salted almonds
fino sherry, manzanilla sherry

crisps
crémant, champagne – bubbles and acidity are great with salt

prosciutto and breadsticks
anything goes, but particularly good: prosecco (add some slices of pear to the plate, and Pecorino too if you have it), Provence rosé, petite arvine

olives
gin, manzanilla sherry (especially good with the big green manzanilla olives), dry Greek reds with kalamata olives

gougères (aka cheese puffs)
chardonnay of all types but especially Chablis

bagna cauda and raw veggies
pigato (aka vermentino and favorita), arneis, verdicchio

On toast

The first glass of the day is always the best and so many of the matches I love are simple snacks that can be squeezed into time-poor evenings, or this or that on toast that you eat in the kitchen as you chat with friends and prepare the main course.

avocado
unoaked or lightly oaked chardonnay from a warmer climate; Marlborough sauvignon blanc (especially if you're dressing the avo with lemon); sauvignon blanc from Adelaide Hills, Australia, or from Chile; pinot grigio

baked beans
smooth, fruity, very slightly sweet but pretending to be dry and fruity supermarket red

skagen toast
Gavi, young semillon, barrel-fermented sauvignon blanc and sauvignon-semillon blends, young bordeaux sauvignon blanc, cooler-climate chardonnay, vermentino, aquavit

chorizo and caramelized onions
Rioja (white or red)

broad bean and Pecorino
rosé, verdicchio, Gavi (cortese), arneis, vermentino, gamay

duxelles of mushrooms with lemon thyme
sauvignon-semillon blend (for instance from Bordeaux or Margaret River) either unoaked or oaked

anchovies
fino or manzanilla sherry; dry pedro ximénez; rosé; verdejo; arneis; cava; young, unoaked tempranillo, Langhe Nebbiolo

crab and coriander mayo
albariño

tomatoes
raw, with olive oil and garlic manzanilla or fino sherry, rosé, cava, unoaked sauvignon blanc, verdicchio, arneis, young Loire chenin blanc, carricante
grilled, on buttered toast pinot grigio, Loire sauvignon blanc, verdejo, vermentino, grüner veltliner, South African chenin blanc, barbera

Plant-based plates

Many of the classic food and wine matches are carnivorous. One reason for that is that the tannin in (especially young) red wines goes well with meat protein. Here are some excellent plant-based food and wine combinations. And a tip for veggie red wine drinkers: adding smoked paprika to a dish (where appropriate!) can help it to go with red wines, especially mencía or tempranillo (the Rioja grape) from Spain.

PASTA

pumpkin, pine nut and sage ravioli
Soave, chardonnay, lighter sangioveses, xinomavro

broccoli and garlic orecchiette
pinot grigio, cortese

pomodoro crudo
crisp, unoaked whites like sauvignon blanc, verdicchio, pecorino

truffle and tagliolini
nebbiolo

cacio e pepe
Frascati, Vernaccia di San Gimignano, verdicchio, sangiovese

pasta-pesto
vermentino, cortese, pinot grigio, vernaccia, verdicchio

RICE

mushroom risotto
chardonnay, cabernet-based claret, South African pinot noir

beetroot risotto
cabernet sauvignon from a warmer climate like Margaret River or Chile

Spanish cauliflower rice (paella rice cooked with tomato, onion, paprika and cauliflower)
tempranillo, Rioja (red or white), mencía

bean chilli
New World cabernet sauvignon, carmenère, pinotage

vegetarian Thai green curry
medium-dry riesling, off-dry pinot gris

avocado sushi rolls
rosé, orange wine, pinot gris, crémant

stuffed peppers
(*with rice, courgettes, garlic, tomatoes, olives, thyme*) whites, reds and pinks from Provence, the Rhône and the Languedoc; Rhône blends from South Africa
(*with rice, oregano, feta*) sauvignon blanc, assyrtiko, gouveio, xinomavro

PLANTS

green asparagus
grüner veltliner, unoaked Bordeaux Blanc, sauvignon blanc, arneis, verdicchio, vermentino

aubergine parmigiana
reds from the Dão or Douro in Portugal, agiorgitiko from Greece, Lebanese blends, malbec. Most Italian reds are also a good shout, eg Valpolicella, Rosso di Montalcino, primitivo, aglianico, nero d'avola

roasted butternut squash with pine nuts and Parmesan
South African chenin blanc, chardonnay, Soave, sangiovese, primitivo

blue cheese, pear and endive salad
dry Jurançon, oaked sauvignon blanc, sauvignon-semillon blends

beetroot & goat curd salad
sauvignon blanc, Bordeaux blanc, sauvignon-semillon blends

Puddings

In general, I am not hugely into drinking wine with dessert. One usually spoils the other. But there are a few exceptions: brilliant combinations where the wine and food sing together. Here are some favourites.

fresh strawberries
dry wines: claret, cabernet franc, Brut champagne
sweeter wines: demi-sec champagne, Moscato d'Asti

ice cream (vanilla, praline, stracciatella)
PX sherry, Rutherglen Muscat

ice cream (coconut) with roasted pineapple and physalis
Sauternes

tarte tatin
sweet riesling, sweet chenin blanc such as Coteaux du Layon

mince pie
cream sherry, Passito di Pantelleria

pecan pie
Rutherglen Muscat, malmsey

crème caramel, pastel de nata
tawny port, Muscat de Rivesaltes

chocolate: rich, dark chocolate mousse; chocolate tart; chocolate Nemesis, plain chocolate truffles
spirits: Armagnac, cognac, rum
wines: young vintage port, LBV port, Maury, Muscat de Rivesaltes, tawny port

caramelized oranges
amontillado sherry, cream sherry

seed cake
vintage Madeira

Chardonnay

Versatile chardonnay can be twangy, citrusy and refreshing or nutty, creamy and rounded. It loves fish, dairy, chicken and the sunny taste of roasted root vegetables. Tweak the dish to suit the wine: for instance, by adding toasted hazelnuts to go with the toasty oak of the wine.

dairy
creamy/buttery/eggy/cheesy sauces – mayonnaise, béchamel (think fennel, tomato and other vegetable gratins; parsley sauce), hollandaise, cheese soufflé, eggs Benedict, good Cheddar cheese with crackers

sweet root vegetables and sweetcorn
pumpkin risotto with lots of cheese stirred in, roasted squash, pumpkin pie, butternut squash and Pecorino ravioli, roasted sweet potato with butter

fish
with buttery or creamy accents, such as sole meunière, chowders, salmon with buttery potatoes

roast pork

nuts
especially cashew, almonds, hazelnuts

mushrooms
mushrooms on toast, creamy chicken and mushroom casserole, mushroom risotto, mushroom omelette

chicken
roast chicken, chicken and avocado salad, smoked chicken with basil mayo

crustaceans
grilled lobster and chips, prawns with lemon and garlic, crayfish, crab, fried scallops

Riesling

Riesling is the answer for so many otherwise tricky food matches, especially when chilli is involved. The hotter the chilli the more sweetness you need.

DRY AND OFF-DRY RIESLING

white asparagus, fennel, dill, capers and gherkin
think of salads, vegetable, fish or chicken dishes with these accents, for instance smoked salmon with dill on rye

creamy or rich
tartiflette, baeckeoffe (pork slow-cooked in a white wine sauce), sausages and choucroute, tarte flambée (bacon and onion tart)

coq au riesling

fish
plain white fish barbecued, steamed, fried with salt, pepper and butter, or cooked en papillote

lime
snapper or sea bream with guacamole and a coriander, lime and tomato salsa; chicken marinated in lemongrass, chilli, garlic, lime and Thai fish sauce

pig
pork chops, roast pork, roast gammon

lemongrass, ginger, coriander (and not too much chilli)
fish, noodle and chicken dishes such as soba noodles with snow peas, carrots, edamame and ginger sauce; sea bass cooked en papillotte with lemongrass and ginger; steamed white fish with ginger, torn coriander and makrut lime leaves

OFF-DRY AND MEDIUM-DRY RIESLING

South-East-Asian food and other dishes influenced by those flavours
Som tam (green papaya salad), larb gai (Laotian chicken salad), crunchy Vietnamese noodle salads, pork banh mi (pulled pork sandwich), rice noodles with sticky prawns, stir-fried prawns with chilli and tomato

fatty meats
pork belly, roast pork with crackling, goose

spicy rubs
jerk seasoning or ras-el-hanout

sweeter dressings
peanut butter and lime slaw, salads whose dressings are sweetened with honey, maple syrup or pomegranate molasses

mango, peaches, stewed apple sauce, caramelized apple slices
Fruity salads or noodle dishes benefit from a sweeter wine: think mango and prawn noodles. Likewise meats cooked or served with sweet fruit: roast pork and apple sauce, smoked goose with caramelized apple, chicken and mango curry

Pinot noir

Pinot noir is a wonderful wine when it comes to food matching. As always try to think about the weight of the wine and the flavours it needs to contend with. A bright and juicy pinot noir can be refreshing against a richer dish – but add in too many spices and it can be drowned out.

duck
pinot noir is the ultimate match for duck. Think roasted duck with roasted root veg, magret with peas cooked in lettuce with pancetta – anything

salmon, tuna, red mullet, cod wrapped in prosciutto

cherries, cranberries, redcurrants, raspberries
not on their own but as accents. For instance, duck with cherry sauce, turkey with cranberry stuffing

mushrooms, truffle
mushrroms on toast, in a risotto, or as a side. Or think truffle-layered dauphinoise potatoes with a piece of beef

figs
tagliatelle with ricotta, mint and figs; fig and prosciutto salad

chicken, turkey and goose
but hold the butter and cheese; think instead along the lines of chicken roasted with olive oil and thyme, chicken and mushroom pie, turkey with chestnuts and cranberry stuffing, chicken and bay kebabs

thyme

beef, veal, calves' liver, sweetbreads

potatoes
think earthy new potatoes with thyme and a simple piece of meat or a salad

roasted root vegetables
squash, pumpkin, red onions, carrots and sweet potato

game birds
pheasant, partridge, quail

teriyaki, sesame, soy, hoisin, star anise
not all at once, but pinot is great with, say, a Thai beef salad or Peking duck. Be careful not to overwhelm the wine with too much strong flavour though. A young, more intense pinot can take more flavour in the food than something older or more delicate

juniper
spiced red cabbage, pork stuffed with juniper, thyme, coriander and lemon zest

burgers

Tempranillo

Tempranillo is the red grape of Rioja and Ribera del Duero. It works well with many meat and slow-cooked rice dishes but in Spain it's often also drunk with fish. Choose lighter styles with less or no oak for more delicately flavoured dishes.

paprika
chorizo; Spanish rice dishes such as paella, aubergine and tomato rice; chickpea, paprika, tomato and spinach salsa; roasted cauliflower with paprika and garlic

rich, unctuous meat dishes
such as oxtail stew, braised beef cheeks, goat kid

cumin, nutmeg, coriander, cinnamon and cloves
think lamb chops rubbed with cumin, paprika, garlic and coriander seeds or cinnamon and cumin spiced lamb shank with aubergine and mint

chorizo
chorizo in red wine, hake cooked with chorizo, chickpea and chorizo soup

tapas
pan y tomate, slow-cooked artichokes, croquetas

corn
nachos, polenta, grilled sweetcorn

lamb
slow-cooked lamb shoulder with date and almond couscous; lamb with rosemary and garlic

pork
pork chop, slow-roast pork shoulder, pulled pork on a toasted roll with barbecue sauce, cured hams, lechon al horno

fish
meaty fish like swordfish or tuna and other fish cooked with red wine, tomato and/or paprika/chorizo accents, e.g. hake with tomato, garlic and clams; squid, chorizo and red pepper stew

Spanish rice dishes
aubergine and tomato rice, slow-cooked artichoke rice, paella

Manzanilla and fino sherry

Sherry is one of the world's ultimate food wines. The two lightest styles are manzanilla and fino and they are as nifty with sushi as they are with seafood, tapas and almost anything fried.

seafood and fish
smoked salmon, nigiri sushi, sashimi, California rolls, cod wrapped in pancetta, garlicky prawns fried in butter with lemon, razor clams, oysters, chargrilled squid with rocket and red peppers, bouillabaisse (fino is heavier, so more appropriate with richer flavours or dressings)

fried things
croquetas, vegetable tempura, fritto misto, calamares fritos, deep-fried artichokes

small bites
green manzanilla olives, marcona almonds and other salty, roasted nuts, tortilla, pan con tomate, gazpacho, crisps

chicken liver pasties

MANZANILLA

soft-shell crab nam rolls

citrus-marinated raw fish – ceviche of sea bass or sea bream

green asparagus

FINO

white asparagus or green asparagus with aioli or hollandaise

mushrooms on toast

smoked and cured meats
mojama, smoked duck, jamón

Acknowledgements

So many people helped with the original *The Wine Dine Dictionary* and I owe all of them equal thanks for this volume. You know who you are. Especial thanks are due to my agent, Lizzy Kremer, and to the team at Granta, in particular my editor, Laura Barber, copy-editor Francine Brody and desk editor Christine Lo.

Index of recipes

Index

Page numbers in **bold** denote a main entry or description. Page numbers in *italics* denote a food as a game-changer ingredient.

bacchus, 27, 88, 135, 171, 190, 200
bagna cauda, **31**, 98, 218
Baileys, 107
baked beans, **31–2**, 219
Bandol, 42, 72, 78, 81, 102, 118, 131, 157,
    163, 165, 172, 186, 196
banitsa, **32**, 52
Banyuls, 64
Barbaresco, 78, 79, 103, 111, 128, 157,
    191
barbecues, 15, **32–4**, 113, 116, 158, 172,
    174, 180
    barbecue sauce, 33–4, 37, 45, 151,
        210, 227
    barbecued fish, 159, 165, 168, 171,
        224
barbera, 46, 79, 84, 85, 117, 118, 123,
    135, 141, 144, 156, 157, 159, 160,
    161, 192, 195, 196, 197, 219
Bardolino, 24, 50, 52, 70, 78, 127, 140,
    144, 147, 168, 187, 193
Barolo, 36, 79, 103, 111, 128, 133, 191
Bartoshuk, Linda, 25
bean chilli, 221
Beaujolais, 26, 29, 32, 45, 70, 79, 80,
    95, 123, 130, 172, 187, 193
    Beaujolais Blanc, 161
    Beaujolais Cru, 49, 68, 70, 78, 80,
        89, 117, 142, 144, 160, 161, 185,
        196
    Beaujolais Villages, 43, 50–1, 117
Beck, Graham, 49
Beckett, Fiona, 180
beef, **34–8**
    accompaniments, 37–8
    beef cannelloni, 48
    beef wellington, **38**
    boeuf à la gardiane, **40–1**
    boeuf bourguignon, **40**
    burgers, **45**
    steak with peppercorns, 143
    Thai beef salad, **184–5**
beer (and ale), 28, 47, 52, 59, 60, 75,
    112, 146, 147, 151
    Black Sheep Best, 149
    dark beers, 196, 197
    Harviestoun Bitter & Twisted, 33
    London Pride, 172
beerenauslese, 121, 184

beetroot, **38–9**, 149, 209
    beetroot and goat curd salad, 38, 221
    beetroot purée, 83
    beetroot risotto, 39–40, 221
Bergerac, 32, 38, 40, 78, 79, 80, 115,
    144, 209
beurre blanc, **40**, 46, 173
Bianco di Custoza, 162
Bierzo, 24, 43, 54, 56, 67, 70, 80, 127,
    128, 137, 138, 141, 156, 168, 193,
    195, 199
Biferno Rosso, 120, 146
biltong, 51
bitterness (taste), 7–8, 17, 18
Blakeslee, Albert, 25
blaufrankisch, 138, 156
blinis, **40**
Bloody Mary, 176
bobal, 78, 80, 85, 149, 171
bonarda, 47, 58, 59, 85
bone marrow, **41**
bonito flakes, 19
Bońkowski, Wojciech, 144
bordeaux, 34, 36, 38, 40, 41, 50, 51, 54,
    55, 69, 70, 71, 78, 115, 116, 117, 118,
    119, 123, 125, 142, 145, 155, 163,
    169, 170, 174, 195, 207, 208–9,
    210, 217, 219
    Bordeaux Blanc, 27, 32, 124, 168, 221
    white bordeaux, 40, 116, 118, 128,
        129, 141, 170, 173, 184, 195
bottarga, **42**
bouillabaisse, **42**, 165, 228
bourboulenc, 148
Bourgogne Blanc, 132, 138, 139, 150,
    161, 190
Bourgogne Rouge, 50, 54, 62, 70, 84,
    102
Bourgueil, 36, 97, 145, 155, 172
Boxing Day leftovers, **42–3**
Brachetto d'Acqui, 64, 66
brandy, 33, 63, 66, 107
Brebis, 53
bresaola, 17, 35, 52
Brindisi, 141, 147
broad beans, 40, **43–5**, 155, 161, 219
    broad bean, pea shoot, asparagus and
        ricotta bowl, 44
broccoli, 139, 220

FRIED EGGS AND RIOJA

grillo, 72, 87, 193
grouse, **102–3**
Grover Zampa, 109
grüner veltliner, 27, 40, 43, 51, 69, 71,
    88, 95, 121, 160, 168, 169, 172,
    177, 182, 190, 200, 219, 221
Gruyère, 71, 74, 95, 101, 134
guacamole, 51, 59, 87, 98, 200, 224
Gyngell, Skye, 29

haggis, **105**
ham, 51, 70, 97, 199, 207
    Bayonne ham, 50–1
    ham salad, 162
    ham terrine, 111
    jambon persillé, **111**
    melon with air-dried ham, 126
    Teruel ham, 51
    with lentils, 121–2
    see also charcuterie; gammon;
        prosciutto
hangovers, **105**
Harding, Julia, 139
harissa, **105–6**
Hawkins, Craig, 168
Henry, Diana, 118, 199
herbs, 17, **106**
Hermitage, 196, 212
    see also Crozes-Hermitage
hoisin sauce, 75, 78, 212, 226
hollandaise, **106**
horseradish, 38, 83, 169, 200
hummus, 56, 81, 116, 119
Hunter Valley (Australia), 16, 24, 27,
    51, 73, 74, 89, 141, 142, 217

ice cream, **107–8**, 222
Ikeda, Kikunae, 7
Indian food, **108–10**
    see also curry
Insoglio del Cinghiale, 145
Irouléguy, 70, 133, 155

jacquère, 23, 95, 112, 156
Jansson's frestelse, **111–12**
jerk, **112**, 225
Johnson, Hugh, 53, 73
Jones, Roger, 192
Julius, David, 56

juniper, 163, 195, 226
Jurançon, 51, 133, 163, 200, 201, 221
    Jurançon Moelleux, 94, 181

Kapoor, Sybil, 187
kebabs, **113**
kedgeree, **113**
kékfrankos, 138, 181
Keller, Thomas, 55
Kellett, Ian, 90
Kent, Marc, 33
kidney beans, 59, 60, 61
kidneys, lamb's, 117
King George whiting, **113**
Kir, 148
kirsch, 64, 95
koshu, 62, 63, 139, 170, 172, 181

lager, 59
lagrein, 26, 52, 156, 171, 193, 195
Lam, Martin, 83
lamb, **115–19**
    khoresh gheimeh, 122–3
    lamb with herb crust, 118, 217
    slow-cooked lamb shoulder, 117, 217
Lambrusco, 35, 49, 156, 171, 193
Lancashire hot pot, **119–20**
Languedoc pink, 56
lasagne, **120**
lassi, 57, 58
lemon, 17, **120–1**
    lemon juice, 18, 25, 28, 35, 37, 121,
        150, 166
    preserved, **151**
lemon tart, **121**
lemongrass, 71, 73, 74, 94, 100, **121**,
    151, 159, 168, 174, 176, 177, 224
lentils, **121–2**
    see also dhal
Leyda (Chile), 30, 43, 159
lime, 7, 73, 75, 100, **122**, 124, 149, 159,
    173, 174, 179, 185, 224, 225
    dried limes, **122–3**
    lime juice, 51, 71, 93, 94, 100, 121,
        142, 166, 176, 178, 184, 185,
        206
    lime leaves, 176, 224
Limoux, 25, 40, 87, 128, 132, 161, 205
Lindo, Bob, 62